'*LoveSex and Relationships* takes the readers on an all-round tour of the brain, mind, body and emotions, in a jargon-free yet in-depth exploration of human sexuality and intimate relationships. Written in a warm tone and with a sex-positive philosophy, this book is the essential guide for anyone who wants to know more about sex and relationships. Cabby Laffy and Polly McAfee offer many reflective exercises that will help readers improve their sex lives and relationships. The authors expertly lift the lid on sensitive subjects that are often unspoken'.

Silva Neves, *COSRT-accredited and UKCP-registered psychosexual and relationship psychotherapist, speaker and author*

'*LoveSex and Relationships* is an inclusive, up-to-date, accessible and engaging book about how sex and intimacy work. Drawing on a wide range of relevant theory and research, the authors present a compelling understanding of how mind, brain, body, and feeling work together - within our social and relational context - to shape our experience of love and desire. This book is a must-read for all sex and relationship practitioners and will be very helpful to share with clients who are grappling with these issues too'.

Meg-John Barker, *author of a number of popular books on sex, gender and relationships, including graphic guides to Queer, Gender, and Sexuality, How To Understand Your Gender, Life Isn't Binary, Enjoy Sex (How, When, and IF You Want To), Rewriting the Rules, and Hell Yeah Self Care. They have also written a number of books for scholars and counsellors on these topics, drawing on their own years of academic work and therapeutic practice*

'This book contains a systematic but delightful guide full of information and a model to work with for both students and qualified therapists looking for information on love and sex. Not only does the updated information provide solid knowledge but also embraces the nuances of the modern-day issues that affect mental and physical health. The texts and diagrams specifically help therapists to keep easy note of how to work with sexual dysfunctions and relationship issues. This book has already added a wealth of knowledge developing this field and the update will make a huge difference to the newcomers in the profession not forgetting those who will be encouraged to join the profession having read this book'.

Rima Hawkins, *AccCOSRT Psychosexual & Relationship Psychotherapist (Individuals, Couples & Polycules) AccCOSRT Supervisor Trauma Therapist – (EMDR Europe Accredited Practitioner – MEMDRAssoc - UK) Response to Domestic & Sexual Violence Specialist – Accredited Expert Witness in*

'I would describe this book as beautiful. It offers an accessible and inclusive way to think about human sexuality in the contemporary context, uniquely and deftly integrating science based information with an acute awareness of and sensitivity to the impact of dominant social systems. It navigates the multidimensional human experience of love, sex and relationships across cultures and identities, with the depth of consideration reflective of the authors' extensive psychotherapeutic experience. It is beautiful and important and will immediately go to the top of our recommended reading list'.

'So much of how we talk and learn about sex is from a limited perspective, which further limits our capacity for sexual wellness and getting to our best sexual relationship with ourself and others, and *LoveSex and Relationships* is the antithesis of that. Using the homeodynamic model, it examines sex through a holistic lens encompassing the huge breadth of factors that are influencing us and making us the sexual person that we are today. Most importantly *LoveSex and Relationships* is pleasure-focused and sex-positive meaning that it pushes back against so much we are taught about sex which is through a shame-based model. It's a must read for all, but especially for clinicians working with those in mental health and psychological contexts'.

LoveSex and Relationships

LoveSex and Relationships introduces a pleasure-focused rather than reproductive model of sex, exploring how our brains, minds, bodies and emotions interact to create our experience of sexuality.

This book challenges the cultural commodification of sex and sexuality, and it encourages the reader to experience 'being sexual' rather than 'doing sex' or 'looking sexy'. This is crucial to our development of sexual self-esteem, particularly in the digital era of pornography, dating and hookup apps. Bringing the material of the first edition up to date, chapters include anatomical diagrams and social commentary with a focus on trauma and Polyvagal Theory. Diversity and cultural changes are also addressed, including a more expansive understanding of gender identity, and greater awareness of the impact of power and rank in sexual relationships. Lastly, each chapter features a new partnered exercise alongside every solo exercise from the first edition.

The book's accessible language makes it a valuable resource for sex and relationship therapists and trainees, general mental health and sex/relationship professionals, and clients themselves.

Cabby Laffy, UKCP, COSRT, NCIPm accredited, author of the first edition, is an experienced psychosexual therapist who is passionate about inspiring people to have the most satisfying sexual life that they can.

Polly McAfee, mBACP, mCOSRT, is a trainer, group facilitator and sex and relationship therapist helping people love their bodies, delight in their sexualities and be true to themselves in relationships.

LoveSex and Relationships

An Integrative Model for Sexual Education

Second Edition

Cabby Laffy and Polly McAfee

Illustrations Tessa Gaynn and Gerry Laffy

Routledge
Taylor & Francis Group

LONDON AND NEW YORK

Designed cover image: © Getty Images

Second edition published 2023
by Routledge
4 Park Square, Milton Park, Abingdon, Oxon, OX14 4RN

and by Routledge
605 Third Avenue, New York, NY 10158

Routledge is an imprint of the Taylor & Francis Group, an informa business

First edition published by Karnac 2013

British Library Cataloguing-in-Publication Data
A catalogue record for this book is available from the British Library

Library of Congress Cataloguing-in-Publication Data
Names: Laffy, Cabby, author. | McAfee, Polly, 1974- author.
Title: Lovesex and relationships : an integrative model for sexual education / Cabby Laffy and Polly McAfee ; illustrations [by] Tessa Gaynn and Gerry Laffy.
Other titles: Lovesex
Identifiers: LCCN 2022058317 (print) | LCCN 2022058318 (ebook) | ISBN 9781032344935 (hardback) | ISBN 9781032344911 (paperback) | ISBN 9781003322405 (ebook)
Subjects: LCSH: Sexual ethics.
Classification: LCC HQ32 .L34 2023 (print) | LCC HQ32 (ebook) | DDC 176/.4--dc23/eng/20221227
LC record available at https://lccn.loc.gov/2022058317
LC ebook record available at https://lccn.loc.gov/2022058318

ISBN: 978-1-032-34493-5 (hbk)
ISBN: 978-1-032-34491-1 (pbk)
ISBN: 978-1-003-32240-5 (ebk)

DOI: 10.4324/9781003322405

Typeset in Times New Roman
by MPS Limited, Dehradun

Contents

Illustrations

Acknowledgements

We would like to thank all the clients, students and supervisees who have helped us sharpen our thinking in developing this book.

Also, the colleagues who have supported and encouraged us in our work, especially Anita Sullivan, Kate Moyle, Sarah Paton Briggs, Rima Hawkins, Meg-John Barker, Dominic Davies, Silva Neves and Julie Sale.

We would like to thank artists Tessa Gaynn (https://www.tessagaynn.com/) and Gerry Laffy (https://gerrylaffyart.com/).

Deep appreciation to our families and friends for all their support in getting this update written, particularly Rose McAfee, Shana Laffy, Aleine Ridge, Carole Ingram, Lizzie Ruffell, Nomi McLeod and Boo Armstrong.

Finally a big shout out to Kate Goldenberg for her amazing admin at the Centre for Psychosexual Health (CPH) and excellent editing of this book.

Introduction

Introduction to the Updated Edition

The first edition of this book was published in 2013, seven years after Cabby set up the Centre for Psychosexual Health and created its two-year Diploma in Integrative Psychosexual Therapy. Polly graduated from the Diploma in 2008, joined the faculty in 2009 and has worked with Cabby ever since. Over the years, we have taught hundreds of students an integrative approach to working therapeutically with sexual issues. Between us we have also supported many clients – through individual and relationship therapy, and group work – to address sexual issues and reclaim their sexual pleasure. Then as now, three guiding principles have shaped our work:

1. The Homeodynamic Model

We are complex beings, and our sexual experiences are affected by many different factors. Cabby developed the Homeodynamic Model to conceptualise this by separating human experience into four different quadrants: mind, body, brain and emotion. Each of the quadrants is given a chapter of its own to allow us to explore it in depth. Understanding all these parts – which in reality are constantly impacting and being impacted by each other, i.e. 'homeodynamic' – gives us much more choice and freedom when it comes to enjoying sex (Figure I.1).

2. Deconstructing Social and Cultural Messages

As well as all of this going on inside us, our sexuality is also much influenced by social context. We believe that the position we hold in society, our cultural privilege or lack thereof, the way our sexuality is perceived by those around us, the messages we receive from family and culture about what sex is or should be – all of this affects us a great deal. Deconstructing and deciding which beliefs we want to claim for our own is one of the most impactful things we can do for our sexual lives.

DOI: 10.4324/9781003322405-1

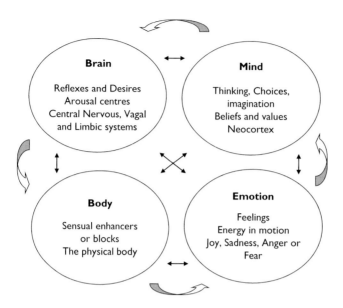

Figure I.1 The Homeodynamic Model for Sexuality.

Nowhere is this more important than in recovery from sexual violence. A 2018 study[1] showed that 'a third (33%) of men in Britain think it isn't usually rape if a woman is pressured into having sex but there is no physical violence'. This kind of myth leads to self-blame and difficulties in recovery for survivors. Education about the fawn and freeze trauma responses and how these cause us to act in situations of threat is crucial for the reclamation of sexual self-esteem.

3. The Pleasure Principle

Our approach is not just about fixing or solving sexual problems, so people can 'perform' better. It is about celebrating pleasure as our birthright, as a healing, joyous and potentially transformative experience. Following and claiming what gives *us* pleasure (physical, relational, even spiritual pleasure) rather than fulfilling obligations or adhering to a social script has the potential to make sex an expression of our very selves.

Why an Updated Edition?

While these principles have remained constant over the ten years since this book was first published, the world has changed a lot in that time. Let us not forget we have experienced a global pandemic and widespread lockdowns that drastically increased social isolation, showing us just how important touch and social contact are for our mental and physical health. In addition, the following changes in particular led us to create an update.

Tech Revolution

Although this was underway in 2013, the last decade has seen the popularisation of both smartphones and unlimited data phone plans, making online porn, social media and dating via apps constantly available to a lot of people. Many get smartphones when they start secondary school, and although there are some age controls, today's teenagers are pretty adept at finding what they want regardless. This increasing online aspect of life has had many effects on our sexual lives; some positive, like access to more information, and assistance with maintaining and eroticising long-distance relationships, others harder, like greater difficulty being embodied and in the present moment, shorter attention spans, less 'offline' time for example in the bedroom, more and earlier use of porn, body image pressures and a tendency to keep more dating options open for longer. This edition speaks directly to these challenges, with a focus on embodiment and sexual nourishment that feels more important than ever.

Diversity and Non-normativity

The last decade has seen much greater acceptance of non-binary and queer gender identities, and a more fluid conception of gender. In this update we have tried to separate out body parts or sexual behaviours from the person or gender of the person. We have also tried to include trans, intersex and non-binary research and voices where we could find them, and speak to those identities. This decade has also seen more interest in calling out other areas of normativity and privilege, such as the whiteness inherent in much psychotherapeutic thinking. We have seen more work prioritising black and minority ethnic, disabled, neurodiverse and other voices. Within the sexual field this critique of normativity has included the depathologisation of kink, asexualities, aromanticisms and consensual non-monogamy. Again, we make an effort to celebrate and signpost these voices.

Polarisation

In counterpoint to this celebration of diversity and critique of the misuse of power, the last decade has also seen a rise in political conservatism, populism, attacks on 'woke' culture and women's reproductive rights, and movements to decrease the rights of vulnerable minorities. This increase in polarisation stifles discussion and debate, which is disastrous on many levels, given we live on a planet under threat, with weapons of mass destruction, and power increasingly concentrated in the hands of a few. We need to move away from an Us and Them ideology if we want to embrace difference and diversity. We are aware that some of what we say in this book might offend; we do this to encourage discussion and debate so as to foster deeper understanding.

Our updated edition, *LoveSex and Relationships* responds to the threats of polarisation by putting more emphasis on relationships, and the skills needed to conduct them successfully. Leading relationship research body The Gottman Institute has found that 69% of relationship problems are perpetual,[2] and that the key to a thriving relationship is learning to communicate effectively about these irreconcilable differences, thus developing empathy and collaboration. Easier said than done, for sure! But so important. This edition is packed full of support for navigating differences within your sex lives and personal relationships, whatever they may look like, and also, hopefully, for addressing the challenges of our wider world.

Notes

1 End Violence Against Women (2022). *Attitudes to Sexual Consent, Research by YouGov, December 2018.* Available at: https://www.endviolenceagainstwomen. org.uk/wp-content/uploads/1-Attitudes-to-sexual-consent-Research-findings-FINAL.pdf. (Accessed: 11 September 2022).
2 Gottman, J. (2015). *The Seven Principles for Making Marriage Work.* Random House.

Chapter 1

LoveSex and Relationships

Who This Book Is For

LoveSex and Relationships has been written with the many clients and students we have worked with in mind. Also, a range of other people:

- you may be someone with a general curiosity about sexuality who wants to explore and re-evaluate your sexual beliefs and behaviour to build a more conscious sexual self-esteem;
- you may have a specific sexual issue or difficulty that you would like to find out more about and be looking for ideas on how to change things;
- you may be in a relationship where you want to explore your sexual lives together. This edition includes an introduction to sexual healing and growth with a partner, or partners if you are non-monogamous, and a new set of exercises to guide you. This is explained further in the following section on how to use this book;
- you may be one of the many people who have experienced childhood sexual abuse or sexual violence as an adult. You may wish to explore some of the effects this has had on you along with ideas and insights for recovery;
- you may be a therapist or other practitioner working with clients' sexual issues. We recommend that you do any exercises yourself, and discuss them in supervision, before you suggest them to clients.

How to Use This Book

This book is divided into chapters. This first chapter outlines who this book is for and how it can be used, and provides a social and cultural context for exploring sexual issues.

Chapter 2 is an overview of different ways of thinking about sexual difficulties. We describe the traditional medical perspective, and then 2001's 'New View',[1] which takes into account social, cultural and relationship

DOI: 10.4324/9781003322405-2

factors as well. We then introduce our own Homeodynamic Model for Sexuality.[2] This trauma-informed model explores our reactive brain and our thinking mind, as well as our somatic experiences and our emotions.

Chapter 3 discusses areas to be considered before undertaking the Sexploration exercises; for example how to create a safe space for the work and how to look after yourself. This may be particularly helpful for those with trauma in their history. This chapter also contains a section on Working with Partners, and presents ideas to maximise relationship robustness, including effective communication skills.

We then move on to explore the four sections of the Homeodynamic Model where each chapter provides information and asks pertinent questions, inviting you to explore and evaluate the many different topics addressed:

Chapter 4 Mind
Chapter 5 Body
Chapter 6 Brain
Chapter 7 Emotion

With easy-to-read text, illustrations and diagrams, these chapters describe the body and brain physiology of sexuality, and explore how what we believe and have experienced about sex in the past informs our desires and sexual behaviour in the present day. Difficulties with current language and thinking are identified and our implicit reproductive model of sex is explored. We honour that for some, love and sex are a package, while others prefer to keep them separate. However you engage with your sexuality, we invite you to be in loving relationship with yourself, foregrounding consent and pleasure. We advocate being conscious, respectful and creative with our sexual energy – making love, not war.

Rather than offering answers, tips or techniques about performance, this book asks many questions. You are invited to investigate your own answers by participating in a series of self-discovery exercises that have all been tried and evaluated throughout years of clinical practice and experiential training. You may want to explore on your own, or with partner/s. There are exercises for both.

Through this self-discovery, you are able to clarify feelings, values and beliefs about what turns you on and what turns you off – physically, emotionally and mentally. You can explore who you want to be as a sexual being, how you want to express your sexuality and who with. You can find out what nourishes you sexually by becoming more mindful of your own sensual and sexual desires, tastes and appetite.

We do not need to understand the workings of our bodies to have a good relationship with our sexuality, just as we do not need to understand the metabolism of digestion to eat well. However, most people who want to eat a healthy diet do want to understand what their nutritional needs are, what foods provide proteins, carbohydrates, vitamins, minerals, etc. They want to know how to prepare and cook foods to maximise their benefits.

Most of us are surprisingly uneducated about ourselves sexually: what we need and how we 'work'. *LoveSex and Relationships* offers an opportunity to learn more about and re-evaluate your sexual life. It aims to empower you, the reader, of any level of education or professional training, ethnicity, age, culture, race, religion or spirituality, physical ability, gender or sexual orientation, to consciously create a nutritious sexual life, one to be pleased with and proud of.

From our clinical experience, we are aware this work can have a profound impact, sometimes more than we expect. We are not suggesting extremes like repressed memories, though this can happen, just that consciously exploring our sexuality, a powerful and vulnerable aspect of our humanity, is something that culturally, we tend to keep hidden and shrouded in shame. Gentle explorations can and often do, trigger uncomfortable feelings. We recommend you read the introduction to the Sexploration Exercises before embarking on them.

Social and Cultural Context

Nobody has sex in a vacuum – all of us are deeply influenced by the social and cultural norms we grew up with around sex and sexuality. And nearly all of us have experienced a general level of sexual shaming and lack of celebration about sexuality, given that most societies, cultures and religions denigrate or exploit sexuality. Even when sex seems to be 'everywhere', there is a flip side presenting challenges for many. Very few people report growing up with a confident and celebratory attitude towards sexuality and this influences many of our difficulties surrounding sex and sexual relationships. We will explore our social sexual shame and how it hinders our ability to develop a positive sense of sexual self-esteem.

We receive and internalise these messages about sex from our families of origin, our communities and the media we consume. This can be particularly challenging if our desires do not conform to what is culturally sanctioned. Figure 1.1 shows some *Dimensions of Diversity and Culture*. Individuals will be positively and negatively impacted by these different dimensions, uniquely. Moreover different areas of oppression tend to have a cumulative effect, see work on Intersectionality introduced by Kimberle Crenshaw.[3]

Robinson-Wood (2017)[4] reminds us that people who do not subscribe to Western individualism may experience enormous conflict, guilt and/or shame about having a sexual identity or making reproductive choices that differ from their social, cultural or religious collective beliefs.

Class too can have an impact on our reproductive and sexual well-being. For example in 2015,[5] it was reported that high teenage pregnancy rates in the UK correlate with socio-economic issues, particularly living in areas of higher deprivation, being in care or having lower educational achievement.

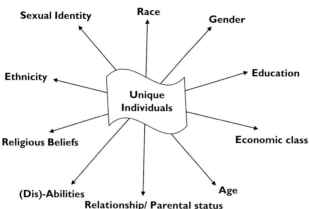

How do our **Dimensions of Diversity and Culture(s)** influence our experiences, values and beliefs, attitudes and behaviours?

Adapted from Amal Saymeh (2021)
https://www.betterup.com/blog/multicultural-competence

Figure 1.1 Dimensions of Diversity and Culture.

Teenage mothers are more likely to be unemployed or have lower salaries and educational achievements than their peers, and therefore to live in poverty – all of which may add up to challenges in developing adult self-esteem and sexual assertiveness and well-being.

Take a moment to see where you are within these diversities, and to notice how some of these privileges and/or marginalisations influence your values and beliefs about sex, your attitudes and sexual behaviours, and your sexual experiences.

Another crucial factor to consider is the shadow side of sex – sexual abuse and sexual violence, the scale of which is shocking. It is a central tenet of this book to speak to survivors of sexual trauma, with guidance offered in future chapters. We believe the Homeodynamic Model can help survivors reclaim a sense of sexual self-esteem. Conversely social norms such as societal 'blaming' of victims can impede recovery and increase sexual shame. Challenging these myths can be both empowering and healing.

When we feel ashamed of our sexuality we might react in numerous ways. We might have an increased need to stay in control sexually, or to avoid feeling vulnerable. We might avoid sexual encounters altogether, or sexual intimacy within an ongoing relationship. We might pretend to others that we are much happier with our sexual lives than we really are. On the other hand, we might reject this shame and take the other polarity, that of shamelessness, a sort of empty pretence of liberation and ease, a performance of 'great sex'. In shamelessness, we do not really contemplate the possibility of saying no. Instead, we try everything, have a willingness to do anything, the more outrageous the better, regardless of how it might actually make us feel.

Ours may seem to be a liberated sexual environment, with sexuality widely displayed. It is assumed that everyone (else) is having an amazing sex life with no problems, so individuals with difficulties can often feel inadequate and ashamed. However, the Natsal-3 study, conducted in 2011 and 2012, revealed 42% of men and 51% of women in the UK report experiencing sexual difficulties.[6] Bringing these issues to light, understanding them individually and as a society, can help to alleviate the fear and anxieties often associated with discussing these subjects.

In this book, we suggest that it is not what we do, but how we feel about doing it that makes up a nutritious and satisfying sexual life. Do you wake up the next day thinking, oh no, what did I do? Or wow, that was great, I feel so good? To understand how we feel, we need to consciously enquire into our sexuality, rather than treat it as something that 'just happens'. You might fear this will interfere with the spontaneity of sex. We argue just the opposite: by knowing ourselves, we are free to initiate and receive the kind of sexual contact we truly desire.

Notes

1 Kaschak & Tiefer (2001). *A New View of Women's Sexual Problems.* Routledge.
2 Laffy, C. (2013). *LoveSex: An Integrative Model for Sexual Education.* Routledge.
3 Crenshaw, K., & TEDx Talks (2016). *The Urgency of Intersectionality: Kimberlé Crenshaw at TEDWomen.* Available at: https://www.ted.com/talks/kimberle_crenshaw_the_urgency_of_intersectionality (Accessed: 16 August 2022).
4 Robinson-Wood, T. (2017:367). *The Convergence of Race, Ethnicity and Gender.* Sage.
5 Cook, Sinead M. C. et al. (2015). 'Social issues of teenage pregnancy', *Obstetrics, Gynaecology and Reproductive Medicine*, 25 (9), pp. 243–248.
6 Davis, N. (2019). 'Sexual dysfunction cuts risk "leaving thousands in UK without help"', *The Guardian*, 22 April. Available at: https://www.theguardian.com/society/2019/apr/22/sexual-dysfunction-cuts-risk-leaving-thousands-in-uk-without-help (Accessed: 16 August 2022).

Chapter 2

A New Model for Sexuality

Understanding Sexual Issues

Human sexuality is a vast and intriguing subject, affecting and being affected by so many things. It is unique, specific to each and every individual, and it is also universal. Most humans have sexual desires and urges that move them both physically and emotionally. Not everyone chooses to express this desire in sexual behaviour, as we will discuss later. At its best, sexual energy is a free, potent life force that can be used to enhance and heal, bring great joy, pleasure, self-esteem, physical and emotional well-being. It is a creative force, our fire energy and a source of power.

However, socially, we think and talk about sex as something we do, rather than sexuality being something that we have and being sexual as something that we are. We talk little about feeling sexual, or the emotional and relational reasons for sexual desire – about the fact that it is usually an 'other' that we want to be sexual with. Our focus seems to be on how much sex we can have rather than how we want to express ourselves sexually.

This book is a culmination of many years of personal and professional experience. It is a comprehensive sexual education resource offering an opportunity to explore a range of areas and issues that are crucial to creating positive sexual self-esteem. It presents a new paradigm for professional thinking in psychosexual therapy by focusing on sexual health and on us all being sexual people, rather than on dysfunctions that are defined around performing sexual acts. It explores many relevant issues and discusses what sexual self-esteem could look like if we were to celebrate and explicitly value our sexuality. *LoveSex and Relationships* offers an integrative model for sexual education where you, the reader, can learn more about the richness of sexuality and be encouraged to experience 'being sexual' rather than 'doing sex' or 'looking sexy'.

Two common sexual issues people seek help for are a lack of sexual interest or a different level of interest from their partner/s, and physical difficulties with sexual arousal. These latter might be self-diagnosed online as for example

DOI: 10.4324/9781003322405-3

'vaginismus', or 'erectile dysfunction'. It is useful to distinguish between sexual *interest* and sexual *arousal*, although they are often related and can exacerbate each other. It is useful to know whether a lack of arousal is because there is no desire to be sexual, for example, with a specific person or to partake in specific sexual activities. If there is desire but you are having difficulties with physical sexual arousal, this can, in time, lead to a lack of desire, because wanting to be sexual but not being able to can bring feelings of distress and/or pressure about developing or sustaining relationships.

A good starting point for understanding the root causes of sexual diffi-culties is to ask some questions to clarify what helps or hinders the situation and to uncover more about the meaning. Physical issues will be happening within your framework of beliefs and values, and feelings and emotions, so it is also worth exploring the exercises in those chapters.

- If there is a complete lack of sexual desire, is it connected to other physical or psychological symptoms? Is it being affected by the side effects of medication? Antidepressants, epilepsy medication and others can inter-fere with desire, arousal and/or orgasm. Have there been hormonal changes due to menopause or ageing? If none of these factors, what are the circumstances in which desire is more present or less available? Are there any sexual daydreams or interest in masturbation? Is there a 'relationship challenge' like bereavement, fertility issues or conflict in the relationship?
- Some people experience an involuntary tightening of the muscles of the vagina (vaginismus), which hinders penetration. This difficulty can also affect the muscles of the anus. There may be pain during penetration. Others experience a lack of or unreliable erections, which can make penetration difficult. In both these circumstances it's worth asking whether this always happens? If not, which situations or scenarios make it better or worse? Is there adequate arousal and lubrication before attempting penetration? Does this happen during masturbation or only during sex with a partner?
- Any of the above issues may also impact on experiences of orgasm and/or ejaculation so these are worthy of the same questions about circumstances and the quality and levels of arousal. If ejaculation is experienced as happening prematurely, we could ask, too soon for what? Is it pleasurable when it does occur? At what stage of arousal or sexual behaviour does ejaculation happen, is there anything which helps to delay it, or which makes it worse? Does this also happen during masturbation or only with a partner?
- With regard particularly to difficulties with erections, is this total or partial? When or during which activities, does the situation improve or what makes it worse? Does the arousal begin but is not sustained?

It is important to understand or discover whether there is a medical or organic (physical) cause to a sexual difficulty, and whether a problem is 'situational' (only happens in some situations) or 'universal' (always happens) as these will influence the way forward. For example, if there are no morning erections or if there are no circumstances in which the person feels desire or is able to become sexually aroused, a medical investigation by either a GP or a doctor at a sexual health clinic may help identify why. It can be worth checking about side effects of any current medications. It is a good idea to get a medical check-up for physical sexual difficulties as they can sometimes be indicators of other health problems such as diabetes or a heart condition.

Some people suffer with the hormonal rollercoaster of the menopause or with other issues due to ageing. They may have physical impairments or be suffering from chronic or long-term illnesses. There can sometimes be physical difficulties due to injuries sustained during the birthing process, from accidents, or through sexual violence. Some may be experiencing long-term gynaecological complications after undergoing Female Genital Mutilation or Cutting, as it is often called (FGM/C). There may also be physical issues with the size or shape of the genitals making some sexual behaviour difficult or impossible.

For these circumstances there are sex aids designed to support a sex life and make it as fulfilling as possible. These can be discussed with a psychosexual therapist or through investigation of dedicated websites.[1] It is often useful to consider counselling to address any psychological issues associated with these difficulties and/or to support incorporating the use of sex aids into people's sexual life. All the above issues may require new ways of thinking about sex and new ways of behaving sexually to incorporate the physical needs of individuals.

A New View

Historically, psychosexual therapy has considered sexual difficulties from a purely individual perspective, as bodily dysfunctions with organic (physical) and/or inorganic (psychological) causes. These can be addressed in the ways previously discussed. However, many sexual difficulties are also issues of relationship, or internalised shame. In 2001 the publication of *A New View of Women's Sexual Problems*, edited by Kaschak and Tiefer,[2] provided a radical new conceptualisation of women's sexual problems which considered the impact of socio-cultural, political and economic influences, as well as influences relating to the particular partner and/or relationship. This model can be considered biopsychosocial – biological, psychological and taking into account social factors. It is very much in line with our approach, and we consider it applicable to all genders.

This perspective on sexual difficulties means that we consider the impact of belonging to any group that diverges from the most societally accepted and valued norm, for example, being a person of colour, or disabled or working class, or older. Gender, Sexual and Relationship Diversities (GSRD) are some of the most directly impactful stresses on people's sexual lives, although all minority stress can have an impact on self-esteem, sense of safety, experiences of shame, withdrawal and rage.

Exploring the broader context of people's sexual difficulties has been crucial to how we have approached working with a wide range of other psychosexual issues, including:

- fertility problems, unwanted pregnancies, abortions or living with sexually transmitted infections, all of which can affect experiences of sexuality and sexual relationships;
- questions about gender or sexual identity, including asexuality, or seeking support to deal with social and cultural homophobia or transphobia;
- the exploration of sexual desires, tastes and preferences. This may include exploring thoughts, beliefs and values, and how they may conflict with social, religious or cultural backgrounds;
- difficulties with body image and sexual self-esteem;
- other consequences of sexual shame, such as getting involved in compulsive sexual behaviours that make the person feel bad;
- challenges around porn, including exposure at a young age, shame or worry about performance;
- dealing with the relational legacy of difficult or traumatic childhoods;
- negotiating sex as a single person – hookups, dating apps, etc.;
- opening up relationships, exploring consensual non-monogamy or polyamory;
- dealing with betrayal in relationships;
- developing communication and intimacy skills to sustain marriages or long-term relationships;
- recovery after sexual abuse and violence;
- challenges with sex during life transitions, including gender transition, early parenthood, menopause, ageing and chronic illness.

By far the most common difficulty we have encountered is the impact of sexual violence. There are far too many people who have experienced sexual abuse as children or sexual violence as adults. Childhood sexual abuse confuses our brains and bodies as well as our minds and emotions. Sexual violation as an adult can be devastating too, particularly because of societal attitudes towards victims of sexual violence. Some commonalities include physical and emotional trauma, not trusting self or other, self-harm or compulsivity, intimacy and relationship difficulties. Many physical sexual difficulties are associated with a history of sexual violence or exacerbated by social or cultural issues.

This model for sexuality is sex-positive; it promotes the pleasure principle, and challenges sexual shame. Rather than feeling uncomfortable or embarrassed to talk about sex, *LoveSex and Relationships* recommends that we get comfortable exploring things that are, after all, done and felt by the vast majority of people. Throughout this book we will be offering you exercises, information and suggestions that are:

- Educational – providing knowledge to stimulate your curiosity and desire. You can learn more about your fascinating and amazing body, your intelligence and creativity. Through this, you can explore your sexual potential and reflect, discuss, ponder and evaluate.
- Experiential – encouraging you to get intimate with yourself, your body, your uniqueness and delights. Feel into your nerves and muscles, your fingertips and lips; find out what really turns you on and what turns you off; revel in your sensuality.
- Ecstatic – helping you discover your core erotic themes, experience the free serotonin highs of pleasure and bliss through touch and intimate sexual play.
- Empowering – challenging you to choose what ways of being sexual you really want and value. Choose your own sexual nourishment diet, one to suit your preferences, tastes and desires. Experience the difference between 'power over' and 'power with' models of thinking and behaving.
- Existential – redressing our cultural shaming of sexuality so you can feel pleasure and well-being and have a good sense of sexual self-esteem, one where you value, honour and celebrate this gift you have. Reclaim your sense of sexuality from the consumerist dictates of the media, advertising and sex industries.

The Homeodynamic Model

The Homeodynamic Model was presented ten years ago in the first edition of *LoveSex*. Its trauma-informed view was innovative then and is now, appropriately, more mainstream. Most psychotherapists and counsellors would agree that trauma affects the more primitive, survival aspects of our brains. Our psychology and mental abilities, as well as our bodies and emotions, are also impacted. All need to be considered.

As a concept to help us understand some of the different elements that are at play in any human sexual moment, the Homeodynamic Model expands on the body-mind paradigm and uses the four distinctions of Mind – Body – Brain – Emotion. We are familiar with the idea of the head or the mind being the part of us that is rational, our thinking part, and the body being the more irrational or emotive part of us. With regards to our sexuality, it can be helpful to distinguish what goes on in the **Brain**, the back brain, which triggers our reactions, reflexes and urges, from the **Mind**, the front of our brain, our rational thinking ability. We could think of this as the back part of the skull and the forehead. Also to consider the differences between our **Body**, our physical sensations and sexual responses, and the feelings and **Emotion** we may experience.

In reality, human experience is a continuous relationship between all of these different aspects: our instincts, our physiology, feelings and thoughts are affecting and being affected by each other, and they are all operating in unison in a continual feedback loop. We cannot separate them out or place them in any hierarchy, as all are equally important.

The phrase 'homeostasis' is used in science to describe how organisms rebalance in reaction to stimuli and responses, to come back to stillness. To understand human sexuality more deeply, we've adopted the phrase 'homeodynamic', coined by Rose[3] in 1999, to indicate the constant feedback loop of responses and interactions that happen in human beings.

This new integrative model for sexuality incorporates research from neuroscience, complementary and alternative health therapies and cognitive behavioural therapy, along with psychotherapy and traditional eastern and western approaches to psychosexual therapy. It considers our sexuality with regards to these four different aspects, and also how they impact and are impacted by each other.

- The **Mind** can be thought of as the front brain and is home to our sexual values and beliefs. Humans have evolved with frontal lobes which allow us to reflect on our reactions; to think, weigh up options and make choices about our behaviour. We have imagination, the ability to anticipate and dream about the future.

   We are starting here as our beliefs and social cultures deeply inform our sexuality. Having an opportunity to question and re-evaluate our explicit and implicit belief systems allows us to identify issues for concern and to make more conscious choices. We can review what we believe, where we learnt these ideas and whether they still serve us. By analysing our unique history and our current social and cultural opinions about sexuality, we can contextualise our thinking. We can become clearer about what we really value about our sexuality and sexual relationships, and what suits us now as adults. We can gain some tools to change any outmoded ideas and sharpen our current belief system.

- Our **Body** has a sexual anatomy and physiology that is little understood. By separating our reproductive and sexual functioning, we can learn more about sensuality and more fully understand and enjoy our physical sexual potential. For example, that ejaculation and orgasm are distinguishable from each other and that all genders are capable of multiple orgasms (Chia & Abrams).[4] Sexual arousal on a physical level is sensual arousal, stimulation of the senses. Some sights, sounds, tastes, smells, touches and ways of being touched turn us on and others turn us off.

We can find out more about ourselves sexually by exploring sensuality in-depth, and including all the various body systems, not only our genitals, that are involved in sexual arousal. This is particularly useful where there are obstacles to sexual arousal like erectile difficulties, lack of clitoral arousal or lack of vaginal lubrication. We can develop a more intimate connection to our own body and thus discover and become more conscious about what arouses pleasure and what does not; a subjective experience of feeling sexual rather than what we look like to others.

- The back **Brain** triggers our reflexive, survival abilities, like the adrenaline rush of fight and flight or our desires and urges, for sex and food. It is home to our limbic system: the name given to a cluster of organs in the brain which are activated when we react to any stimulus to our system. It includes our vagus nerve and memory centres, which process reactions by using our knowledge; our history, to evaluate responses in any given moment.

Understanding the neurochemistry of sexual arousal allows for a wider view of our imperatives for being sexual and also, helps us understand the impact of sexual trauma. We can see passion and desire as impulsive reactions from our back brain, as distinct from the thinking abilities of our frontal lobes, our mind.

We can explore issues concerning sexual desire to help clarify our own sexual identity: who we are attracted to, what behaviours we wish to express with them, and also when, how and why. We can discover more about our 'reactivity' and the triggers which turn arousal on, or turn it off, and how this links with our personal history.

Such explorations are useful to address sexual difficulties which impact both arousal and desire, like rapid or delayed ejaculation, orgasm difficulties, unconscious tightening of vaginal or anal muscles or where there is pain during intercourse.

- The **Emotions** and feelings are our experience of the energy that gets set in motion through the body by any triggers that have stimulated any of the other quadrants. A feeling can be an emotion like love, grief, fear or anger or it can be expressed as physical sensations like feeling hot or cold, tightness in the stomach or a headache. A feeling might be a hunch, a guess or maybe a thought. Sometimes it is a combination of all of these.

We can explore the myriad feelings and emotions which surround human sexuality and their impact on our experience of sexuality. A focus on social issues provides a wider context for some of the sexual issues people contend with. This includes sexual shame, compulsivity and the impact of sexual violence.

Many people have concerns about seeking sexual relationships or sustaining current relationships. Relationship issues are discussed, such as communication skills, managing difference and conflict. Sexual health is explored in terms of physical, emotional, mental and spiritual well-being.

The Homeodynamic model is a way of understanding what may be happening within an individual person, while taking into account that humans do not exist in isolation, we are also social beings. We experience ourselves and behave in ways that are influenced by our society and culture. We are constantly in a relationship, not only with ourselves (and all our internal body systems) but also with our external environment and other people including our families, friends and lovers. We need to consider all these factors and how they interact in relationship to our sexuality.

Chapters 4–7 of this book explore the dynamics of mind, body, brain and emotion, individually and in-depth, with a focus on sexuality. They are presented in no particular order of importance, as all are interrelated and interdependent.

In reality, all elements are triggering and responding to all the others, all the time. There is a constant dialogue and communication between our brain, our body systems and body organs, and back again, all in nanoseconds. Our thinking, brain chemistry and physiology are constantly online, reacting and responding back, creating a circular and interacting flow. Every reaction in our brain causes physiological change, which in turn triggers emotions and thoughts, which again, trigger more reactions.

This could be seen as a circle, as a circuit of arousal which can be switched on or be broken and switched off. By drawing all these aspects together and examining how they affect and are affected by each other, we can uncover the preciousness and fragility of our lived human experience of sexuality and begin to develop a new framework and model for sexual self-esteem. With the knowledge and confidence of this self-esteem, we can more consciously create a model for psychosexual health, individually and societally.

Notes

1 Several examples: SPOKZ (2020). Available at: https://www.spokz.co.uk/sex-aids. html (Accessed: 16 Aug 2022); ABLEize (2019) *Disability & Special Needs Products & Services*. Available at: https://www.ableize.com/ (Accessed: 16 August 2022); Disabilities-R-Us (2022) *Disability Sexuality Resources*. Available at: https://www.disabilities-r-us.com/sexuality-resources/ (2022) (Accessed: 16 August 2022); My Pleasure (2022). Available at: https://mypleasure.com/ (Accessed: 16 August 2022).
2 Kaschak & Tiefer (2001). *A New View of Women's Sexual Problems*. Routledge.
3 Rose, S. (1999). *The Chemistry of Life*. New York: Penguin.
4 Chia, M., & Abrams, D. (2002). *The Multi Orgasmic Man*. London: Thorsons; Chia, M., & Abrams, D. (2002). *The Multi Orgasmic Couple*. London: Thorsons; Chia, M., & Carlton Abrams, R. (2005). *The Multi Orgasmic Woman*. Emmaus, PA: Rodale.

Chapter 3

The Sexploration Exercises

The exercises in this book are within the format of the Homeodynamic Model for Sexuality, exploring in sections the Mind, Body, Brain and Emotion. They do follow a flow, but you can choose to start or focus where you like. You may like to consider each exercise as it is presented, or read each chapter and then go back over the exercises, or read the whole book and then consider which if any exercises appeal to you.

First, some preparation:

Exercise: Create a Safe Sexploration Space

Identify a room or physical space where you feel private, comfortable, warm, relaxed, undisturbed and whatever else is important to you. Think about the words, 'privacy' and 'secrecy'; what do they mean to you, how are they different and how similar? Create a safe private space for yourself, consider the physical space, the lighting and ambiance. Do you like candles or aromas? Notice what you like and want, and what you don't want.

Make this space emotionally safe too, where you can do this work at your own pace, where you feel comfortable and relaxed.

Self-care

We are aware that there may be physical, practical or emotional impediments to completing this or other exercises. If so, we would encourage you to adapt our suggestions in any way that would work better – be creative, if there is some other way you wish to think about or explore a topic.

You may be disabled, have chronic illness or be in recovery, limiting your physical movement. Take the time to find the most comfortable physical situations for yourself and maybe, reduce the time limit on any exercises to suit your pace.

DOI: 10.4324/9781003322405-4

You may be homeless or not have access to physical privacy. In the UK in 2020, 47% of males and 36% of females aged 15–34 live with their parents, mainly due to economic reasons.[1] Some people live in multi-generational housing arrangements, suiting their class, religion or social culture; perhaps with less access to privacy.

You can always have the privacy of your own thoughts. If you don't have a physical place, find somewhere public, like a park or a cafe where you can take some exploration time. Use your imagination to visualise a safe space, in as much detail as possible, what you would want and how you want it to be. When we imagine an activity or behaviour, our inner world responds as if it is actually happening, so you can explore what you think and how you feel about something, without actually doing it. Having said that, we are aware that the more touch-based sexual exercises would require privacy.

If you find an exercise becoming difficult emotionally, be kind and gentle with yourself. Take a pause; decide if you want to continue now or perhaps later, when you have had time to consider what is difficult and why.

It can be useful to set a time limit, especially if you know a particular exercise may feel difficult. It can be helpful to get support; tell a friend or therapist what you are doing and how you are feeling, maybe ask them to be with you while you do a specific exercise or ask if you can speak to them afterwards about it. This can help create a 'container' for strong emotions – just knowing someone else is there to care and support you.

A Note for Survivors of Traumatic Histories

If you know or believe you have experienced childhood sexual abuse or physical punishment, sexual violence as an adult, or invasive medical procedures, the impact of doing this work may be more profound. The body does indeed remember, and can react to certain touches, smells, sounds, etc, often on a sensory level, rather than cognitive, perhaps outside our conscious awareness. Issues of self-care become even more important in these circumstances.

Recovery and reclaiming a sense of sexual self-esteem may involve several stages depending on each person's unique needs. Psychotherapeutic support is invaluable for the 'relational' aspects of betrayal and violation, and for the confusing and complex physical and sexual survival responses that people often experience during abuse.

By learning more about your own 'psychosexual processes' through these exercises, you can identify and remedy disruptions to your sexual ease. It may be helpful to do this work within a therapeutic relationship or with the support of friends, someone you feel safe with, to share any thoughts and feelings which may be evoked during your explorations.

Bodywork and a variety of complementary health therapies and spiritual practices can also help. Sexual healing can help people to thrive once again;

to reclaim a sense of sexual joy and playfulness and an enjoyment of intimacy and sharing, sexual love and pleasure.

One legacy of sexual violence is that strong feelings can get easily triggered; we can feel scared, confused or enraged if old traumas are re-stimulated. Through these exercises you can discover where you may still have disharmony due to your past. Memories will affect brain responses to stimuli. Physical sensations in your body or certain emotions may trigger you back into trauma. What goes on in your mind may cause distress. Usually, a combination of all of these! It is therefore useful to know how to check in with your nervous system; to understand a bit more about what is happening and to learn to 'apply the brakes'; taking some time to relax and soothe yourself. Triggers will cause automatic scanning of your memory centres; there may be a re-stimulation of any 'horrible history'. Learning to understand and manage your responses to your reflexes brings a reclaiming of your body.

It can be helpful to think about a 'Traffic Light' system, where at our most primal level we move in and out of three colour modes[2]:

Red: I'm in danger, I'm feeling numb, spacing out
Amber: I'm in fight or flight
Green: I'm feeling safe, calm and in connection with other/s

This is explained in more detail in Chapter 6 and there is more information about recovery from sexual trauma in Chapter 7.

First, we recommend you create your safe space as outlined earlier. Another idea is to create anchors to support your therapeutic work. Choose something or someone you associate with a feeling of safety, relief and well-being, physically and emotionally. For example, a favourite pet or person, a special object, a hobby or a place. Take some time to notice this sense of safety in your physical body and your thinking process. Imagine that if you feel unsettled or wobbly, this anchor can help to restabilise you and help you feel grounded again. You could do this before starting an exercise or go back to it during an exercise if you feel the need.

The next exercise has been developed by Rothschild (2000)[3] around working safely with recovery from trauma and is now a central aspect of trauma-informed therapy. If we get flooded by feelings, stress hormones activate the sympathetic nervous system. This can send us into overdrive causing 'hyper arousal' - an increase in heartbeat, rapid breathing and muscle tension (the word arousal can be used in the context of sexual arousal, but there are other arousal responses we will be exploring, like thirst or hunger, or anger, fear, sadness or happiness, joy, ecstasy; all part of the human sexual and relational experience). We can feel 'frozen', unable to move or speak. Our thinking process is impaired, and we may feel exposed and at risk (red traffic light).

We recommend you read through this exercise and practice *Applying the Brakes* before 'driving this car' – doing these sexploration exercises. This can then be used whenever the need arises. If you know or think you have trauma in your history, it is useful to practise until you can contain your anxieties, emotions and body sensations, *at will*.

It takes longer to bring the relaxing part of the nervous system back online than for the nervous system arousal to trigger – you need to slowly apply the brakes. You will not be able to think clearly, to choose the next step until you calm your body.

Exercise Applying the Brakes

You can start exploring this now. Just the fact of reading these pages probably means that the curiosity circuit in your brain has fired, causing an arousal of energy in your nervous system. Put your hands over your heart area and notice your heartbeat. And breathe –if you are holding your breath!

As you are doing the exercises pay attention to your heartbeat and breath, as they indicate levels of physiological arousal (which also happens when we feel joy or pleasure). If you are experiencing difficult or intense feelings; panic or anxiety, you need to 'apply the brakes'.

Imagine your feet firmly on the ground. It may help to sit down and take some deep breaths. Just keep focussing on breathing in and out, long slow out-breaths. You could imagine you are blowing the breath out through a straw. You will see how this slowing down can soothe how you feel. It can take some practice.

Narrowing your focus to the here and now helps to calm also. Notice your body sensations. Look around and notice what you see. Maybe say words out loud. Remind yourself you are in your safe space. Remember your anchor(s). Just keep focussing on your breathing; allow the breath in and slowly out, releasing any tension you are holding, particularly in your jaw, neck or shoulders.

Notice your thoughts – are they calming and soothing? If not, consider why you are saying mean things to yourself and try to be more kind. When you are ready, go back to the previous exercise and re-consider your safe space; make any alterations you may need. If necessary, it can be useful to consider this exercise again before you start each new chapter of the book.

Therapist Pat Ogden[4] offers a short exercise to help if you are feeling triggered. First, she recommends shaking; start with your hands and arms, then legs and torso, shake-shake-shake it out. Now stretch up, arms out and wide, fingers wide open, stretch, and stretch again. Now rock or sway, gently, slowly, side to side. This practice helps to bring the body back to physiological, and therefore emotional, regulation, helping you be able to think again.

Working Solo

Preparation

Imagine for a moment that you want to cook a nice meal. First you would decide what to make, then check you had the ingredients or shop for them. You may want to marinade, or chill or defrost something.

What would be the equivalent of preparing to start doing the exercises in this book?

- We have suggested the 'Creating a Safe Space' exercise above.
- Make yourself available – switch off phones and put aside other distractions.
- Attend to any bodily needs first (a drink, snack or the loo).
- Before you start, allow yourself a few deep breaths, a moment to arrive at your body and your feelings.
- You might want to set yourself an intention for a particular exercise – is there a question you have or a particular aspect of the exercise you would like to focus on?

Doing the Exercises

- Read the text and just notice what happens in your body, how does it make you think and feel?
- Try to catch your very first responses and be curious about them.
- During the exercises, allow yourself to wander into any thoughts and feelings, lean into them bringing an attitude of compassion and enquiry.
- If you feel overwhelmed at any point, just stop and take a few breaths. If you don't feel calmer after five minutes or so, go back to the exercise on *Applying the Brakes.*

Reflecting on the Exercises

You may want to make or buy yourself a special journal to write about the exercises in this book. Choose something that represents your sexuality. It may be about the cover, a picture, the colour or design. It may be about the paper inside, whether it has a lock or not or about how much it costs.

- You may prefer to express yourself through art, dance, music, sculpture or other creative means. Collect or buy the art and craft materials you may want to use.
- After each exercise sit back and spend some time thinking and reflecting on your experiences. Then write, draw or phone a friend, whatever feels right to you.
- Review what you have done; reflect on the words or phrases, colours or shapes. Does anything surprise you? Write about what you think and feel about what you have written.

Working with Partners

A major addition to this updated version of *LoveSex and Relationships* is the inclusion of exercises for those in relationships who wish to explore their sexual lives together. We would like to draw your attention to some of the challenges of doing such work and offer some suggestions to make this journey as smooth as possible. Many theories about intimate relationships were developed in regard to a two-person couple relationship. However, the principles can generally be extrapolated to those in consensual non-monogamous or polyamorous relationships, and we aim to include these relationship styles in this book.

Relationship Challenges

One of the biggest trials in relationships is managing our differences. These may be in many areas of our lives together, from seemingly incompatible desires about our shared sexual life to where we go on holiday, to what take-away to order. We may find that what was endearing in the early stages of getting to know someone has become deeply irritating. Frisson and passion are vital elements in romantic relationships, but we can find these energies hijacked into conflict.

John and Judy Gottman describe what they call *The Four Horsemen of the Apocalypse*[5] as detrimental elements in a relationship: criticism, contempt, defensiveness and stonewalling. High levels of criticism between partners are seen as a major predictor in relationship breakdown, and conversely, happy relationships have a high ratio (5:1 in Gottman's research) of positive to negative interactions.

Why Does This Happen?

Goldhor Lerner (1990)[6] describes intimacy as a dance: that we need to be two separate beings, able to tolerate our differences and trust that we will not be abandoned when we are in the place of separation. We need to be able to move together to make contact, and at times merge. In this place, we need to trust that in time we will separate and not become engulfed by the other. As partners dance their intimacy, they move in and out and between these three places, feeling comfortable (enough) in all. And clearly, this is not always easy.

Relationship therapist Esther Perel[7] says that eroticism thrives in the space between – that is, in the separateness between people. She posits that the current setup for many partners – being flatmates, and/or co-parents, and/or best friends (all Contact or Merger places, as shown in Figure 3.1) – makes it more difficult to be in the separation place needed to be lovers.

We know that our early childhood experiences set up an internal blueprint about relationships. Difficulties in attachment can undermine many aspects in intimate relationships, such as trust and jealousy, intimacy and commitment.[8]

There are four attachment styles:

- Secure – we may have learnt that in general, relationships are safe and secure, and others can be relied upon.
- Dismissive-avoidant – we may have felt unloved or rejected so we become more avoidant of contact with others.
- Anxious-preoccupied – we may have sometimes felt we could rely on our caregivers, and other times not, giving us a preoccupation with our relationships, and an anxiety about them.
- Fearful-avoidant (disorganised) – our caregivers were frightening; we may have very little stability in the way we relate to others.

Although these blueprints are set in childhood, other relationships will influence us and attachment patterns can change. Most adults will have some of all of these patterns in varying degrees. To understand more about this for yourself, you might want to do Diane Poole Heller's adult attachment quiz.[9]

Bader and Pearson[10] say that after the initial merger phase of a relationship, where we are hopefully creating a secure foundation, we then need to move into *differentiating* – we need to become more comfortable with our

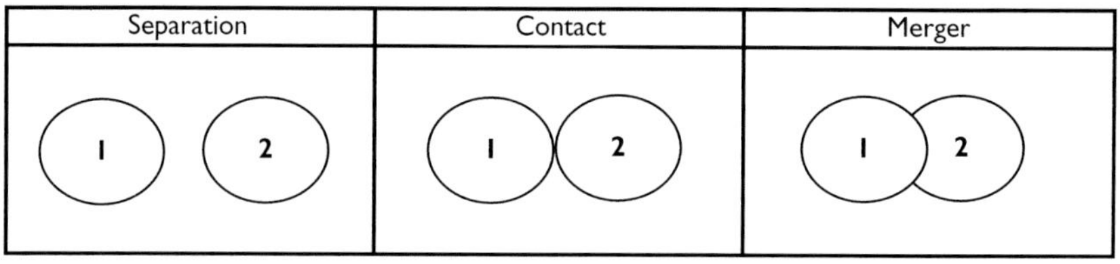

Separation	Contact	Merger
① ②	① ②	①②

Figure 3.1 The Dance of Intimacy.

differences again. They believe that if we don't manage to differentiate, we will become stuck in one of two predictable ways:

- Conflict avoidance – where we avoid intensity and conflict (not good for sex); or
- Hostile dependence – where we get stuck in anger and conflict (and use our fire energy for fighting rather than the erotic).

They remind us that relationships also face challenges due to life events. This could be around children: fertility issues, birth, adoption, ill health, parenting differences, children leaving home, etc. It could also be around change: moving house, gender transition, new work; or around loss: the death of a parent or child, or other significant bereavement, serious illness or the loss of a job or a home. As a dance of intimacy, being in a relationship requires movement and adaptation to change. On a day-to-day basis many relationships are in the throes of, or adjusting to, changes like those mentioned earlier or sexual difficulties, menopause, illness, medication, work, extended family/caring responsibilities, money struggles, redundancies. Consensually non-monogamous relationships potentially both demand and foster a particularly high degree of differentiation and self-responsibility. For more on this, see Kauppi (2021)[11] who builds on the Bader-Pearson differentiation work with particular regard to non-monogamy.

We like the Orange Example from the Conflict Resolution Network.[12] Two people are in a kitchen where there is only one orange left and both of them want it. Does one have to win, and one lose? They might compromise and have half each. Or they tell each other more: one wants to grate the rind of the orange to flavour a cake, the other wants to squeeze it to make orange juice. By sharing their needs with each other, they may find they are complementary, and they can both have what they want.

Hendrix and LaKelly Hunt[13] say that a power struggle is an inevitable element in relationships, and further, that on an unconscious level, we choose partners who will trigger our childhood wounding. Many therapists believe that as these wounds develop in relationship (with our caregivers), they can be best healed in relationship: we are adults now, who have the power of communication and the right to negotiate, which we do not have as (emotionally) dependent children. This offers an opportunity for personal development and for a deepening of our abilities for intimacy. So, rather than seeing our partner as 'the problem', we are offered the challenge to address our own difficulties with intimacy.

We could consider a relationship as a vessel that holds people within it. We may be out on the sea in a beautiful lagoon, on a calm day. We may drift and find ourselves out in a choppy sea, or indeed with a storm brewing. We may need to hunker down and survive. The robustness of our vessel will be important.

Exercise Relationship Quiz

Separately, each of you respond to the statements below with your first thoughts as either:

Rarely/Never, Sometimes or Usually/Often

> *I am a good listener*
> *I am able to express my needs*
> *I am good at negotiating*
> *I have good empathy and compassion*
> *I show appreciation to my partner/s*
> *I am critical of myself*
> *I am critical of my partner/s*
> *I don't like to show my vulnerability*
> *I get angry and fight with my partner/s*
> *I get defensive when people ask me questions*

Then sit back and individually look over what you have answered and notice how you think and feel about your answers. After ten minutes, share your answers and talk about what you think and feel.

What Can We Do?

Eric Fromm[14] declared that love is an art which must be developed and practised with commitment and humility, requiring knowledge, courage and effort. He says it requires the practice of four essential elements[15]:

- **Care** – a concern for the welfare of the relationship, including a commitment of time and effort.
- **Responsibility** – a willingness to respond to physical and psychological needs of our partners.
- **Respect** – the need for differentiation – the ability to experience love is based on the individual's commitment to the freedom and autonomy of both [all] partners.
- **Knowledge** – of the other, not of our own perspectives or concerns.

There are many online resources to support this. Take a look at the websites of the Gottmans,[16] Bader and Pearson,[17] and Harville and Helen Hendrix,[18] the latter having developed the Imago Dialogue[19] to help couples communicate.

Conscious Communication

We have taken the Imago Dialogue as a basis and developed it to create the 'Conscious Communication' tool for you to use in your relationships, or if you are a relationship counsellor, with your clients. The idea behind this tool is that people are taking it in turns so both/all will get heard, and listening to listen, rather than to respond.

Conscious Communication has two roles: the *Speaker* and the *Listener.* If there are three of you, you can add an Observer role and swap around. Whatever time you have for this process should be divided equally. If you have an hour and two people, thirty minutes each in the Speaker role, or three people, twenty minutes each in that role.

At first, this may seem formulaic and contrived. The ultimate goal is to keep things structured enough that each party feels heard and understood. Once people understand and are able to use the core skills, the actual wording/sentence become less important.

The Speaker is the one who has a topic they want to discuss, and asks someone to be their Listener. They should first ask, *are you available for a chat?* The potential Listener replies, *Yes, ok,* or *not now but I will be ... .*

The Speaker talks from the perspective of *I feel ..., I think ...* rather than *You ... .* This minimises the need for the person listening to be defensive. Ultimately each party can hear the other and begin to uncover the unmet need underneath any upset, so it eventually becomes possible to assertively and lovingly, make a request for change.

Conscious Communication has three stages:

1   **Mirror** – where the Listener echoes back what they've heard from the Speaker and checks they have heard correctly.
2   **Validate** – where the Listener bears witness by verbally acknowledging the Speaker's experience.
3   **Empathise** – where the Listener offers empathy to their partner – that they understand why the Speaker (being who they are) thinks and feels the way they do. For example: *I imagine you may be feeling scared/ angry/ hurt......*

Once this is complete, swap over and the new Speaker now gets to share what they were thinking and feeling *while listening to and focussing on their partner.* They do not introduce a new topic.

The empathy and validation from the Listener can feel so reparative. They don't have to fix anything; they just have to be there. This kind of active listening is a good skill to develop. When we listen attentively and reflect back without judgement and advice, other people feel not only heard but valued. This allows us to move onto Requests for Change, which are realistic and more likely to be implemented.

If you consider that your relationship is not robust enough yet for these sexplorations, you could practise learning Active Listening skills in stages. We recommend you start with an appreciation of each other.

Exercise Sharing an Appreciation

Practice the first stage until you are both good at it, then move onto the second stage.

Stage 1

Have five minutes each where the Speaker says one sentence about what or how they appreciate the other. The Listener repeats back. Then the Speaker adds another sentence, 'Because what it makes me feel/think is ...'. The Listener repeat back. Continue until the time is up. Swap roles.

Stage 2

Have ten minutes each to share a Frustration that you have – but NOT with or about each other. This time the Speaker shares no more than three sentences at a time, and the Listener repeats back and asks, 'Did I get the gist of what you were saying?' If not, the Speaker clarifies until they do, or time is up. Continue until the time is up. Swap roles.

Talk about what this was like – to offer an appreciation and to receive one. How easy or difficult was each role for you?

Figure 3.2 is an example of how to use the dialogue.

Summary of Working with Partners

- Each do the solo exercises separately.
- For a day, each think over what you experienced doing the exercise and what you have learnt about yourself.
- Read the Partner exercise and choose what is most important to share or focus on with your partner.
- Explicitly agree when and where you will do an exercise together. Agree on time frames before you start and set an alarm.
- Read and apply the Preparation section for Working Solo above.
- Use the Conscious Communication dialogue format to share your thoughts and feelings, especially if any exercise becomes difficult.
- Be compassionate towards yourself and your partner/s, especially towards your vulnerabilities.

SPEAKER

Are you available for a chat?

LISTENER

Yes, what do you want to talk about?

SAYS ONLY 2 OR 3 SENTENCES AT A TIME

I felt upset yesterday when you didn't message to say you would be late. We had agreed to have dinner together at 7, and I'd rushed to do extra shopping for a nice meal. And you didn't get home till 11 pm. No message. I was scared something had happed.

---

1. MIRROR

REPEAT BACK LITERALLY WHAT THE SPEAKER SAID - (NOT INTERPRETATIONS, RESPONSES, OR OWN CONTENT)

WHEN YOU HAVE FINISHED MIRRORING ASK

Did I get the gist of that, did I get it right?

Yes, mostly right but I want you to get most was that I felt scared when you were so late with no word from you.

IF CORRECTED, THEN REPEAT MIRRORING STAGE AGAIN

Then after you have confirmed you heard and mirrored correctly, ask

Is there more about that?

Yes, when that happens, I also feel so unsure what to do. I want to just keep calling you, then I get angry and don't want to see you, then I'm terrified something happened to you.

So, what I heard that time was…

Did I get that correctly?

Figure 3.2 Conscious Communication Dialogue.

**IF THERE IS MORE, MIRROR AS ABOVE AND CONTINUE UNTIL IT IS TIME
TO SWAP OR SPEAKER DOESN'T HAVE MORE TO SHARE**

> Is there more about that? Does that remind you of anything from your childhood?

> *Yes, it reminds me of ...*

*Repeat previous stages of mirroring and checking out until there is no more
to share or you have reached the time allotted for each person*

SUMMARISE

*SHORT OVERALL SUMMARY OF
WHAT THE SPEAKER HAS SHARED*

> Did I get everything?

> Yes - OR-You missed the bit about.... – OR - Yes, mostly but also.….

---

2. VALIDATE

*SPEAKER ACCEPTS THE
VALIDATION OR CLARIFIES*

> I can understand why you feel the way you do, it makes sense to me because...
> – OR, *if you still feel confused ask*
>
> Can you tell me more about…, clarify…

(*continued*)

3. EMPATHISE

SPEAKER LISTENS AND RECEIVES THE EMPATHY

I can imagine that you might be feeling... or have felt....or wanted....

Is that right?

Yes, you got that all thanks.

OR - I think I felt more.....

CONTINUING MIRRORING, VALIDATING AND EMPATHISING UNTIL IT IS TIME TO SWAP OR SPEAKER FEELS HEARD

Thank you for really listening and understanding

Thank you for sharing

WHEN YOU SWAP THE NEW SPEAKER TALKS ABOUT WHAT THEY FELT AND THOUGHT ABOUT WHAT THE OTHER HAS JUST SHARED. IF YOU WANT TO TALK ABOUT A DIFFERENT TOPIC THEN ASK FOR ANOTHER DIALOGUE

- Leave out any exercises that don't feel right for you. Feel free to adapt them in any way that suits you better.
- These exercises will be specific to the moment when you do them. You may want to regularly review or update any shared lists or agreements you make.

Overall, this series of sexploration exercises is about our relationship to our own bodies and our own sexuality, to our own sexual beliefs and behaviours. This informs us, and so allows a more conscious choice about the sexual relationships we engage in. Doing this in partnership with a lover or lovers can really take your relationship to a new depth.

At the heart of these exercises is a model for psychosexual health, where we can feel proud about our sexuality and have a nutritious and healthy sexual self-esteem. This includes mental, physical, social and emotional aspects of sexuality. When we have a sex affirmative attitude that honours our sexual capacity and abilities, we can see our human sexual potential as a life force which offers love, creativity and pleasure; all vital aspects of being human. These exercises are an opportunity to update your sexual knowledge, both generally and personally, and to evaluate your relationship to your sexuality.

Notes

1 Grigg, K. (2021). 'Record Rise in Young Adults Living with Their Parents', *Richard Nelson LLP*, 20 April. Available at: https://www.richardnelsonllp.co.uk/record-number-young-adults-living-with-parents/ (Accessed: 29 August 2022).
2 Spring, C. (2015). 'The Trauma Traffic Light', *Carolyn Spring*, 1 June. Available at: https://www.carolynspring.com/blog/the-trauma-traffic-light/ (Accessed: 29 August 2022).
3 Rothschild, B. (2000). *The Body Remembers*. New York: W. W. Norton.
4 Ogden, P. (2021). *The Pocket Guide to Sensorimotor Psychotherapy in Context*. US: W.W. Norton; Sensorimotor Psychotherapy Institute. (2022). *Pat Ogden, PhD*. Available at: https://sensorimotorpsychotherapy.org/therapist-directory/pat-ogden-phd/ (Accessed: 19 August 2020).
5 The Gottman Institute. (2022). *Couples*. Available at: https://www.gottman.com/couples/ (Accessed: 6 September 2022); Lisitsa, E. (2013). 'The Four Horsemen: Criticism, Contempt, Defensiveness, and Stonewalling', *The Gottman Institute*, 23 April. Available at: https://www.gottman.com/blog/the-four-horsemen-recognizing-criticism-contempt-defensiveness-and-stonewalling/ (Accessed: 16 August 2022).
6 Goldhor Lerner, H. (1990). *The Dance of Intimacy*. Ontario, Canada: Pandora.
7 Perel, E. (2007). *Mating in Captivity*. USA: Hodder & Stoughton.
8 Wu, J. (2020) 'How Does Your Attachment Style Impact Your Relationships?', *Psychology Today*, 8 April. Available at: https://www.psychologytoday.com/us/blog/the-savvy-psychologist/202004/how-does-your-attachment-style-impact-your-relationships (Accessed: 4 September 2022).
9 Poole Heller, D. (2022). *Attachment Styles Test*. Available at: https://dianepooleheller.com/attachment-test/ (Accessed: 16 August 2022).
10 Couples Institute. (2022). *For Couples*. Available at: https://www.couplesinstitute.com/for-couples/ (Accessed: 19 August 2020).
11 Kauppi, M. (2021). *Polyamory: A Clinical Toolkit for Therapists (and Their Clients)*. Rowman & Littlefield.
12 Conflict Resolution Network. (2020). 'Conflict Is the Stuff of Life'. Available at: https://www.crnhq.org/cr-kit/ (Accessed: 29 August 2022).
13 Hendrix, H. (1993). *Getting the Love You Want: a Guide for Couples*. London: Pocket Books; Hendrix, H. (1995). *Keeping the Love You Find*. London: Pocket Books.
14 Fromm, E. (1995). *The Art of Loving*. Thorson: New Ed edition.
15 O'Dwyer, K. (2011). 'Can We Learn How to Love? An Exploration of Eric Fromm's The Art of Loving', *Self and Society*, 39(2).
16 Lisitsa, E. (no date). 'The Four Horsemen: The Antidotes', *The Gottman Institute*, no date. Available at: https://www.gottman.com/blog/the-four-horsemen-the-antidotes/ (Accessed: 19 August 2022).

17 Couples Institute. (2022). *For Couples*. Available at: https://www.couplesinstitute. com/for-couples/ (Accessed 19 August 2020).

18 Harville and Helen. (no date). Available at: https://harvilleandhelen.com/ (Accessed: 19 August 2022).

19 Imagoworks. (no date). *Imago Dialogue: The Basic Steps*. Available at: http:// imagoworks.com/the-imago-dialogue/steps/ (Accessed: 19 August 2022).

Chapter 4

Mind

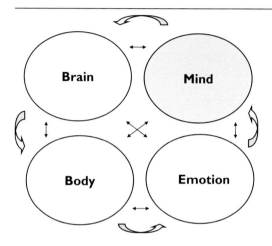

The Thinking Brain

Sex educator Emily Nagoski[1] says the most common theme in all the questions she is asked about sex is basically, 'Am I normal'? Or in other words, 'Is it OK to like what I like, and want what I want'?

This book – and the Homeodynamic Model on which it is based – responds to these questions by addressing the interplay between our biological urges and our social conditioning, our bodies and our feelings. Clearly, all these facets inter-relate with one another. However, it is easier to understand them if we first separate them out.

In the Homeodynamic Model, we distinguish between the **brain** and the **mind**. What we refer to as the brain is the reactive or limbic system, devoted to survival reactions like fight and flight. These are our instinctual defensive reactions, programmed from back when humans shared the planet with sabre-toothed tigers. If in danger, we needed a quick-fire response. The Brain is explored in Chapter 6.

As humans we also have frontal lobes in our brain, developed to give us the capacity to think; to reflect on our feelings and urges. This is what we

DOI: 10.4324/9781003322405-5

refer to as the mind. To understand the difference, consider the following example: we see a tiger. Our reactive brain causes our heart to beat faster. Once the frontal lobes (mind) process the fact that we are in a zoo and the tiger is fenced off, our heart will begin to slow down. Of course, all of this happens in nanoseconds.

This chapter focuses on the mind – our beliefs, values and social conditioning around sex. By becoming more mindful and more aware of our thinking, we can make more conscious choices as sexual beings. This ability to reflect gives us a consciousness and allows us to choose and decide on our behaviour, as in Figure 4.1. We make many decisions every day, mediating between how we feel; our urges, and what we do; how we act. We may not feel like getting up for work on a chilly morning, but we do; we may feel like crying or shouting at someone but decide for various reasons not to; and we

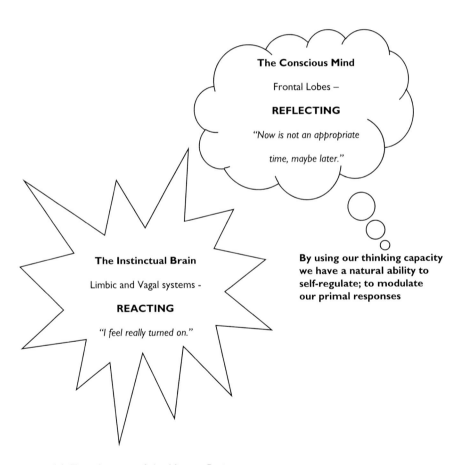

Figure 4.1 Two Aspects of the Human Brain.

may feel a sexual urge but be aware that it is not an appropriate time or place to act on that desire. This is an important distinction for psychosexual work as the sexual arousal process is a reflexive reaction from the instinctual brain. This is mediated by many aspects of the reflective mind, explored and discussed in this section.

First Thoughts

Solo Exercise

*What do you **think** about sex? Write down the first three words that come to mind when you think about sex and sexuality. Try to catch, not censor your very first thoughts – your mind talk.*

Sex:

1

2

3

Sexuality:

1

2

3

Reflect on what you have written.

Exercise with Partner/s

When you have each done the solo exercise by yourselves, chat together about the words you have each used. Has anything surprised you? Discuss what you like or do not like about what you have written, and each choose three words for sex and for sexuality that suit who you are now and/or would like to become.

Internal Dialogue

By becoming more conscious about our mind-talk or internal dialogue, we become clearer about what we do think, why we think it and also the quality of how we speak to ourselves. Do we talk to ourselves in a bullying voice, constantly moaning and telling ourselves off, or in a wise voice, gently guiding, helping us to see our mistakes and giving advice about how to improve things for next time? For example, if we ask for something we want but get rejected, do we tell ourselves that we were stupid for wanting it in the first place or crazy for believing we deserved it; or do we feel our disappointment; re-evaluate whether we do still want this thing, and if we do, perhaps go somewhere else to ask for it? We will discuss in more detail in Chapter 6, how child developmental phases are the building blocks of healthy self-esteem and supportive inner dialogue, and how our own specific histories will have supported or damaged our perceptions and abilities as adults. A critical inner voice is often a greater source of distress than the emotions; what we tell ourselves about what we are feeling and whether it is acceptable to have such feelings causes more anguish than the emotion itself.

There are many psychological models for understanding inner dialogue. One of our favourites is the Transactional Analysis Ego States model developed by Eric Berne (1961).[2] The idea is basically that we have three aspects to our personality: **parent**, **child** and **adult**. The parent includes conditioning and socialisation; beliefs about what we *should* do. The child is seen to include our natural spontaneous reactions – emotions, feelings, needs and desires – and is related to our past, our childhood. The adult aspect is seen as the part of us capable of making informed choices: we are able to process the information from our parent and child parts; think and reflect and make decisions about our behaviour.

The parent part can have two aspects: **nurturing**, which is educative, caring, supportive and helpful, or **controlling**, which is critical, bullying and judgemental. Children who grow up in nurturing environments, with their basic needs met, will develop a strong free child, who loves to play, feels free to be a child but who will also respect boundaries and co-operate with the adults in their lives. Children who do not grow up in nurturing environments will become 'wounded' and their child part can become **adapted** – either **withdrawn**: passive, conformist and manipulative in order to get their needs met, or **rebellious**: angry, fighting and anti-authoritarian.

How we dialogue internally between the reactive and reflective aspects within ourselves will also be mirrored in our interactions with others. If we have a strong inner critic, we will often be quite critical of others and probably lack the good negotiation and communication skills vital for maintaining sexual relationships. In contrast, the adult position is being assertive, having self-awareness and an ability to 'manage' our feelings.

We need to know what we feel and think before we can communicate and negotiate with others.

The good news is that this can change, with awareness and personal development. A sense of empowerment and inner self-esteem can come from being more mindful; choosing our beliefs, accepting our feelings as reactions and responses and using our mind to reflect, evaluate and then choose, as much as possible, how we want to behave.

Inner Critic

Solo Exercise

Take five minutes to think about your 'mind talk' in a general sense. Notice your internal dialogue and how it is you talk to yourself. What sort of words do you use; are they kind or critical? What about the tone of your words? Say some common phrases that you use out loud, what is it like to hear them? Evaluate whether you think the quality of your self-reflection is useful or bullying and critical.

Choose one thing you criticise yourself about sexually and see whether there could be a different phrase or comment, or way of thinking about it that could be more helpful to you.

Exercise with Partner/s

Each do the exercise alone about yourselves. Then consider (alone) your mind-talk about each other – the words, language and tone of voice.

Each think about how you could be more assertive and clear, and also kinder and more compassionate with each other. Discuss what you have discovered.

Beliefs

We have many social, cultural and religious belief systems about human sexuality, which have historically been steeped in shame and taboo. Until very recently the influences of the major monotheistic religions have limited approval of sexual expression to within (heterosexual) marriage. We have religious beliefs and laws about sexual behaviour which traditionally espouse a reproductive model of sex – that real sex *is* heterosexual intercourse, to be practiced within the institution of marriage. Many people define loss of virginity as having experienced heterosexual intercourse and in slang, 'doing it' means experiencing penetration. Until 2003, the crime of rape was defined solely as non-consensual penis-to-vaginal penetration. It now includes any type of non-consensual penetration to any orifice.

Most children's first introduction to the world of human sexuality is about reproduction; about something that adults do to make babies. Sex education in schools has, certainly until recently, focused on avoiding pregnancy and sexually transmitted infections (STIs), rather than on pleasure and consent. This again supports the belief that sex is heterosexual intercourse or penis-in-vagina (PIV) sex. A notable exception to this kind of sex education is found in the books of Corey Silverberg[3] and websites such as bishuk.com[4] and scarleteen.com.[5]

Not reflecting on what we believe, where we got those beliefs from and how they influence us can lead us to think that others share our beliefs and that they are actually facts rather than opinions. What we were taught and what we believe now will be unconsciously influencing our sexual behaviour. So, let us stop and think about our sexual values: what each of us really finds valuable about our sexual desires; what we want emotionally and relationally from sex; how we would like to express ourselves as sexual beings; what makes us feel good, not just in the moment, but ongoingly.

Sexual Beliefs

Solo Exercise

Write down something/s that you believe about the following – go with your first thoughts:

> *My Sexuality ...*
> *Women and Sex ...*
> *Men and Sex ...*
> *Trans/Non-binary People and Sex ...*
> *Sexual Identity ...*
> *Sexual Relationships ...*
> *Straight People ...*
> *Gay People ...*
> *Bi- and Pansexual People ...*
> *Asexual People ...*

Review what you have written; reflect on the words or phrases. Does anything surprise you? Explore how you feel about your comments.

Exercise with Partner/s

Together, create a new page outlining what you choose to believe together now.

Sexual Language

How we think about sexuality is also influenced by language; the language we were taught as children and the words and concepts we use culturally. Even though sex seems to be everywhere in our culture, we are still surprisingly embarrassed and uneducated, not at ease with acknowledging and discussing this aspect of our humanity.

Our first introduction to the word sex is probably in response to us asking where babies come from. School sex education starts with the biology of reproduction; about grown-ups 'making love'; about a man and a woman having sexual intercourse. With children, we may reflect our discomfort with sex by using euphemisms for sexual body parts, such as willy and fanny. As adults, sexual organs can be described in a clinical, medical way (penis, vagina, clitoris), by using a more porny kind of language (pussy, cock) or with swear words (dick, cunt). It is interesting that calling someone a prick or a dickhead implies (somewhat affectionate) stupidity, while 'cunt' implies serious contempt. Calling a woman a whore or a slut is still a way to police her sexual expression, whereas for men, 'slut' or 'stud' is often perceived as a good or at least a funny comment. However, things are changing, through cultural challenges to 'slut-shaming' and the reclamation of this and other slurs and swearwords.

To complicate things further, we have words that are used interchangeably but mean different things to different people. For example, the word *sex* may be used to mean biological sex or a sexual act. The word *sexuality* is often used regarding minority sexual orientations, as if everyone did not have a sexuality. The phrase *sexual health* usually refers to sexually transmitted *infections*. It can be hard to talk about sex when you do not have a language you feel comfortable with, so it is worth thinking about what language feels good to you.

We implicitly teach our children that sex is for procreation; that sex is something that we *do* – we have sex; we make love *to* someone. Thinking about 'our sexuality' allows us to see it as an expression of ourselves and our personality; as something that we *are*. It is important to be able to separate our sexual feelings and our sexual behaviour, where feelings come from the reactive brain and choices about our behaviour emanate from our mind. Seeing our sexuality as something we can express in many more ways than sexual intercourse allows us to explore our sexual desires and attractions in a new way.

Sexual Knowledge

Solo Exercise

Explore the following statements:

What I learnt about sex as a child was …

Please note: *If you have experienced sexual abuse and/or inappropriate sexualisation as a child – or teenager – this may be a complex and upsetting question. Give yourself time.*

Instead you may want to explore what you wish you had learnt.

What I learnt about sex as a teenager was …

What I have learnt about sex as an adult is …

Reflect on what you have written and then write:

What I want to know about sex is …

Exercise with Partner/s

Compare the lists you have written individually. Notice the differences and similarities and discuss what you have discovered.

Each identify one thing you want to know about sex and research together.

Together, create a new page outlining what you choose to believe together now.

Sexual Culture

We all have a sexual culture inherited from our family and community. However, white culture is often portrayed as the (idealised) norm, when we actually live in a multi-ethnic, multi-racial and multi-cultural society with diverse beliefs and attitudes. That cultural diversity can include ideas about marriage, relationships, gender roles and sex. In *Black Identities & White Therapies: Race, respect and diversity*, Charura and Lago[6] remind us how white thinking permeates much psychotherapy theory, for example, with its focus on the inner life of the individual. Dwight Turner[7] points out how this serves to therapise social issues and keep them out of the political arena.

Hawkins and Neves[8] identify seven elements of culture, all of which may affect how people of colour view their sexuality differently than those from a western, individualistic perspective:

- Social organisation
- Customs and traditions
- Religion
- Language – bi+ lingual/dialects
- Arts and literature – heritage (national heritage)
- Forms of government
- Economic systems

McKenzie-Mavinga (2016)[9] describes how the sexuality of Black people has been pathologised, stereotyped and demonised by white patriarchal views, and that Asian sexuality has been perceived on the basis of exoticism and religious mythology. She reminds us that many Asian families uphold taboos about virginity, sex before marriage, common law relationships and intermarrying outside of cultural norms and traditional laws, and how this can cause emotional conflict for those at odds with their peer group.

In Britain, we live in a highly sexualised culture where images are widely displayed in our media and sex is alluded to often. We are also, paradoxically, still very shame-bound as a culture with a pervasive lack of ease about our sexuality. One reaction to this background, and perhaps an attempt to overcome it, is a new cultural shamelessness; a notion that really liberated people are having a wild time sexually, doing everything and anything, all the time. It is a quite different thing for people to consciously choose as expressive a sexual life as they want and for them to feel ashamed or frigid for not wanting to engage in certain sexual behaviours.

Over the last fifteen years, there has been a revolution in adolescent access to online pornography due to the proliferation of smartphones. Surveys of the effects of porn consumption on young people paint a complex picture. A 2020 NSPCC report[10] found that about half of sixteen to seventeen-year-olds had recently viewed pornography, although the researchers stated this was likely to be a major underestimation due to their awkwardness in answering the question. Pornographic material is being accessed more through social media platforms like Snapchat and Instragram than through dedicated porn sites.

Many studies find that heterosexual pornographic material portrays problematic relationships between the sexes. For example, Davis et al. (2018)[11] found that 70% of scenes viewed showed men being dominant over women, and 11% featured non-consensual violence towards women. This may spill over into behaviour and sexual scripts, with Dr Elly Hanson (PHSE, 2020)[12] stating that 'longitudinal controlled studies following adolescents or young adults over time have found pornography consumption predictive of subsequent sexual coercion and aggression'.

Many teenagers now report getting their primary information about sex from internet pornography and taking these unrealistic impressions as 'normal'. The bodies displayed in most porn are incredibly unrealistic – for example, abnormally large penises which are always erect. There are rarely views of flaccid penises or foreskins, what they look like or their more realistic size. Breasts are large and silicone enhanced, and vulvas look like they belong to a prepubescent girl. The focus on penetration in pornography encourages the myth that 'real sex' is penetration and undermines the fact that the clitoris is a woman's sexual organ. The depiction of women being orgasmic through the penetration of various orifices is also highly unrealistic. The focus on sexual acts rarely addresses safer sex, nor educates people about negotiating sexual encounters or relationships. A campaign spearheaded by the US AIDS Healthcare Foundation resulted in a 2012 Los Angeles County law requiring that condoms be used during porn film shots; however, in 2016, a move to extend this across the state was voted down.

On the other hand, many young people are somewhat porn-literate and often aware that the material they are watching is not 'realistic', understanding it as a form of entertainment and fantasy. Also, some studies indicate that for LGBTQ young people, porn can provide a means of representation and validation of their sexuality. Sex educator Justin Hancock takes the view that young people are bound to watch porn, and what is important is how they understand it. His website[13] has great guidance for teens on becoming porn-literate.

What impact does all this have on our experience of our sexuality, our sexual practices and our sexual self-esteem? How realistic are our current beliefs and images about looking, and therefore being sexy? A chronic lack of self-esteem about body image is expressed by both men and women,[14] in comparison to the images of ultra-thin celebrities and air-brushed glamour models. In 2020, a meta-analysis by Paslakis, Bractis and Mestre-Bach[15] found that 'Compelling evidence shows that frequency of pornography exposure is associated with negatively perceived body image and sexual body image'.

Who Taught You?

Solo Exercise

Think about what you have written above and consider more explicitly who helped to inform you about sex and sexuality.

> *What I learnt from my parents or carers …*
> *What I learnt from extended family …*
> *What I learnt from religion …*
> *What I learnt from my siblings or peer group …*
> *What I learnt from porn, social media, the movies, books …*
> *What I have learnt from my own experience …*

Reflect on what you have written. Has anything surprised you? Contemplate and re-evaluate. Which of your beliefs feel right for you now? Are some outmoded? Identify one belief you want to change.

> ### Exercise with Partner/s
>
> *Share with each other the lists you have written individually. Tell your partner/s one belief that you now want to change. Ask them what they think about your belief. Ask for their help/support/ideas about how you could change this belief. You may want to accept their thoughts, or not.*

Sex and Reproduction

As we have said, the distinction between our sexual and reproductive functioning is not made explicit. Yes, humans do reproduce through having sexual intercourse, but humans do not have sex just to reproduce.

Humans frequently engage in sexual intercourse when conception is not even possible; adult females are not fertile for most of their adult life, as we will explain in Chapter 5. There is also a huge repertoire of sexual behaviours other than intercourse that people engage in which include kissing, cuddling, playing, masturbating yourself or another, oral and anal sex and same-sex activity.[16] A quick analysis of any average one hundred sexual acts on any one day shows us that our biological reproductive chances are surprisingly low. Since the 1950s, researchers[17] have claimed that probably only one in nine sexual acts have been heterosexual intercourse. This would leave only ten sexual acts that could have resulted in a conception. A recent study[18] showed that in 2017 around 75% of people in Great Britain use contraception, lowering the odds to two and a half chances of a conception from any average one hundred sexual acts.

Clearly people have benefited from contraception by being free to have intercourse at any time without much risk of pregnancy. However, rather than utilising our knowledge that women are only fertile for a brief time each cycle, we have developed a range of contraception to interrupt the natural hormonal cycle, many with side effects. Bennett and Pope (2008)[19] explore many of the physical health and psychological issues surrounding the contraceptive pill, including a range of wider social issues. They raise the question: how do we regard and respect our fertility? Shapiro[20] argues that women get to feel that their fertility is a liability, in the way of sexual availability. She says the best contraceptives are seen as those which do not 'interfere' with lovemaking, perhaps part of our romantic view that sex should be 'spontaneous'. It also promotes the idea that sex should include PIV intercourse and ejaculation. One consequence is to push aside conscious choices around sexual behaviours that could lead to pregnancy. Another is to undermine our awareness of practicing safer sex to reduce the chances of STIs.

Your Fertility

Solo Exercise

Think about your experiences of your fertility.

Have you been pregnant when you did not plan to be? How did you feel, what did you do, how do you feel now? Are you wanting to conceive and finding that difficult or undergoing fertility treatment? What is your experience of this? Have you lost a pregnancy or had a stillbirth? Are you experiencing menopause? What has been your experience of using contraception?

And for those with male reproductive capacities, how do you feel about your fertility? What experiences have you had of someone becoming pregnant with your child or with any of the issues mentioned above?

Explore your current feelings about your experiences and what impact they have had on how you currently view your fertility.

Consider how your views and experiences of fertility impact your sense of your sexuality and your sexual behaviour.

Exercise with Partner/s

Discuss together how your individual views and experiences of fertility and contraception impact your relationship now. Think about how you could care for this aspect in your relationship, if relevant.

The Pleasure Principle

If we think about how many thousands of babies are being born daily, we can get a scale of how many millions of sexual acts humans are engaging in. What are the motivations or needs of all these other non-reproductive sexual acts?

In an article called, *Why Humans Have Sex*, Meston and Buss[21] identified two hundred and thirty-seven reasons why people have sex. These were ranked as physical reasons, including stress reduction, pleasure, physical desirability and experience seeking. There were goal attainment factors including resources, social status, revenge and utilitarianism. The emotional factors included love, commitment and expression. There were also three insecurity subfactors including self-esteem boost, duty/pressure and mate guarding.

What we are taught about pleasure, sexual intimacy and our sexuality, as distinct from reproductive abilities, is limited. Our goal-orientated view of sex implies a progression through activities; some desirable, some only to pave the way and allow for penetration/intercourse and thrusting, which should lead to (male) ejaculation/orgasm. This marginalises other sexual orientations and minimises the many other satisfying sexual behaviours people engage in, as 'just foreplay' or somehow lesser than the real thing. It encourages the belief about sex as something we do, rather than about being a sexual person. A circular view of sex (see Figure 4.2) allows us to flow in and out of whichever behaviours we are in the mood for, in whichever order we choose, bringing and allowing for creativity and spontaneity in our sexual encounters. In this way, we might think of sex as a delicious buffet of tempting 'foods' (activities, ways of being sexual), rather than a three-course meal.

Having 'a sexuality', being a sexual being, includes a desire for pleasure and often a desire for other. It hooks our curiosity and our desire to play and have fun. Sexual desire is a reflex; a sexual energy charge in the body, causing many physiological changes and feelings and emotions. By becoming more conscious of our desires, what turns us on and what turns us off, physically, emotionally and psychologically, we become more aware of our feelings about these desires. When we are also more conscious about our values and beliefs about sexuality, we can consider options and make choices about which ways of expressing ourselves and which sexual behaviours will enhance our sexual self-esteem. Connecting more with the idea of being sexual and of sexuality as a subjective experience, we can see how objectifying our current perceptions are.

In The Erotic Mind, Jack Morin[22] contends that attraction plus obstacles equals excitement. His book gives us permission to explore our peak sexual experiences and favourite fantasies for what it is that most turns us on. His 'sexual excitement survey' and the responses he received helped him set out four main 'cornerstones of eroticism', namely: longing and anticipation, violating prohibition, searching for power and overcoming ambivalence.

Figure 4.2 Circular View of Sexual Play.

Best and Worst Experiences

Solo Exercise

*Please note: this exercise may trigger memories, thoughts and feelings about non-consensual experiences. If so, take some time to address this by going back to the exercise '**Applying the Brakes**'. Take time to think and choose if and when you want to do this exercise.*

*Note down your three best **consensual** sexual experiences:*

1

2

3

*Note down your three worst **consensual** sexual experiences:*

1

2

3

Notice the memories; what images are triggered, what body sensations and what feelings? When you have noticed your reactive responses, take your attention to what you are thinking. Take some time to think about the differences. Is it about where you were, who you were with, what you did and what happened to you? Is there anything that you realise now that you did not then?

Write down three things about your best sexual experience that made it so good:

1

2

3

Exercise with Partner/s

Using the Conscious Communication dialogue, tell each other about one of your worst consensual sexual experiences; specifically what it was about it that made it not good for you.

We suggest you limit this to thirty minutes each. Make sure you Validate and Empathise with each other.

Have a break of at least twenty minutes, then tell each other about your best sexual experiences and what made them so good.

Consent

Consent is a word in many conversations these days. There were updated legal understandings of the complexities of consent with regard to sexual offences by the Crown Prosecution Service in 2021.[23] However, a survey on public opinion on sexual violence in 2018[24] found that:

- A third of people in Britain think it is not usually rape if a woman is pressured into having sex but there is no physical violence
- A third of men think if a woman has flirted on a date it generally would not count as rape, even if she has not explicitly consented to sex (compared with 21% of women)
- A third of men also believe a woman cannot change her mind after sex has started

Thames Valley Police[25] are more enlightened in outlining what does not constitute consent. They say on their website: *Consent – it is simple as tea,* which is explained in a now popular video clip[26]:

'Understanding consent is simple, responsibility for rape rests solely with the perpetrator. The below attributes do not automatically mean consent to sex.

- Dating, flirting, kissing or being friendly or intimate does not mean consent
- Consenting in the past or being in a relationship does not mean consent is automatically given in the future
- Being married or in a relationship does not mean automatic consent
- Both parties have to agree to sex. When someone is asleep or unconscious they cannot give consent. Someone on drugs or too drunk to make decisions does not have the mental capacity to give consent
- If someone is on drugs or is too drunk to consent, stop. Wait until they are sober and ask again'

In their work on Rewriting the Rules,[27] Meg John Barker offers a more in-depth eight-point Consent checklist[28] about what consent is, or could be, through a series of questions to explore:

1   Consent as the aim: have we made consent the explicit aim of our interaction rather than something happening?
2   Informed consent: is everyone fully informed about what is being asked for, offered, etc., why and where everyone is coming from?
3   Ongoing consent: is consent ongoing before, during and after an encounter, or throughout a relationship?
4   Relational consent: is this a relational interaction where everyone can bring their needs, limits, wants and boundaries to the table?
5   Consent and wanting: are people able to clearly express and be heard about what they want and do not want, and what they consent to and do not consent to?
6   Multiple options beyond a default script: are we aware of the default script for 'success' in this situation, and have we shifted this to multiple options and an agreement to default to the lesser one on the table?
7   Power awareness: are we aware of the cultural and personal power imbalances between us and their potential impact on capacity to feel free enough and safe enough to consent?
8   Accountability: can we notice when we have been non-consensual, name that with the person concerned (if they are up for it), hear the impact and offer to make reparations?

The macro-historian Riane Eisler says humans create two types of societies.[29] One is 'dominator cultures', like ours, where hierarchical models of power persist, along with beliefs that humans are essentially violent, selfish and greedy and that suffering is the 'human condition'. The other is 'partnership cultures', with more power sharing and collective responsibility, where social structures are created to support life as an essentially joyful and connected experience. A society like ours invites a cynicism about the possibility of change, of us becoming less abusive and more honouring and respectful of many things, including our sexuality. Our economic model of relentlessly pursuing growth, until the inevitable bust and depressions, is similar to the eating disorder, Bulimia. Our consumer society encourages an addiction model where we should always want more, so we never get to feel satiated. The social costs include rising rates of stress, emotional and physical ill-health.

Amy and Arny Mindell[30] have written for many years about *Deep Democracy*. They outline the differences between Power, Rank and Privilege where:

Social Power comes from a range of characteristics and capabilities, some earned through our efforts, others unearned – we were just born with them or given them.

Rank is multi-dimensional – there are many criteria or domains in which we can have high or low rank. It is rare to only have high or low rank in any given context; usually, we have a combination of both.

Privilege is bestowed on us through our rank/power, in that:

- It makes our lives easier than those without our rank(s)
- It protects us from pain or oppression that those without our rank(s) are not protected from
- It gives us opportunities that those without our rank(s) cannot access

We considered issues of Social power (both physical and structural), in Chapter 1, with regard to Diversity and Intersectionality. We can see the challenges to marginalised and disadvantaged groups in our current *social power* inequalities. This may be the practicalities of inadequate housing and access to basic food and warmth; inadequate salaries and terrible working conditions – it can be difficult to think about the quality of our experiences when our basic needs are not being met. It may also be the daily strains of racism, trans or homophobia, sexism, ableism, etc. How might a lack of social power compromise our ability to freely consent in a sexual context?

Importantly, the Mindells say there is not just Social power but also Personal power, which has both a Psychological and Spiritual element: it is seen as an internal source of power, independent of the values of the culture and is mostly built from developing self-knowledge and growing from difficult experiences.

Psychological power:

- Self-awareness
- Being at ease with conflict
- Insight and capacities from having worked through or healed from a traumatic life event
- Resilience (the capacity to 'bounce back' from failure and disappointments)
- Feeling loved as a child and having your ideas and opinions supported and validated in childhood
- Valuing your own opinions and perceptions
- Being able to notice and articulate emotional states – your own and others

Spiritual power:

- Feeling like you belong
- Knowing your purpose in life
- Having been close to death
- Contact with 'the ineffable'
- A deep faith and trust that life is meaningful
- A relationship to something divine or transcendent

We believe this model helps us to recognise our own power and agency when we may not have Social Power; to see the power we have that is not necessarily valued in our current economic focussed society. And crucially, to use it to take responsibility, and express our consent and our dissent, in our sexual relationships.

Personal Power

Solo Exercise

Consider each of the points in the lists above about both psychological and spiritual power and identify areas where you experience yourself as empowered or disempowered.

How do your experiences of disempowerment in the psychological and spiritual realms impact your experiences of consent in your sexual life?

How can you use your psychological and spiritual power to support yourself in your sexual life?

Exercise with Partner/s

Discuss your experiences of the solo exercise. What do you think about the ideas of psychological and spiritual power?

What strengths and challenges do your differences with regard to these types of power bring to your relationship? Are there ways in which you could support each other?

Principles of Sexual Health

People are turned on by all sorts of different things. As long as you are not harming another person (or creature), and your desires and sexual behaviours are not impinging on your health or ability to enjoy and participate in other areas of life, we see no reason to pathologise. In this, we find Doug Braun-Harvey and Michael Vigorito's Six Principles of Sexual Health[31] a very useful guide. The six principles are as follows: consent; non-exploitation; honesty; shared values; protection from HIV, STIs and unwanted pregnancy; and pleasure.

A note on fantasies. Sexual fantasies are just that – fantasies. Having a fantasy about being coerced does not mean you want to be coerced in real life. Some fantasies you may want to play out, others you may absolutely not. That is fine. Returning again to Nagoski's most common enquiry, 'am I normal?', the research of Justin Lehmiller[32] suggests that for men, the most common sexual fantasies include group sex, and for women, bondage, domination/discipline, sadism and masochism (BDSM). A 2020[33] study comparing the sexual fantasies of cis-gender and non-binary people found that fantasies were generally comparable, with the exception that the fantasies of non-binary people 'were significantly more likely to contain references to non-normative genitals, and less likely to refer to themselves as the object of desire'.

One important skill in following the 'principles of sexual health' is the ability to communicate assertively. People who have experienced abuse of power can find it difficult to step into their own authority, fearing that they too may abuse their power. Others replay power abuse, which, from a psychotherapeutic perspective, could be an unconscious compulsion to repeat or to normalise – or to try to heal – previous experiences. Assertive communication requires us to acknowledge our own and others' vulnerabilities and to have compassion and empathy for others, but also for ourselves. An assertive person is aware of, and can separate out, their own thoughts, feelings and motivations, and can distinguish between 'can't' and 'don't want to'. They can say 'no' as well as 'yes'. They can manage conflict and weigh up contradictions; they can think and reflect before taking action. They can stay with their own opinion without needing to criticise or become defensive. Being assertive includes being willing to negotiate and share skills and resources. A useful framework for understanding the difference between assertiveness and persecution, caring and rescuing, vulnerability and being a victim, is Karpman's Drama Triangle[34] and the counterpoint positions of the Winner's Triangle, see Figure 4.3. The Drama Triangle outlines three implicitly learned roles that are commonly unconsciously played out, especially in our current power-over

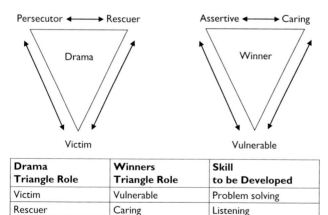

Drama Triangle Role	Winners Triangle Role	Skill to be Developed
Victim	Vulnerable	Problem solving
Rescuer	Caring	Listening
Persecutor	Assertive	Assertiveness

Figure 4.3 Drama and Winner's Triangles.

social model: winners and losers. The Winner's triangle recommends a more power-with model, aiming to create win–win encounters.

Any technique that the **vulnerable** person can use to get themselves thinking about options and consequences is valuable. In the **caring** role, the development of **listening** skills that involve empathising with the **vulnerable** person is required. **Listening** is frequently the only **caring** response needed. **Assertiveness** is about getting your needs met without punishing. Self-awareness is essential in all three roles.

Sexual Timeline

Solo Exercise

Think about your sexual experiences from your first **consensual** *experience up until now. Draw a timeline and identify up to ten experiences. Do not go into details but briefly note what has brought each one to mind. Was it the place, the person and/or what happened that has made it memorable?*

When you have written your timeline look at it overall; can you see any patterns? Did most events happen at a particular age? Was it with a specific person or types of people? Was it what happened mostly that has made these events significant? Notice which of these things is most important to you (where, who or how?).

Exercise with Partner/s

Take it in turns to share your individual timelines and tell each other about three of the most significant events to you. When you have done this, discuss the impact these events may be having on your relationship now. Explore how you could look after yourselves; each other and your relationship.

BDSM and Kink

BDSM or kink is a popular form of sexuality, participated in by about one in five people. We decided to place our BDSM section here, just after information on assertive, effective communication, as good communication is crucial in kinky play.

For the uninitiated, BDSM may conjure lurid scenes of whipping, spanking, torture and degradation. However, kink or BDSM is any erotic play that involves intense sensation and/or psychological power play. It may or may not involve sexual contact, it also needn't involve pain. It can be helpful to think of BDSM as intense sensation seeking; just as some people enjoy extreme sports like bungee jumping or marathon running, some enjoy more intense forms of erotic play. In fact, the high or altered headspace reported in BDSM play is very similar to the rush of endorphins created by heavy physical exertion. It can also be seen as a form of roleplay or theatre, as evidenced by the use of words like 'scene' and 'player'. Finally, some people report considerable healing from psychological or sexual trauma in reparative BDSM scenes, where they have control over the outcome.

Kink and BDSM have until quite recently been pathologised by much of the mental health profession; the current Diagnostic and Statistical Manual is the first to distinguish between paraphilias (atypical sexual interests) and paraphiliac disorders (atypical sexual interests causing harm or distress to self or others). This is not necessarily as straightforward as it may seem – for example, Maltz (2012)[35] describes how victims of incest, violence and sexual abuse may experience compounded feelings of pleasure, pain and shame whilst being sexual and may find it difficult to know fear from sexual excitement. For this reason, we find it helpful to think about Braun-Harvey and Vigorito's Six Principles of Sexual Health[36] in regard to kink – is it consensual, non-exploitative, honest, are there shared values, is there protection from unwanted pregnancy and STIs, and is it pleasurable for all involved?

Numerous studies have explored links (or lack of) between childhood sexual abuse and participation in BDSM. A small Finnish study of attendees of a BDSM club[37] found a higher rate of self-reported childhood sexual abuse than in the general population, whereas an Australian national survey of nearly 20,000 people[38] showed that those engaged in BDSM were not overall more likely to have ever been coerced into sexual activity, as children or adults. Another study[39] showed that compared to the control group, BDSM practitioners were less neurotic, more extraverted, more open to new experiences, more conscientious, less rejection sensitive, had higher subjective well-being, yet were less agreeable. There were slightly less favourable scores for those with a submissive than a dominant role, although still more favourable than the control group.

In his study of 19,000 adults in 2007, Brett Kahr[40] found that kinky fantasies are the most popular form of fantasy reported by women, and multipartner fantasies the most popular for men. He discovered no links between those with violent fantasies and experiences of childhood sexual abuse. However, further in-depth psychotherapeutic interviews showed strong links between those who had experienced neglect from their childhood caregivers and having violent fantasies. Similarly, Justin Lehmiller's work on fantasy[41] does show a correlation between a history of sexual victimisation and *fantasising* about BDSM, and also fantasising about gender bending, sexual fluidity and both emotional and emotionless sex.

Over the years, kink communities have developed various ways of advocating for best practice, including Safe, Sane and Consensual, and Risk

Aware Consensual Kink. Consent includes safe words, and clarity before-hand about what is on and off limits. There should also be provision for aftercare, in particular looking after submissives who may be feeling very vulnerable. In our view, BDSM-related problems are most likely to stem from two things: firstly, people seeing kinky sexual activities in porn and trying to copy them without the necessary negotiation and consent creation, and without appropriate awareness of any physical risks (this has become quite prevalent with the practice of choking or restricting air flow, a highly risky activity that can potentially result in death); secondly, people entering a 'fawn' trauma state in which they may be saying yes (consenting) or continuing to submit, but are actually not in a position to make that decision. Therefore, considerable pre-play negotiation and communal rather than individual responsibility for con-sent are essential. We also like the concept of enthusiastic, positive consent (setting out what you do want to happen) rather than relying on safe wording. We highly recommend Meg John Barker's work on BDSM, both on their website and in the book they co-edited in 2007.[42]

BDSM

Solo Exercise

Think about the term BDSM. What do you know about this subject, what have you heard about it, are you curious or not?

Write for five minutes about what BDSM means to you. Notice how you feel while doing this. If you want to, take a break and at another time come back and think about what this means about getting involved in any BDSM activities, or not.

Exercise with Partner/s

Yes/Safe Word/Maybe
Happy BDSM is all about being able to confidently and easily say no as well as yes. This comes easier to some of us than others, and particularly if you have trauma in your background, it may be tempting to 'go along with' or 'get through' something you do not want to do, rather than being able to say no. Therefore, our first BDSM exercise is about developing that ability to say no. Because BDSM is primarily a relational activity, this is a partnered exercise. You can do it with a good friend though, not necessarily a lover, just someone you trust and enjoy spending time with.

Partnered Exercise 1
First, choose with your partner for this exercise a safe word, something that means 'stop'. We encourage you to find another word than stop, something out of context like 'yellow' or 'dinosaur'. Then, take turns

being the toucher and the recipient for five minutes each. The toucher should start touching the recipient, following – and this is important – their own wishes rather than trying to please or turn on the recipient. The recipient should regularly – as in every ten to twenty seconds – say either 'yes' (meaning carry on, I love it), 'safe word' (meaning stop and do something else) or 'maybe' (meaning I am not sure, carry on a little bit but pay close attention to my body language. Within the five-minute turn, the recipient should say their safe word at least five times. This means that the toucher should take some risks, doing things the recipient might not like (but obviously stopping as soon as the safe word is said). This exercise will help the recipient become more aware of how difficult or easy it is to speak up and give the toucher practice in both following their own desires and listening to the recipient's responses.

After each turn, take five minutes to each privately write about your experience before swapping roles.

If it was hard for you to say the safe word (i.e. get your partner to stop), reflect on why, and keep practising until it is easy. You should not take part in any BDSM activities until this is easy for you and you are confident in your ability to use the safe word.

Partnered Exercise 2
Think of a scene you would like to try out with a partner or partners, which involves some taking or giving up of power. This might involve restraint, and/or psychological or physical dominance or submission. Do you trust your current partner to do this with you? Write out the scene in advance. Think about what is important to you. Then share with your partner or partners what you would like to do and negotiate with them to reach a place of full, informed and enthusiastic consent.

Looking Good

There is obviously great pleasure to be found in expressing our sexuality through attending to our appearance with clothes, make-up and accessories. Many people get immense pleasure playing with materials, different fabrics, colours and shapes. They may enjoy designing outfits, trying unique styles and fashions and having fun in the hours spent with others 'getting ready' to go out, swapping ideas, clothes and accessories. Yet there is a dark side to this too. It is one thing to get glammed up because you want to; it is another to have to wear make-up and walk around in high-heeled shoes all day, because of the gender-expression beliefs of your employer.

Culturally we are bombarded with media and images about looking good and what looks good. We are encouraged to think more about what we look like to others; how we might appeal to them, than about what makes us feel sensual and sexual. We are encouraged to use (and abuse) sexual power; our power to attract, to get what we want.

Most people have a low opinion of their body image, and many are caught in cycles of dieting and eating disorders. Our current sexualised image for women is quite distorted. Despite the average British woman being a size sixteen, most female mannequins in high street shops are representative of a 'very underweight woman'[43] and would be considered medically unhealthy in humans.

It is almost like what is admired as beauty in women is a very thin girl with no body hair but a very large bust, like our Barbie dolls, whose proportions are ridiculous. In ratio to the average woman's waist size, Barbie's bra size is thirty-eight EE and she is eight foot and ten inches tall! There is a great deal of pressure on men these days too, around body image and sexual prowess. Writers like Zilbergeld (1999)[44] have challenged the idea that men are supposed to be 'hard as steel and go all night' and Biddulph (2004)[45] has discussed the pressures of rigid sex role stereotypes and their impact on male physical and emotional health. Barry and Emily McCarthy's[46] *Contemporary Male Sexuality: Confronting Myths and Promoting Change*, published in 2020, offers an update, showing that many of the same pressures are still on men. Trans and non-binary people may also have their own struggles with body image and dysphoria – as described for example in Juno Roche's *Queer Sex*.

There is a great deal of commercial focus on our imperfections and hundreds of products to buy to improve our sexual attractiveness. We are encouraged to feel ashamed rather than proud of the bodies we have, which do, after all, come in many different shapes and sizes. This may compound the difficulties for disabled people where it may be hard enough to deal with the physical challenges of limitation, without feeling you are less than. Internalised beliefs may say if relatively healthy and *beautiful* people are not sexy enough, what chance do I stand? The lengths to which we are encouraged to go for the sake of beauty have become increasingly severe, like extreme dieting and cosmetic procedures. Obviously, being physically healthy improves our feel-good factor but we think that being attractive stems mostly from feeling physically and emotionally good about yourself.

You will notice that the principles of sexual health referred to above contain no reference to a person's looks or levels of 'attractiveness'. Adults of all ages, looks, abilities, ethnicities, orientations and genders have the right to consensual, honest, non-exploitative, pleasurable, sex. It is, however, easy to internalise society's implicit communication through media of all kinds that sex belongs only to 'the beautiful (straight) people'. Powerful ways to counteract this internalised criticism include representation – consuming media that shows people like you as sexual beings – and community – surrounding yourself with people you identify with, having happy sexual relationships.

One of the aims of this book is to show you that sex belongs to all of us that want it, whatever we look like and however we identify.

Ironically, there are also significant questions about the potential health risks of many 'health and beauty' products because of some of the ingredients. The Women's Environmental Network[47] has done research to indicate the most worrying examples and also to highlight how commonly they are used. There are between thirty and a hundred thousand chemicals used in cosmetics, with 95% of them displaying little or no health or environmental safety information. The two most widely used compounds are parabens and phthalates.

Parabens are used in many cosmetics and products like shampoos, bubble-bath, shower gels, make-up, lotions and deodorants. Take a look at the ingredients in items that you have. They have been detected in human breast tissue and, although they cannot yet be conclusively linked as a possible cause of breast cancer, evidence now suggests they can act as oestrogen mimics. There is concern about the huge rise in breast cancer rates; the numbers have doubled in twenty years, with the causes of 50–70% of cases classed as 'unknown'.

Scientists have said that sperm counts and concentrations have been undergoing an alarming decline in western countries for decades, with sperm counts halving over the last forty years. Other male sexual disorders such as penis malformation, breast cancer and undescended testes have been increasing. Hormone-disrupting chemicals are a prime suspect and this study[48] sheds new light on the potential for chemical cocktails to cause harm.

Phthalates are linked to reproductive damage, and some have been banned because of this. They are commonly found in products such as deodorants, fragrances, hair gels, hair sprays and mousses and hand and body lotions. Many couples now suffer with fertility problems and many females have diseases associated with hormone disruption, such as irregular menstrual cycles, polycystic ovaries, endometriosis and fibroids. There has also been a huge rise in prostate cancer incidence over the last twenty years. Cancer Research UK[49] says it is now the most common cancer in men in Britain – accounting for nearly a quarter of all new male cancer diagnoses. There is concern that these issues are correlated not just to lifestyle factors but also to toxicity in foods and our environment. A recent study[50] declared that more than three thousand potentially harmful chemicals are found in food packaging.

Beautiful Body

Solo Exercise

Use your safe space. Make it warm.

Sit for a few moments and close your eyes. Allow your breath to settle. Allow sounds and distractions to just come and go. Think about your body, your breathing lungs, your beating heart, your brain and bones, muscles, torso and limbs. Feel any sensations in your body, consciously tense and then relax.

Put your left hand on your heart area and your right hand on your stomach and give yourself a chance to relax your body and breathe. Imagine you have just woken up in your body. For the first time, you realise you are inside this body. You are excited and curious. You are told you are the first person ever. You are the prototype that all future humans will be modelled on.

Get up; take your clothes off, look at yourself naked in a full-length mirror. What do you see? Look front and back and from the side, take your time. Look at yourself from all angles as if you have not seen a human body before. Move yourself, your limbs. Be aware of what you, this body is and what it can do.

Notice if there are any aspects of your body you do not like and any that you do like.

Be aware of your feelings and thoughts about yourself. Notice if you are kind, appreciative and accepting of your body or whether you are critical.

If you are critical, consider whether you would prefer to - and can - develop love for yourself just as you are, or would you like to plan some dietary or exercise alterations.

Exercise with Partner/s

Do this exercise together. Tell each other five things you like about seeing their naked body.

Notice your responses while your partner/s are sharing their comments. If you find it difficult to hear your partner/s' appreciations, try saying to yourself, 'I am willing to hear their appreciation of me. I delight in my uniqueness'.

Sexual Identity

We commonly use the phrase sexual identity to mean a person's sexual orientation. Because we implicitly use a reproductive model of sex, it implies a heterosexual model also; therefore, people who are not heterosexual have been defined and labelled as 'other'. Scientists have tried to discover why people are sexually attractive to, and attracted to some people and not others, and why some are attracted to the same sex and some not. They have tested many theories exploring whether sexual attraction may be based on facial shapes, hormones, pheromones, psychological profiling or on reproductive qualities. None seem to be proved, except that a spark of attraction happens within seconds of people meeting. It seems that the reflex in the brain just happens; – who we see, fancy or respond to, is a reaction. This spark of attraction sets off a whole neurochemical, hormonal and physiological reaction in our bodies.

There are many labels like straight, lesbian, gay, bisexual, transgender/ sexual, kink, queer, asexual, polyamorous and so on. They serve to identify sexual orientations and lifestyles other than the culturally valued heterosexual, cis-gender, monogamous, vanilla, coupled norm. However, these subgroups are not homogenous and vary massively in interpretation and expression. For some, identifying with a group or with a particular sexual identity is particularly important: it is about belonging, a political statement or a vital part of their self-identity. It can also be an important way of counteracting the marginalisation or 'othering' minority groups experience. For example, the rise in people identifying as asexual (or ACE) and/or aromantic. It is important to realise that there are many forms of asexuality. Individuals may or may not want many of the aspects of being 'in relationships', but do not experience a desire to be sexual. They may want to be intimate and affectionate, or be into BDSM. Or not. Rather than seeing themselves as 'suffering' from low sexual desire, they are claiming a sexual identity or orientation of being asexual (and/or aromantic). This challenges our social assumptions around sexual desire; that everyone wants to be sexual, or at least should want to. Also worthy of mention is Lisa Diamond's[51] study of female sexual desire, showing that for many, love and desire are not rigidly heterosexual nor homosexual but fluid and changeable through various stages of life and social groups and most importantly, different love relationships. In 2011, the annual Integrated Household Survey[52] (Sherwin) featured a question giving a choice of sexual identities; the largest increase was in the 'don't know' answers.

Figure 4.4 shows the changes over the generations in how people in the UK define their sexual orientation. In the 2021 Sexual Orientation Global survey,[53] the percentage of people defining themselves as heterosexual has decreased from 87% for so called 'baby boomers' to 68% for 'Gen Z' (generally meant to refer to those born between 1997 and 2012). Lesbian and gay same-sex attraction appears to have reduced from 12% to 4% with bisexuality orientations increasing from 2% to 9%. Those identifying as trans/non-binary/non-conforming have increased fourfold and the numbers preferring not to say or 'don't know' have increased from 9% to 14%. This might in part be due to gains in human rights for sexual and gender minorities since the turn of the millennium.

Folx considering themselves transgender, non-binary and/or gender expansive (and the terminology in this area is changing fast) may or may not wish to address this through gender expression (how they dress and present to the world, including the pronouns they use), hormonal treatment and/or surgery. It is important to note that this is not purely a modern phenomenon – historically,

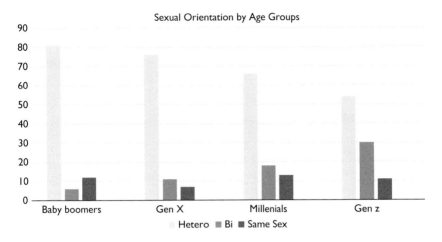

Figure 4.4 Sexual Orientation by Age Groups.

some gynocentric, rather than patriarchal societies, have included gender and sexual orientation diversity within their cultural beliefs and practices. For example, some Native American peoples hold a sacred place for non-heterosexuals and for people who are gender non-conforming.[54]

However, others do not accept diversity and pathologise any sexual identities that are not heterosexual. This leads to a power differential with social and legal implications. Non-hetero, non-cisgender people have to 'come out' to family, friends and colleagues, not knowing whether they will be accepted or rejected or whether they may be at risk of losing relationships or jobs. Others are at risk of bullying or violence.

Kaufman and Raphael[55] believe that sexual orientation is affected by three factors: firstly, a person's erotic attraction, who it is who catches your eye. Secondly, who do you yearn to touch and hold; in that affection communicates protection and security, the foundation for trust. And thirdly, identification, who you wish to be intimate with, share fusion and merging: whose eyes do you want to gaze into?

Swami and Furnham[56] have explored a wider idea of what they call 'dynamic attractiveness', where they found people are actually more interested in a person's conversational and social skills, personality and sense of humour. How we think and feel about our reflexive reactions will also influence our response to our attractions. Sometimes we act on our sexual feelings, and sometimes not. Some people choose celibacy as a lifestyle and some feel socially or culturally uncomfortable with their sexual orientation so do not express this aspect of themselves at all. Moving away from a heteronormative view would reduce the need for labelling and lead to a situation where sexual identity could be understood more widely as describing our desire, sexual tastes and preferences. It could include what we believe and identify with to suit our sensuality and feelings and our sexual values. Our sexual identity is also about our experience of our passions and creativity as well as our choices of behaviour and lifestyle.

Sexual Preferences

Solo Exercise

Write down five things that you are easily aware of that you prefer sexually. They might be who you are attracted to or sexual behaviours you like.

1

2

3

4

5

Write down five more things that you have discovered are part of what you prefer sexually from the earlier exercise about your best sexual experiences.

1

2

3

4

5

Reflect on what you have written. What is it like to see a list stating your sexual preferences? Any surprises?

Exercise with Partner/s

Share your answers to the solo exercise. In turns, ask each other to tell you more details about the sexual preferences they have written.

Each identifies three most important preferences. Tell each other more about what you think and feel about them and why they are important to you.

Safer Sex

This is one area where cultural beliefs – in this case, the reproductive model of sex – get us into trouble. For example, until 2013, 'Family Planning' Clinics, often within a doctor's surgery, provided a variety of contraceptive methods to control fertility and allow heterosexual intercourse with a supposedly minimal risk of pregnancy. However, most of these contraceptive methods do not protect against STIs, which are a huge sexual health problem for us now and may have other health implications. Until recently, oral sex, anal sex and mutual masturbation were considered to belong to a separate, often hospital-based clinical setting, the 'Sexual Health' Clinic. There is now a more integrated provision.

Condoms, which address both reproductive and STI concerns, are available for free from Sexual Health clinics, some GP surgeries, some youth projects and the Terrence Higgins Trust. You can find out where free condoms are available in your area by searching for 'free condoms' on the main NHS website.

Safer sex practices include the following:

*   Using condoms for vaginal and anal sex
*   Using barriers such as dental dams for oral sex
*   Washing and/or using condoms on sex toys
*   Taking care to practice safer sex when under the influence of alcohol or other drugs
*   Effective communication about sexual partners and practices

There are those who always practice safer sex and those who consider they do not need to as they are not sexually active, are in an exclusive, monogamous relationship where both partners know they carry no risk, or have been clear about their sexual health status. It is now possible with treatment to reduce HIV markers to 'untransmissible, undetectable' levels, and also to take PrEP (pre-exposure prophylaxis) proactively to protect against possible HIV transmission if risks are to be taken (this will not protect against other STIs). Some people act to protect themselves against pregnancy but not against STIs, and some do neither. Why might this be? There are people who like the thrill of engaging in risky behaviour and others who inadvertently do so whilst under the influence of alcohol or other drugs. Others seem oblivious to all the risks; a morning after pill may reverse the risk of pregnancy but not of catching an STI.

There is also the cultural context; we rarely see safer sex being practiced or referred to during 'lovemaking scenes' on the TV, in films or in pornography. It is as if we prefer not to see ourselves consciously choosing to be sexual. Do we want to just get so carried away that we do not think about consequences till later? This may be part of our romantic view of sex or our belief that the sex urge is so strong nothing can (or should) get in its way. It could also be an indicator of the degree of shame we feel still about owning and honouring our sexual desires. Coming out of shame would necessitate witnessing our desire, admitting in advance that we may well behave sexually and being prepared so we can practice safer sex. We do not have to 'stop' to put on a condom; it can totally be part of sex play. Some people think others will not like them being prepared; that it is presumptuous for a man or slutty for a woman, neither of which are true. Acknowledging your desire and wanting to have safe fun respects yourself and others and indicates sexual self-esteem.

Within a model of psychosexual health, safer sex is not just about the avoidance of STIs and pregnancy, but about emotional and physical safety too. It includes drug and alcohol awareness and how they may undermine safer sex practices or link with risky behaviour. Attention is given to self-care, choices and assertiveness: not just knowing for ourselves what we want and desire but communicating and negotiating this with others. For example, we could teach our girls how to interpret the obvious signs of their brief monthly fertile phase (which will be explained in more detail in Chapter 5); they (and partners) could then make decisions about which sexual activities they may want to engage in at distinct stages of the fertility cycle. This would need a cultural shift in attitudes that have been discussed in this book; it would require coming out of shame. We might think about a 'biopsychosocial' model of safer sex – the physical issues, yes, but also what psychological and/or socio-cultural factors might affect a person's ability to engage in safer sex.

Sexual Health Workout

Solo Exercise

Think about your sexual health in the same way you might consider your physical health if you wanted to get healthier. If you were to review your physical health you might, for example, look at what you eat, what exercise you get, your sleeping habits and your stress levels.

For your sexual health review, you may want to consider having a check-up at a sexual health clinic. You will find details of your nearest clinic via the internet or at your local health centre or hospital.

Do you consider that your current sexual beliefs and values are healthy? Do you consider that your current sexual practices are healthy? Do you practice safer sex? Do you use alcohol or recreational drugs as part of your sexual life? Do some of your practices involve risk or harm to yourself or others? Do you feel good about what you are doing?

What impact do you think any of the above have on your body or your mental or emotional well-being? Write about what you think and feel about your answers to these questions. Identify any changes you would like to make and consider how you may do so.

Exercise with Partner/s

Discuss what you have each discovered from doing your own Sexual Health Workout. Choose one issue to discuss together: perhaps your physical health or your beliefs or sexual behaviours.

Consider what impacts these may be having on your relationship now. Draw up a list together of the Six Principles of Sexual Health that you want for your shared relationship. Discuss how you could move towards these principles if you are not attaining them now.

Food for Thought

Food is a good analogy when talking about sexuality, as both involve our mouths and lips, and both are about our tastes; what we like and what we do not like. Sexual arousal stimulates a desire to use our mouths to kiss and taste, as well as touch. Hunger and the sexual drive are both urges/needs linked to the pleasure centres in the brain and trigger the release of Dopamine and Oxytocin, a feel-good hormone. Both these subjects are also culturally complex and deeply emotive, bringing a range of conditions and health issues. Food means so much more to us than satisfying our need to stay alive; we can derive great pleasure in choosing and preparing food, as well as eating it. We also often share food and eating as a social and bonding experience.

There is a vast range of foods available for us to eat and there are a variety of sexual behaviours. Many people like different foods and we have differing sexual tastes and cultural preferences. Some foods are seasonal, some only grow in certain climates, some are nutritious and great for health and some give us a quick sugar rush that later depletes the body. Is this also true for sexual behaviours and if so, which ones and why? What sort of ingredients would be part of a nutritious sexuality and what sort of sexual nutrition do we want?

To think about the analogy of food and how we express our sexuality, we need to consider the physiology: why we need food/sex; how the body metabolises or uses sexual 'nutrients'; which ingredients may be toxic and why; and how they may affect us. In Chapter 5, we will consider the impacts of sexuality on our whole body, and in Chapter 6, the hormones and neurochemicals involved. In Chapter 7, we will discuss the interplay of all of these factors and how we may begin to answer the question of what constitutes healthy sexual nutrition.

We also need to think about the preparation of food; the choice of ingredients, how we want to prepare and use them; what cooking or seasoning we may want to use. The presentation of food and the ambiance in which we eat, or express ourselves sexually, will also influence our experiences. And, as always, someone has to clean up afterwards! Rather than promoting any particular 'diet', this book encourages the reader to explore the issues and then decide which tastes and choices suit you.

How Do You Nourish Yourself?

Solo Exercise

Think about your favourite meal and what it is you like about it. For example, it could be the foods, how they are prepared or in what combinations. How nourishing is your meal as a food source?

Now imagine this meal was a sexual encounter: what can this tell you about what you like and what you want sexually? Is there any correlation in how you nourish yourself with food and how you feed yourself sexually?

Exercise with Partner/s

Decide on ten things you both want in your shared sexual diet.

Create some menus for your favourite sexual snacks and meals.

Sexual Values

'Sexual values' seems to be an old-fashioned phrase but what if we were to reclaim the concept to ask, what do we actually value? What is valuable to us in terms of our belief systems, our bodies, minds and hearts? We can consider the huge range of behaviours and human expressions of sexuality that we know about and draw up a set of our own values to live by. We can decide individually what we value for ourselves; what we think is OK for others but not to our taste. We can also think more socially and culturally about what we do not think is valuable for ourselves or for others.

Becoming more explicit about our cultural beliefs and assumptions would help to challenge our contradictory attitudes to crimes of sexual violence. On the one hand, rape is considered a serious crime with a long-term sentence; on the other hand, many victims choose not to report, knowing they will go through an arduous process with an exceptionally low prosecution and conviction rate. In the year to September 2021, just 1.3% of rape cases recorded by police resulted in a suspect being charged (or receiving a summons). This compares to a 7.1% charge rate for all other recorded crimes in the same period.[57]

We have a cultural ambivalence towards sexual violence, where we glorify it in pornography and normalise it as entertainment in mainstream cinema and television. It can seem we are more concerned about what victims did or did not do than why so much sexual violence is committed. The natural ability to go through a recovery process after a traumatic event can be compromised by this attitude as victims continue to blame themselves. This can contribute to the development of sexual problems and post-traumatic stress disorders.

By being clearer about our choices and preferences, we can evaluate the full range of sexual behaviours and decide for ourselves what is important for us. We can evaluate our sexual appetite and decide on our own sexual nutrition. We can become prouder of who we are; creatively express our sexuality and develop a good sense of sexual self-esteem.

Sexual Values

Solo Exercise

Write down five ways you have expressed your sexuality in the past week, whatever they may be

1

2

3

4

5

Then read the list given below of some of the diverse ways in which people express their sexuality through sexual acts, behaviours and lifestyles. Add some more to the list if you wish.

Expressions of Sexuality:

- *Masturbating without porn*
- *Masturbating with porn*
- *Kissing with tongues (snogging)*
- *Stroking and looking at each other's naked bodies*
- *Looking into each other's eyes while having sex*
- *Having sex with the lights on*
- *Having your toes sucked and kissed*
- *Your partner taking the lead and telling you what they want you to do*
- *Initiating sex*
- *Being seduced – with words, with partner stripping for you, with wining and dining*
- *Taking the lead and telling your partner what you want them to do*
- *Being fucked/Fucking*
- *Oral sex*
- *Role playing/creating 'scenes' to play out*
- *Impact play – spanking, slapping, etc.*
- *Pain – either giving or receiving*
- *Anal sex – either giving or receiving*
- *Being blindfolded/Blindfolding a partner*
- *Being tied down/restrained*
- *Having sex with someone of the same sex/gender*
- *Having sex with a non-binary or trans person*
- *Having sex with someone of the 'opposite' gender*
- *Consciously breathing together in sex*
- *Choking*
- *Buying sex*
- *Celibacy*
- *Watching porn together*
- *Listening to erotic audio together*
- *Fisting*
- *Self-pleasuring in front of a partner*

- *Continuing to be sexual if someone's erection fades*
- *Making noise during sex*
- *Group sex*
- *Rimming*
- *Being told you like it*
- *Using a vibrator with a partner*
- *Scheduling sex/intimacy dates with a partner*
- *Rough sex – being thrown about, fucked hard*
- *Sex outside in nature*
- *Being watched having sex*
- *Watching others have sex*
- *Wearing a strap on*
- *Having sex drunk/high*
- *Sex with someone you have just met*
- *Casual, out of relationship sex*

Now take some time to really think about the words in the phrase 'sexual values'. What is valuable to you – of importance or useful?

Make a chart and write each of the above sexual expressions in one of the three columns, according to what you think and feel about them. You may want to go by your first reaction or consider each and choose where you want to place them.

What I value for myself	What I do not value for myself but do value for others	What I do not value for myself and do not value for others

Have a look at your lists; what is it like to see these distinctions? How do you feel about what you really do value for yourself? How do you feel about those that you do not think have value?

Of the things that you do not value for yourself, but can see are valuable for others, consider whether this is about your beliefs or preferences, or whether they are behaviours you might like to experiment with in the future.

Your values may change over time; you may want to do this exercise again at the end of the book. You may identify values you have which no longer suit you and wish to set about changing them.

Exercise with Partner/s

Compare your lists of 'What I Value for Myself' and underline all the words on both your lists. Create a new shared list called 'What we value in our relationship'.

> *Now consider your lists for 'What I do not value for myself but <u>do</u> value for others'. Take it in turns to discuss three things that you may move into the 'What I value for Myself', with certain caveats or conditions. Having discussed what they are, create a shared word cloud (i.e. a visual representation showing your most popular, valued expressions biggest and boldest, with the more fringe or 'beige' expressions much smaller). Then, draw a circle around your cloud and put any expressions you might like to consider exploring there. Add another circle around that and place any expressions that you definitely do not want to explore outside the second circle.*

What If ...?

What if we were to begin to think differently about sexuality? What if we were to become more mindful; to re-evaluate and recreate our mindset, our thinking and beliefs and more consciously redefine what we think individually, culturally and socially? For example, sex education could teach detailed sexual anatomy and physiology, as distinct from reproduction, including the stages and processes involved in sexual attraction and arousal. It could include information on the broad range of sexual behaviours and fantasies and teach porn literacy (how to understand porn as a performance and a fantasy, rather than reality, and information about the realities of the porn industry).

Knowing what our sexual processes are helps us to understand what may be happening if something goes wrong; knowing ourselves sexually would give us a clearer idea of what we might need to put things right again. What if we were taught about fertility awareness as teenagers so we could make more conscious choices about our fertility and also about our sexual behaviour with regard to our thoughts and feelings about reproduction? Sexual health could mean more than merely the prevention of pregnancy and sexual infections but could include our feelings and emotional health. Safer sex issues could also address physical safety and emotional well-being and include related subjects like drugs and alcohol. The notion of sexual identity could include our sexual orientations and preferences, along with our beliefs and feelings and our choices about lifestyle and sexual behaviours.

Another advantage to humans having frontal lobes in the brain is the ability to imagine, to contemplate and to make believe. Humans learn not only through the rational mind but also through the memory centre in the back brain. We can think to ourselves, 'if I do this, then that might happen'. We can weigh up consequences; we can heal from trauma; we can and do learn through making mistakes, realising we might want to do something different next time.

Sexual imagination: the ability to fantasise is a crucial aspect of healthy sexual functioning as it enhances the arousal process and fuels the mind–brain–body emotion circuit. Curiosity, anticipation and the excitement of looking forward to something can all be aspects of foreplay. Critical thinking, worry or anxiety can break the circuit of sexual arousal. Thinking about or replaying a previous sexual experience in our minds or in our imagination can, and often will, trigger the sexual arousal reflex. Exploring our favourite or most common fantasies can help to deepen our understanding of our deepest desires. Sexual fantasy is private; we can imagine whatever we like. For some, imagination is a place to explore things we may not want to actually do; for others, we can consider what alterations might be needed if we want to make a fantasy come true in real life.

So what if we were to address our sexual health in the way that we do our physical health? We now understand the need for and the benefits of a good diet, physical exercise and positive thinking and are mostly aware of the deleterious impacts of unhealthy food, constant worrying and modern stress on our well-being. But what do we know or think about a healthy sexual diet or sexual appetite? Nourishment comforts us and provides us with what we need to grow.

What if we were to include a more respectful, perhaps even spiritual or philosophical, approach to our sexuality as well, where we honour our sexuality and cherish our physical bodies and our hearts? Such attitudes embrace love and affection, the subjective experience of relationship: relating to our own sensuality and sexuality and to that of others. The pleasure principle promotes empowerment, encouraging respect for our bodies and our emotional well-being. We are aware these days of ecology and environmentalism, with many being more conscious about what energy sources we have on this planet, what we do to utilise them and what side effects there are. Many are more aware of the short-term and long-term consequences of what and how we consume and are re-evaluating their behaviours. What if we were to consider the ecology of our sexual energy? We could value our sexuality as a precious power resource to be used wisely. Our thoughts, feelings and sexual practices, rather than being polluting or harmful to us, could be harnessed to enhance our well-being.

Review of Chapter 4

Solo Exercise

Read back through the exercises for this chapter and what you have written in your journal. Take some time to reflect on your exploration and to evaluate your work. Which exercises did you like and which ones did you not like? Think about why.

> *What have you discovered about your beliefs about sexuality; your sexual knowledge and where you got it from?*
>
> *What have you discovered about your relationship to your body and how you nourish and value yourself; your sexual preferences and sexual values?*
>
> *Is there anything that has surprised you, if so, how come? What is different than you had previously thought, and how do you feel about that?*
>
> *Is there anything you want to change; if so, how could you do that?*
>
> *Are there any exercises that you would like to do again? If so, notice what is similar or different if you do them a second time.*
>
> *Talk to someone, write or draw something about how you are thinking and feeling having worked on this section.*
>
> ### Exercise with Partner/s
>
> *Give yourselves an hour each and use the Conscious Communication dialogue to explore each other's reviews in detail.*
>
> *Take your time to learn more about yourselves and your partner/s as you discover what has been important about the work on this aspect of your sexuality.*
>
> *Discuss where you feel this leaves your relationship now and identify one aspect that needs your combined attention. Explore how you may want to do this.*

Notes

1 Nagoski, E. (2015). *Come as You Are: The Surprising New Science That Will Transform Your Sex Life.* Simon Schuster.
2 Berne, E. (1961). *Transactional Analysis in Psychotherapy.* MN: Condor Books.
3 Silverberg, C. (2013). *What Makes a Baby.* New York City: Seven Stories Press; Silverberg, C. (2015). *Sex Is a Funny Word: A Book About Bodies, Feelings, and You.* New York City: Seven Stories Press; Silverberg, C. (2022). *You Know, Sex: Bodies, Gender, Puberty, and Other Things.* New York City: Seven Stories Press.
4 BISH (2022) *A Guide to Sex, Love and You.* Available at: https://www.bishuk.com/ (Accessed: 21 August 2022).
5 Scarleteen (no date) *Sex ed for the Real World.* Available at: https://www.scarleteen.com (Accessed: 22 August 2022).
6 Charura, D., & Lago, C. (Eds.) (2021). *Black Identities & White Therapies: Race, Respect and Diversity.* PCCS Books.
7 Turner, D.; Dwight Turner Counselling (no date). Available at: https://www.dwightturnercounselling.co.uk/ (Accessed: 29 August 2022).
8 Hawkins, R., & Neves, S. (2020). 'Integrating Diversity Into Therapy'. *COSRT online seminar*, 26 August.
9 McKenzie-Mavinga (2016). *The Challenge of Racism in Therapeutic Practice.* Palgrave.

10 NSPCC (2022) *How Safe Are Our Children?* Available at: https://learning.nspcc. org.uk/research-resources/how-safe-are-our-children (Accessed: 21 August 2022).

11 Davis, A., et al. (2018). 'What Behaviors Do Young Heterosexual Australians See in Pornography? A Cross-Sectional Study', *Journal of Sex Research*, 55(3), pp. 310–319.

12 Hanson, E. (2020). 'What Is the IMPACT of Pornography on Young People?', *NHS UK*. Available at: https://sexualhealth.cht.nhs.uk/fileadmin/sexualHealth/contentUploads/Documents/What_is_the_impact_of_pornography_on_young_people_-_A_research_briefing_for_educators.pdf (Accessed: 21 August 2022).

13 BISH (2022) *A Guide to Sex, Love and You.* Available at: https://www.bishuk.com/ (Accessed: 21 August 2022).

14 Swami, V., & Furnham, A. (2008). *The Psychology of Physical Attraction.* London: Routledge.

15 Paslakis et al. (2020). 'Associations between Pornography Exposure, Body Image and Sexual Body Image: A Systematic Review', *Journal of Health Psychology*, 27 October. Available at: https://journals.sagepub.com/doi/abs/10.1177/1359105320967085?journalCode=hpqa& (Accessed: 22 August 2022).

16 Masters, W., Johnson, V., & Kolodny, R. (1994). *Heterosexuality.* London: Thorsons.

17 Kinsey, A., Wardell, P., & Martin, C. (1948). *Sexual Behaviour in the Human Male.* Philadelphia: WB.
   Saunders; Kinsey, A., Wardell, P., & Martin, C. (1953). *Sexual Behaviour in the Human Female.* Philadelphia:
   WB Saunders; Hite, S. (1976). *The Hite Report.* New York: Dell.

18 French, R. (2018). 'Sexual & Reproductive Health', *BMJ,* 44(1), Jan. Available at: https://srh.bmj.com/content/44/1/16 (Accessed: 7 September 2022).

19 Bennett, J., & Pope, A. (2008). *The Pill.* New South Wales, Australia: Allen & Unwin.

20 Shapiro, R. (1987). *Contraception: A Practical and Political Guide.* London: Virago.

21 Meston, C., & Buss, D. (2007). *Why Humans Have Sex.* Available at: https://labs.la.utexas.edu/mestonlab/files/2016/05/WhyHaveSex.pdf (Accessed: 21 August 2022).

22 Morin, J. (1996). *The Erotic Mind.* New York: Harper Collins.

23 Crown Prosecution Service, The (2022) *Rape and Sexual Offences - Chapter 6: Consent, 21 May 2021|Legal Guidance, Sexual Offences.* Available at: https://www.cps.gov.uk/legal-guidance/rape-and-sexual-offences-chapter-6-consent (Accessed: 4 September 2022).

24 End Violence Against Women (2022) *Major New YouGov Survey for EVAW: Many People Still Unclear What Rape Is.* 6 December 2018. Available at: https://www.endviolenceagainstwomen.org.uk/major-new-survey-many-still-unclear-what-rape-is/ (Accessed: 23 August 2022).

25 Thames Valley Police (2022) *Consent is Everything.* Available at: https://www.thamesvalley.police.uk/police-forces/thames-valley-police/areas/c/2017/consent-is-everything/ (Accessed: 4 September 2022).

26 Consent is Everything (no date) *Consent – It's Simple as Tea.* Available at: http://www.consentiseverything.com/ (Accessed: 4 September 2022).

27 Barker, M. J. (2018). *Rewriting the Rules.* Routledge; Meg-John Barker (2016). *Rewriting the Rules.* Available at: https://www.rewriting-the-rules.com/meg-john-barker/ (Accessed: 4 September 2022).

28 Rewriting the Rules (2016) *The Consent Checklist.* Available at: https://www.rewriting-the-rules.com/wp-content/uploads/2019/10/Consent-Checklist-1.pdf (Accessed: 4 September 2022).

29 Banks, S. (2011). 'Understanding Despair, Denial, Power and Emotions in the Context of Climate Change', *Transformations.* Winter 2011–2012.
30 Amy and Arnold Mindell (no date) *Process-Oriented Psychology.* Available at: http://www.aamindell.net/process-work (Accessed: 4 September 2022); Amy and Arnold Mindell (no date) *Deep Democracy.* Available at: http://www.aamindell.net/worldwork?rq=Power%2C%20Rank%20and%20Privilege%20 (Accessed: 4 September 2022).
31 Braun-Harvey, D., & Vigorito, M. (2015). *Treating Out of Control Sexual Behavior: Rethinking Sex Addiction.* Springer.
32 Lehmiller, J. (2018). 'The Science of Sexual Fantasy and Desire: Part 1', *Sexual Health Alliance.* Available at: https://sexualhealthalliance.com/justin-lehmiller-science-of-fantasy (Accessed: 22 August 2022).
33 Anzani, A. (2020). 'Sexual Fantasy Across Gender Identity: A Qualitative Investigation of Differences between Bisgender and Non-Binary People's Imagery', *Sexual and Relationship Therapy*, February. Available at: https://www.researchgate.net/publication/339567666_Sexual_fantasy_across_gender_identity_a_qualitative_investigation_of_differences_between_cisgender_and_non-binary_people's_imagery. (Accessed: 7 September 2022).
34 Karpman, S.; Karpman Drama Triangle. Available at: https://www.karpmandramatriangle.com/ (Accessed: 22 August 2022).
35 Maltz, W. (2012). *The Sexual Healing Journey: A Guide for Survivors of Sexual Abuse.* William Morrow Paperbacks.
36 Harvey, D. B., & Vigorito, M. A. (2016). *Treating Out of Control Sexual Behavior: Rethinking Sex Addiction.* New York, NY: Springer.
37 Nordling, N., Sandnabba, N. K., & Santtila, P. (2000). 'The Prevalence and Effects of Self-Reported Childhood Sexual Abuse Among Sadomasochistically Oriented Males and Females', *Journal of Child Sexual Abuse: Research, Treatment, & Program Innovations for Victims, Survivors, & Offenders*, 9(1), pp. 53–63.
38 Richters, J., et al. (2008). 'Demographic and Psychosocial Features of Participants in Bondage and Discipline, Sadomasochism or Dominance and Submission (BDSM): Data From a National Survey', *Journal of Sexual Medicine*, 5(7), pp. 1660–1668.
39 Wiismeijer, A., & Van Assen, M. (2013). 'Psychological Characteristics of BDSM Practitioners', *Journal of Sexual Medicine*, 10(8).
40 Kahr, B. (2007). *Sex and the Psyche: The Truth About Our Most Secret Fantasies.* New York: Penguin.
41 Lehmiller, J. (2018). *Tell Me What You Want: The Science of Sexual Desire and How It Can Help You Improve Your Sex Life.* Robinson.
42 Barker, M. J., & Langridge, D. (eds). (2007). *Safe, Sane & Consensual: Contemporary Perspectives on Sadomasochism.* UK: Palgrave Macmillan. Available at: https://www.rewriting-the-rules.com/ (Accessed: 11 September 2022).
43 Robinson, E., & Aveyard, P. (2017). 'Emaciated Mannequins: A Study of Mannequin Body Size in High Street Fashion Stores', *Journal of Eating Disorders*, 5(1). Available at: https://www.researchgate.net/publication/316631986_Emaciated_mannequins_A_study_of_mannequin_body_size_in_high_street_fashion_stores (Accessed: 6 September 2022).
44 Zilbergeld, B. (1999). *The New Male Sexuality: The Truth About Men, Sex, and Pleasure.* Bantam Doubleday Dell Publishing.
45 Biddulph, S. (2004). *Manhood.* London: Vermillion.
46 McCarthy, B., & McCarthy, E. (2020). *Contemporary Male Sexuality: Confronting Myths and Promoting Change.* Routledge.

47 Women's Environmental Network (2022) Available at: https://www.wen.org.uk/ (Accessed: 23 August 2022).
48 Carrington, D. (2022). 'Cocktail of Chemical Pollutants Linked to Falling Sperm Quality in Research', *The Guardian*, 10 June. Available at: https://www. theguardian.com/environment/2022/jun/10/cocktail-of-chemical-pollutants-linked-to-falling-sperm-quality-in-research?CMP=Share_iOSApp_Other (Accessed: 21 August 2022).
49 Cancer Research UK (2022) *Cancer Incidence for Common Cancers*. Available at: https://www.cancerresearchuk.org/health-professional/cancer-statistics/incidence/common-cancers-compared#heading-One (Accessed: 21 August 2022).
50 Krupnick, M. (2022). 'More Than 3,000 Potentially Harmful Chemicals Found in Food Packaging', *The Guardian*, 19 May. Available at: https://www.theguardian.com/world/2022/may/19/more-than-3000-potentially-harmful-chemicals-food-packaging-report-shows (Accessed: 21 August 2022).
51 Diamond, L. (2008). *Sexual Fluidity*. Boston, MA: Harvard University Press.
52 Sherwin, A. (2011). 'Sex Isn't Such a Straight Choice Anymore for Brits', *iNewspaper*, 29 September.
53 IPSOS (2022) *LGBT & Pride 2021 Global Survey*. Available at: https://www.ipsos.com/sites/default/files/LGBT%20Pride%202021%20Global%20Survey%20Report%20-%20US%20Version.pdf (Accessed: 21 August 2022).
54 Robinson-Wood, T. (2017). *The Convergence of Race, Ethnicity and Gender*. Sage.
55 Kaufman, G., & Raphael, L. (1996). *Coming Out of Shame*. New York: Doubleday.
56 Swami, V., & Furnham, A. (2008). *The Psychology of Physical Attraction*. London: Routledge.
57 BBC News (2022) *Why Do So Few Rape Cases Go to Court?* 27 May. Available at: https://www.bbc.co.uk/news/uk-48095118 (Accessed: 23 August 2022).

Chapter 5

Body

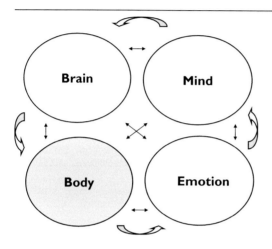

Sex Is for All (Adult) Bodies

If we get our sex education from looking at porn, or the movies, it is easy to think that sex is only for young, able-bodied, slim, hairless, usually white bodies. The 'beautiful people'. And yet all bodies can experience pleasure. Whatever age you are, whether you have a chronic illness, a disability, persistent pain, whatever your weight, you have a right to feel pleasure. Not a responsibility – some people are not interested in sex and do not feel the need to cultivate it. But if you would like sexual pleasure, you can create your own script and your own path to experiencing it.

It is rare to see disabled people represented as sexual, and often assumed that they are asexual, or hypersexual, which could not be further from the truth. Of course, it can be challenging to focus on pleasure if your body is causing you pain, or fatigue, or you have a spinal cord injury or other form of bodily numbness. You may need to make use of sex toys, or aids like swings and slings. Equally you may have a condition that is invisible but makes it harder to communicate with others or feel comfortable and understood when dating or having sex. But if you want it, you deserve it,

DOI: 10.4324/9781003322405-6

and there are resources[1] to help including the website and podcasts of Dr Lee Phillips,[2] an American psychotherapist, who is 'on a mission to crush the myth that people with chronic illness and other disabilities are not sexual'.

It is worth noting that various health conditions and medication can affect sexual function. For example, erections can be limited with diabetes and heart conditions, and conversely if you find yourself unable to get an erection in any circumstances including masturbation, it is worth having yourself checked out for these kinds of health conditions. Antidepressants such as SSRIs can affect sexual interest, and/or make it slower to have orgasms. Other psychiatric disorders and their medications, and illnesses such as cancer and many others can also affect sexual functioning. If this has happened to you and you want to address it, it is worth discussing with your healthcare provider whether you can try alternative treatments that may not have this effect.

A preliminary note about trans and non-binary bodies: this section of the book will explore in some detail bodily aspects of sexual functioning, and while we have tried where possible to focus on the body part, rather than the gender of the person, we do recognise that the names of body parts are closely connected in many people's minds with gender, and that some trans and non-binary people prefer to rename their genitals, perhaps using more gender-neutral words like hole or glans, or whatever feels best. For example, if you are transmasculine and want to call your 'clitoris' your cock, go for it! The key thing here is to use language that makes you feel good, turns you on and helps you feel comfortable. There is no right or wrong, and in general feeling accepted and authentic is highly correlated with sexual satisfaction. For more specific resources and support, we highly recommend Lucie Fielding's *Trans Sex*.[3]

My Body

Solo Exercise

Using the image of the body map in Illustration 5.1 as a guide, create an image of your unique body. You may want to print the map out and draw on it or transfer it into some software to change.

First, alter the outline so that it shows your own body shape more accurately. If you have disabilities, you may want to symbolically show them on the map.

Then add any features (literally or symbolically), which show your own sex characteristics such as bum, breasts, nipples and genitalia. If you are undergoing gender transition or have experienced FGM/C, you may want to show how you are now, or how you want to look.

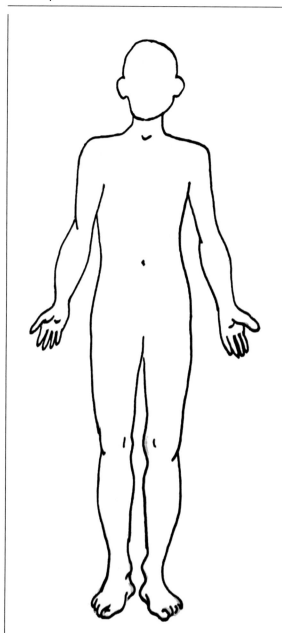

Illustration 5.1 Body Map.

Outside the body outline, add in any words or symbols which are important to you about your sexuality such as your orientation, or other social or cultural factors.

Exercise with Partner/s

Share your images with each other and tell your partner/s what is important to you and why. Share how you feel doing this exercise, what you think and what you think your partner/s may think. Check out your assumptions with each other.

Sex, Reproduction and Pleasure

In this section, we will explore our bodies and our sexual anatomy. Most of us know something about our reproductive functioning, at least a bit about periods, erections, ejaculation and the mechanics of heterosexual intercourse. As children we are introduced to sex as something humans do to reproduce, which is of course true but not the only reason we have sex. This confusion between reproduction and sex can hamper our enjoyment of sex. This is because the clitoris, not the vagina, is the primary female sex organ. Depending on the positioning of the clitoral bud relative to the vagina, there is more or less likelihood of sexual stimulation during vaginal intercourse without additional stimulation of the clitoris. This may help to explain the 'orgasm gap' – the fact that while 95% of people regularly orgasm during masturbation, this drops for heterosexual, cis women during partnered sex down to 65%, and drastically so on a first encounter, down to 16% (Gurney 2022).[4] See Figure 5.1.

Research on the sexual experiences and satisfaction of trans people is still in its infancy; however, a 2020 study of trans women[5] interestingly showed

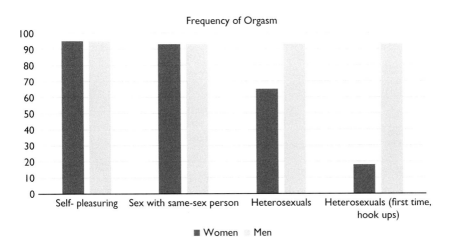

Figure 5.1 Frequency of Orgasm.

that hormonal treatment caused an increase in time to orgasm (with some dissatisfaction about this), and also longer orgasm duration and higher satisfaction. This was true whether there had or had not been genital surgery, which shows how crucial hormones are to orgasm. Genital or lower surgery available for trans men still struggles to both retain sexual sensation and create an erectile penis of sufficient size for intercourse. However, it is not clear how important this is to sexual satisfaction, as it seems generally that a sense of self and bodily acceptance is most central, and this will differ from person to person.

There is a great diversity of human genitalia. Our external genitals come in all shapes and sizes, like our different faces. However, the image in Illustration 5.2 portrays the standard differences of male and female external genitals, for the purpose of contrasting the internal similarities.

Despite the different external male and female genitals, we start out similarly as foetuses, in a primarily female form. If a Y chromosome is present, then at around twelve weeks the seed of the genitourinary system begins to alter to develop as male, if not it continues to develop as female. A proportion of babies are born with indeterminate genitals; this is part of a variety of intersex conditions. Some babies with indeterminate external genitals are allowed to develop until puberty to see what changes emerge, and some undergo surgical operations; this is increasingly campaigned against by intersex adults. The existence of not only indeterminate genitals but also a wide mix of chromosomal and hormonal presentations, and internal sex characteristics in intersex folx shows us that biological sex is much more of a complex gradient than a simple binary of male and female. This is beautifully illustrated by Amanda Montanez's graphic in *Scientific American*.[6]

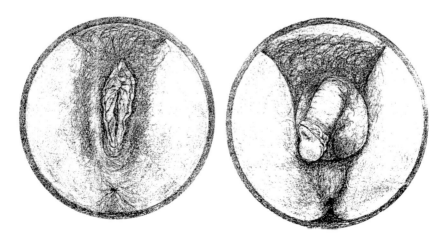

Illustration 5.2 External Genitals.

Traditionally, the penis plays a dual role as both a sexual and a reproductive organ, meaning its owner can be sexual and is potentially fertile all their adult life; from puberty to old age depending on their health. They can experience sexual pleasure regardless of their fertility, for example, after vasectomy or if infertile through ill health. They can also experience orgasms as distinct from their reproductive ability to ejaculate.

Typical biological females, however, have separate sexual and reproductive organs, which work independently of each other. Their sexual functioning is separate from reproduction. The monthly menstrual/fertility cycle is not dependant on or triggered by sexual activity; it happens regardless of whether the person is sexually active or not. Conversely sexual arousal happens regardless of ability to conceive; it is not dependent on or triggered by fertility. Owners of a female sexual and reproductive system can be sexual any time but are actually in a physiological infertile state most of their adult life. This is because between puberty and menopause there are only a few fertile days a month and during these years there may be times of pregnancy or breastfeeding. People can obviously be, and still are, sexually potent after menopause. Virgins and celibate women still menstruate. Trans men who are not on hormone therapy menstruate (for those who are on hormone therapy, this is usually reversible if hormone therapy is stopped, however, the longer a person has been on HT the less likely periods are to return and the longer this may take).

This distinction between sexual and reproductive capacity is an important awareness because it demonstrates that our reproductive model of sex is a social construct and not a biological reality. Understanding the difference between our reproductive and sexual potential is vital. It helps us celebrate our human evolution beyond sex as a reproductive imperative, to see it also as a socialising and pleasure principle, and sexuality as an expression of our fire energy and creativity.

Sensuous Skin

Solo Exercise

Have a bath for the sensuous experience of being in hot water. Prepare the bathroom with candles, bubble bath or music if you want. Lie for at least fifteen minutes, relax and experience your body, letting the water move on you. What does it feel like, what thoughts and emotions are evoked? If you do not have a bath, you could shower but with a similar attitude of experiencing the sensations of the water on your skin.

When you have finished, wrap yourself in warm towels, imagine feeling held and snug.

When you are dry, gently massage your body touching all over your skin. Use lotion or oil if you want. Feel the touch of your skin from outside, how another may experience touching you. What does it feel like inside your body when you are being touched?

Exercise with Partner/s

Using the body map shown in Illustration 5.3, each colour in a front and back body map to indicate places where you like to be touched – in green. Mark in red any areas you do not want to be touched. And any maybe places, can be in orange or amber. Share your body maps with each other and discuss them.

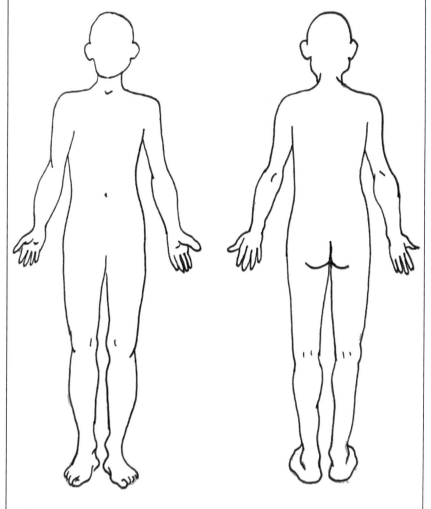

Illustration 5.3 Partner's Body Map.

If you are happy to, have a bath together or a shower. Afterwards massage each other's neck and shoulders –if they are green areas on both your body maps. If not, you may want to massage hands or feet, or a different preferred green area. Tell each other what it is like to touch, and to be touched by each other.

Share how you feel doing this exercise, what you think and what you think your partner/s may think. Check out your assumptions with each other.

The Proud Penis

We have a cultural ambivalence towards the penis; a sort of respect for it as a symbol of power and potency with its ability to stand erect, yet a shaming also. Words like dick or prick are generally used in a disdainful or critical way.

Many feel pressure around the length and girth of their penis, as well as how 'it' performs. It is worth knowing some basic facts: the penis develops until the age of 21. The average flaccid penis is 9.16 cm in length; the average erect penis is 13.12-cm long. The corresponding girth measurements are 9.31 cm for a flaccid penis and 11.66 cm for an erect one. Outliers are rare: a 16-cm erect penis falls into the 95th percentile: out of 100 men, only five would have a penis larger than 16 cm. Conversely, an erect penis measuring 10 cm falls into the fifth percentile: only five out of 100 men would have a penis smaller than 10 cm.[7] It seems that there is more size variation between flaccid than between erect penises.

A penis would be considered unusually small – a micro penis – if it were less than 7.5-cm long when erect. This condition is sometimes the result of a hormonal deficiency that can be treated with testosterone. Other than that, there is no scientific evidence that any treatments promoted in the enormous penile enlargement industry are effective. Penises, like vulvas, vary widely in appearance.

Laura Dodsworth has created some interesting projects – photographing penises and interviewing men to discuss themes of masculinity, gender and sexuality (2017)[8]; and women, talking about how they feel about pleasure, sex, pain, trauma, birth, motherhood, menstruation, menopause and gender (2019).[9]

Physiology

Even though male and female external genitals are quite different, there are many internal similarities. The *testes* and *vas deferens* are similar to the ovaries and fallopian tubes. The *prostate* and *Cowper's glands* are similar to the uterus and paraurethral glands. The penis is an external equivalent of the internal clitoris. Both have a *glans, two corpus cavanosa* and the *corpus spongiosum*. Some penises have a foreskin, and some have had it removed. Illustration 5.4

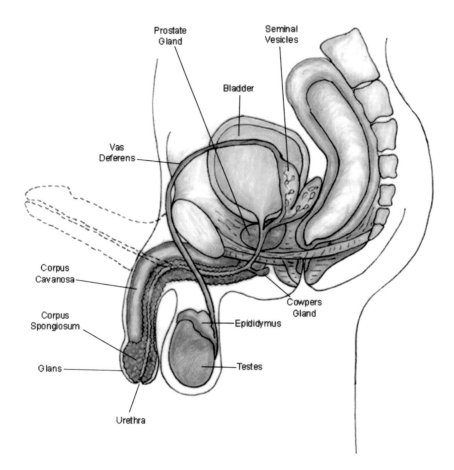

Illustration 5.4 The Internal Structure of the Penis.

shows the internal structure of the flaccid penis within the pelvic area. The dotted lines show how it changes when erect.

Fertility

Every day, millions of sperm are made in the *somniferous tubules* in the *testes*. They move into the *epididymis*, learn to swim and continue up the *vas deferens* to be stored in the *seminal vesicles*. The whole process of sperm production takes about seventy-two days. Because sperm is manufactured in the body, there is the potential for fertility into old age; however, the quality of fertility depends on age, health and lifestyle.

Arousal

Usually the shaft of the penis is flaccid and hangs down over the testicles. The penis becomes erect due to changes in the *erectile tissue*: the corpus cavanosa, the smooth muscle within the penis changes and blood flows into the corpus spongiosum and swells the shaft. This happens in various stages from first excitation through to full erection. It is usual to have three to five erections while asleep, including one upon waking. Getting an erection is not always sexual. It is a reflex, an automatic response in the body.

Ejaculation

Ejaculation is when semen is released from the penis. Sperm mixes with nutrient-rich fluids from the seminal vesicles, the prostate and the Cowper's glands, and is propelled through the vas deferens and out through the urethral opening at the tip of the penis.

Orgasm

Orgasm is a reflex action through the nervous system, due to a surge of hormones. It culminates in a release of sexual energy and pleasurable muscle spasms. Orgasm can be experienced in the genitals or the whole body can be affected. After orgasm, the body returns to a pre-orgasmic state and can orgasm again, and again.

External Genitals

Solo Exercise

Bring a small mirror into your Safe Space, sit for a while and allow yourself to settle. Remove clothes covering your genitals, sit down and open your legs. With the mirror look at your genital area, smile and say hello. Look in detail at yourself and imagine you have never seen a vulva or penis and scrotum before. Make sure to also look at and notice your responses to the anus.

Do a self-portrait or representation of your genitals. It could be a still life or an abstract; a painting, drawing or a collage.

Exercise with Partner/s

Do a drawing of each other's genitals and tell each other what you think and feel about doing this. Tell each other three things you like about their genitals.

The Able Anus

Anal play is common and increasing, for example, in a study of 16–24-year-old heterosexuals in Britain in 2010–2012,[10] approximately one in four men and one in five women reported having had anal sex in the past year. The author of *Gay Men and Anal Eroticism*, Steven Underwood,[11] estimates that about 75% of gay men have at some time participated in anal sex. It is quite possible that the ubiquity of online porn has influenced the popularity of anal sex, particularly among heterosexuals – Pornhub[12] published that in 2021 *anal* was the number 8 'most searched for term', and the number 6 most viewed.

Enjoying anal pleasure does not mean someone is gay. Exploration and stimulation of the anus can be highly pleasurable for all genders and orientations, causing the anal sphincter to twitch and contract, sometimes in unison with other pelvic muscles. Just as you can contract your pelvic muscles voluntarily to enhance arousal, you can do this with your anal sphincter too. In male bodies, the prostate can also be pleasurably stimulated from inside the anus. Many people of all genders enjoy the unique sensation of the anus contracting against something such as a finger, dildo or penis. Always start slowly and gently, and always apply lubrication when inserting a finger or anything else into the anus. Stop if it becomes painful. Explore by yourself first. As with all sexual behaviours, consider your beliefs and feelings about having anal sex and only proceed if you feel comfortable. Water-soluble or silicone lubricants are good overall, whereas oil-based lubes destroy latex if condoms are being used. Note that the pH of the vagina (3.5–4.9) is different to that of the anus (6.0), so you should use different lubricants accordingly.

As for cleanliness, faeces are not normally stored in the rectum for long periods of time as the rectum and anal canal are merely passageways for faeces which, during a bowel movement, are moved by muscular waves out of the colon into the rectum and out through the anal canal. Bathing is usually adequate for cleaning this area, especially if you learn to feel comfortable putting your finger in your anus as part of bathing or showering. If, however you are concerned about cleanliness, you can learn how to give yourself an anal douche.

Anal Exploration

Solo Exercise

Take some time to write down your thoughts about anal pleasure. Perhaps this is already a part of your life, or not. What comes up when you consider exploring your own anus, or incorporating anal play into your sex life with partner(s)? Write about any blocks or inhibitions, any beliefs or values.

Then, while you are in the shower, using some natural oil, experiment with exploring your anus with a finger. This can be a turning point in your desire for anal enjoyment and well-being. Keep in mind that if your anus has been abused in the past, whether through sexual experiences, straining during bowel movements or medical intervention, it may take it a while to trust the presence of your finger. Go slowly, use lube and wait for the body to release and invite in your finger.

Once inside your anal canal, even a little, you will probably encounter new sensations. Some will be pleasurable, while others may feel rather strange. You may experience negative and positive memories and pent-up emotions. Take it easy, and when you have finished, spend some time writing or drawing about the experience.

Exercise with Partner/s

If you would like, take it in turns to give each other an anal massage. The receiving partner should first shower, as in the solo exercise. The giving partner should always use lots of lubrication (either a natural oil such as coconut or almond, or an organic purpose-made lube). Spend time massaging the buttocks, and then more closely around the anus. Be gentle as the skin is very sensitive here. If both of you so wish, experiment with entering the anus slightly with your finger. Never force or push, allow the body to invite you in.

Afterwards, spend some time sharing what that was like.

The Wonderful Womb

Physiology

Female reproductive organs are the *ovaries, fallopian tubes, uterus* and the *vagina*. The *vagina* surrounds the tip of the uterus, the *cervix*, providing a birth canal, to the *entrance within the vulva*. Illustration 5.5 shows the internal structure of the clitoris and the reproductive organs within the pelvic area. The dotted lines show how the clitoris changes when erect.

The uterus and ovaries can be the site of gynaecological problems like endometriosis, polycystic ovaries, fibroids and painful periods, which can interfere with sexual pleasure. If you are experiencing internal pain, please do arrange a gynaecological appointment.

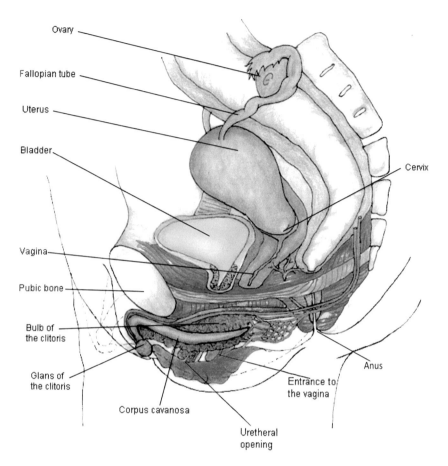

Ovary

Fallopian tube

Uterus

Bladder

Cervix

Vagina

Pubic bone

Bulb of
the clitoris

Glans of
the clitoris

Corpus cavanosa

Anus

Entrance to
the vagina

Uretheral
opening

Illustration 5.5 Female Sexual and Reproductive Organs.

Fertility

The biological female is infertile most of the time, except for a few days
during each monthly cycle. Many of us are not aware of the menstrual cycle
as a fertility cycle. What is actually quite simple, that is, being aware of this
process, is implied as unpredictable; the social narrative is that women are
somehow *potentially* fertile all the time so could get pregnant at any time.
Females are born with a limited number of eggs in their ovaries, making
them potentially fertile from menstruation until menopause. There is usually
one ovulation per menstrual cycle. Just as or soon after menstruation ends,
fertility begins to increase, leading up to ovulation when an egg is released
from the ovary. This egg must be fertilised within twenty-four hours, or it

disintegrates and is reabsorbed into the body. Fertilisation usually happens in the first part of one of the fallopian tubes. If conception does not happen, the egg will disintegrate and there will be a new menstruation in about two weeks, starting a new fertility cycle.

In the same way that the moon cycles vary from twenty-nine to thirty-one days per month, menstrual cycles are not always twenty-eight days but sometimes vary in length. The time from ovulation until the next period is fixed; each individual will have a pattern of between twelve and sixteen days. Once this is recognised (along with an awareness of when ovulation has occurred), one can accurately predict when the next menstruation will start. Some months may be a shorter cycle and some, a longer cycle. This is because the day of ovulation can vary in each cycle, but it will always be preceded with the signs of fertility outlined later. By observing and charting changes in both the cervix and the cervical fluid, one can get to know what one's body is like when it is infertile: the 'basic infertile pattern', and how it changes during the few fertile days.

The basic infertile pattern of the cervix is that it sits into the vagina and can be felt by inserting one or two fingers; it will feel easy to reach and relatively firm. During each cycle, the cervix goes through changes similar to that of the birthing process; it softens and shortens in increments, so that just before ovulation it can feel higher up in the vagina and more difficult to reach, and the Os (the opening of the cervix), has changed from being closed to more open. This may take several days to happen. After ovulation, it returns to its infertile state of feeling firmer and lower in the vagina. In conjunction with these changes, glands in the cervix produce fluids, which change over several days building up to the day of ovulation, and then also change again after.

It is easiest to think of the first day of a menstrual bleed as the beginning of a new cycle (number 1 in Illustration 5.6) and of each cycle having three phases:

- The first phase of these changes is called the *potentially fertile phase* because we are infertile until our fertility begins, which we cannot predict but need to observe cycle by cycle. At this stage (number 2 in the diagram), several ova develop under the influence of follicle-stimulating hormone (FSH) which triggers oestrogen. Following the menstrual period, there may be several days of no visible fluids in the vagina; these days may be absent in short cycles and numerous in long cycles.
- One of the first signs of the *fertile phase* is a sensation or presentation of a moist or sticky fluid in the vagina; it is usually scant, pasty and white or yellow in colour (number 3 in the diagram). The next is a transitional phase where increasing amounts of slightly stretchy, cloudy and thinner fluids may be felt or observed. Highly fertile fluids will become more profuse, giving a sensation of lubrication or slipperiness.

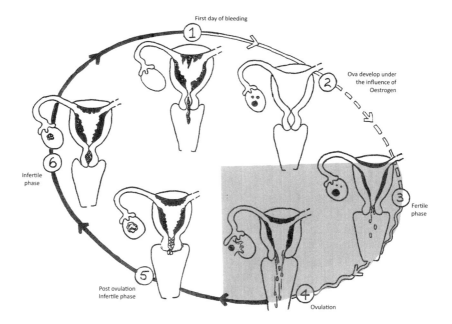

First day of bleeding

①

Ova develop under
the influence of
Oestrogen

②

Infertile
phase

⑥

Fertile
phase

③

Post ovulation
Infertile phase

⑤

④

Ovulation

Illustration 5.6 Changes During the Fertility Cycle.

The appearance will be thin, watery and transparent, and at its peak, stretchy and similar to raw egg white. Triggered by a surge in luteinising hormone, ovulation happens just after the peak of these changes (number 4 in the diagram).

- During the *post-ovulatory phase* (numbers 5 and 6 in the diagram), progesterone is released from the ovary; the slippery sensation of the fluid is lost and there will be a relatively abrupt return to stickiness or dryness again. The cervical fluids will thickened again, forming a plug at the cervix acting as a barrier to sperm, and reducing the chances of infection within the reproductive organs. As the amount and quality of these fluids will vary, charting to get to know one's own 'basic infertile pattern' is the best way to understand your own cycle and the signs of fertility.

Cervical fluids can be distinguished from semen or arousal lubrication; the latter two will dry up quickly upon your fingertips and are water soluble. If confused, test the fluid by dipping it into a glass of water. If it is fertile cervical fluid, it will form a ball and sink to the bottom, if not it will dissolve. Cervical fluids are crucial to fertility, playing several roles, including filtering out any damaged sperm. Ordinarily sperm would die within a few hours after ejaculation but in this fertile fluid they can live for up to five days, occasionally longer. What is clinically called 'discharge' is in fact an alkaline 'sperm-friendly' fluid, providing channels to help them swim the long distance. If the sperm reach a fertile egg, they will be able to fuse with it having been chemically activated and stripped of their outer coating of zinc and proteins by the cervical fluid. Understanding the cyclical changes in fluids can help us know when something is not right and can encourage early detection of a sexually transmitted infection or other gynaecological difficulty.

Other indicators of the ovulatory process include changes in body temperature, breast tenderness and sometimes a sharp twinge in the ovary concerned. The body temperature is basically lower before ovulation and higher afterwards; charting this will show the differences. This is useful to indicate that ovulation has happened but not helpful in indicating the onset of the fertile phase. This *fertile phase* is about five days before ovulation, because of the cervical fluids, and for twenty-four hours after.

First Reproductive Experience

Solo Exercise

*What are your first thoughts when you think about your **first menstruation** or your **first wet dream**? Had you been informed about the biology of what was happening? Were there any adults around to explain things to you?*

How did you feel? Were there any surprises and if so, what were they? What do you think and how do you feel now thinking about this time?

Exercise with Partner/s

Tell each other about your first menstruation or wet dream, and what you discovered in your solo exploration of this exercise.

Share with each other if there are any ways you wish these experiences would have been different.

The Voluptuous Vulva

We have a cultural dislike for female external genitals, which are called the *vulva*. It is confusing that we distinguish the clitoris and the vulva. This probably came about because of the reproductive model of sex; the focus on the vagina as the female sexual organ, yet a need to name and identify the external sexual genitalia. This is like talking about our throat and pretending we do not have a mouth, tongue or lips. By ignoring the vulva, we miss out what is within it – the clitoris – which as you will see in the next diagram is not a 'tiny, hard to find bud'. There are many other colloquial words such as fanny, pussy and cunt that do refer to the whole vulva. Despite being reclaimed by some, the word cunt is also still the most offensive swear word in the English language.

Physiology

The vulva is the outside, oval part of the female sexual organ, the clitoris. Most of the clitoris and the vagina are inside the body. When the clitoral lips or inner labia are open, we can see the glans of the clitoris and the entrance to the vagina. The vagina leads from the opening in the vulva, up to the cervix, the end part of the uterus. Labia may be symmetrical or not, and like penises, they come in all shapes and sizes. Some people are anxious about the appearance of their labia, perhaps from comparison with those seen in porn, and labiaplasty – surgery to the labia – for cosmetic reasons is on the rise.

Genital Geography

Solo Exercise

Bring a small mirror into your Safe Space, sit for a while and allow yourself to settle. Remove clothes covering your genitals, sit down and open your legs. With the mirror look at your genital area, smile, and say hello. Look in detail at yourself.

Gently touch and explore to see all the aspects of your genitals. For those with penises, include the shaft and the tip, move the foreskin back, feel your testicles. For those with vulvas, touch all the outside areas and then open the inner vulva lips and feel the different parts and places, including inside the vagina. Then afterwards, explore the perineum and anus.

What is it like to touch and be touched? Smell and taste your fingers when touching different parts of yourself. Notice any sensations in your body and any feelings evoked.

Using the illustrations in this book, see if you can map out your unique genital geography. Notice different shapes, colours and textures. Can you identify all the different aspects of your genitals?

What do you call yourself: vulva, fanny, pussy, cunt, penis, dick, cock or prick? What do you like to say, what do you like to hear? Is this different in different contexts?

Exercise with Partner/s

Can you allow each other to explore your genitals in the same way you did yourself? Can you bring a sense of awe and wonder to the uniqueness of each other's similarities and differences?

If not, would you prefer to explore yourself and let your partner/s watch and/or talk with you? Or maybe you would just prefer to tell each other about your solo experiences of this exercise.

Either of these is fine –the most important thing is to honour what feels right for you.

The Cunning Clitoris

The clitoris is the only organ in the human body whose sole function is pleasure. The clitoral head contains eight thousand nerve endings, double that of the glans of the penis. In our culture, we cut out the female sexual organ visually and linguistically. In other cultures, this is done literally. The Prohibition of Female Circumcision Act[13] came into force in the UK in 1985, making it an offence to carry out or to aid, or procure the performance by another person, of any form of female genital mutilation (FGM), except for specific medical purposes.

Macfarlane and Dorkenoo's[14] research from 2011 estimated that 137,000 women and girls living in England and Wales were believed to have undergone or be at risk of experiencing Female Genital Mutilation/Cutting (FGM/C), as they were born in countries where it is practiced.

Based on this research, UK government statistics for England and Wales[15] state:

* Around 60,000 girls aged 0–14 were born to mothers who had undergone FGM.
* Approximately 103,000 women aged 15–49 and approximately 24,000 women aged 50 and over who have migrated are living with the consequences of FGM.
* In addition, approximately 10,000 girls aged under 15 who have migrated are likely to have undergone FGM.

Physiology

The *clitoris* is as wide and long as the vulva – from the *pubic bone* to the *anus*. The erectile tissue of the clitoris, the *glans, two corpus cavanosa* and the *corpus spongiosum* also extends inside the body, surrounding the *entrance to*

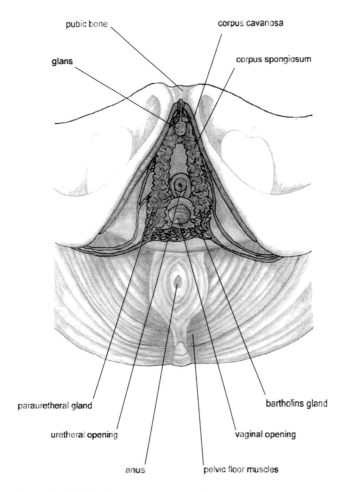

pubic bone

corpus cavanosa

glans

corpus spongiosum

parauretheral gland

bartholins gland

urethral opening

vaginal opening

anus

pelvic floor muscles

Illustration 5.7 The Internal Structure of the Clitoris.

the vagina. Two excellent books with details about the clitoris are *A New View of a Woman's Body*[16] and *The Clitoral Truth.*[17] Illustration 5.7 shows the internal structure of the clitoris.

Illustration 5.8 shows the outline of the external vulva so you can see the clitoral system as it is internally. This clearly shows that the vulva is the primary female sexual organ. There is sexual sensitivity in the first third of the vagina as it is surrounded by the corpus spongiosum, the erectile tissue of the clitoris.

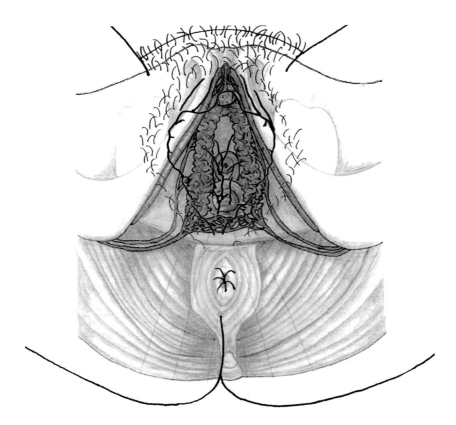

Illustration 5.8 The External and Internal Structure of the Vulva.

Arousal

The *clitoral bud* is similar to the very tip of the penis. When it is erect, the whole clitoris is actually thirty times bigger than the little bud. There are two *Bartholin's glands*, one on each side of the vaginal opening. Sexual arousal causes these glands to produce fluid, making the vulva feel wet and slippery. The *perineal sponge*, between the vaginal entrance and the anus, is also sexually sensitive. The exact distribution of nerve endings between the clitoris, vagina and cervix may differ from person to person. The *pelvic floor muscles* play a crucial role in the sexual arousal process, in all genders, particularly at orgasm.

Ejaculation

The clitoris also surrounds the urethra, creating the *urethral sponge* or *G zone* as it is more commonly called. It makes sense that stimulation of this area tends to only be pleasurable once the person is aroused and the tissue erects. G zone stimulation can lead to ejaculate being released from the *paraurethral glands*. It is now commonly agreed that fluids released are the same as male ejaculate, but without any sperm.

Orgasm

Orgasm is a reflex action through the nervous system, due to a surge of hormones. It culminates in a release of sexual energy, and pleasurable muscle spasms. Orgasm can be experienced in the genitals or the whole body can be affected. After orgasm, the body returns to a pre-orgasmic state and can orgasm again, and again.

Tender Touch

Solo Exercise

Make a time for yourself in your Safe Space. Make it warm. Take your clothes off, sit for a few moments and settle. Close your eyes and put your hands on your face. Touch your face; your forehead, cheeks and chin. Feel your skin being touched. Touch your neck shoulders and both arms.

Experiment with your touch; firmer, softer, slow and fast, longer strokes or circles. Touch with your fingers, palms back of your hand. Try kisses with lips and tongues. Explore and touch your feet, toes, legs and torso but for this exercise do not touch your nipples, breasts, genitals or anus. Notice what touch you like where, why and how. What turns you on?

What ideas, desires, thoughts and imaginations get triggered?

Do you want to go with the flow and want to become sexual? Have you cut off, numbed at the thought of any particular memories or emotions? If so, notice what has turned you off. Maybe it is thoughts or beliefs which may be outmoded now. Remember to 'Apply the Brakes' if necessary.

Reflect on this experience and either talk with someone, write or draw.

Exercise with Partner/s

Each colour in a front and back body map to indicate places where you want to be touched today – in green. Mark in red any areas you do not want to be touched. And any maybe (other places) can be in orange or amber.

Share your body maps with each other and discuss them. Decide how far into the solo exercise you may want to go for now.

> *Take it in turns to explore the green areas indicated by your partner/s, experimenting with touch. Discuss any orange areas to find out if any type of touch, or not, would turn them green.*
>
> *Take ten minutes each after, to share what it was like doing this exercise.*

Life Stages

Menstrual Health

The menstrual cycle can have a profound effect on mood, desire and experiences of sex. Many find that spontaneous desire peaks at certain points of the menstrual cycle. More widely, researchers are studying potential links between the use of endocrine-disrupting chemicals (EDCs) in sanitary products and an increase in reproductive health issues such as fibroids, PCOS and endometriosis. Others campaign about the impact of commercial period products on the environment. See, for example, the Women's Environmental Network's 2018 publication 'Seeing Red: Menstruation and the Environment'.[18] Menstrual cups, period pants and reusable pads are all good alternatives. Some brands have also been at the forefront of making menstruation more inclusive of trans, non-binary and gender nonconforming people. For example, period pants company *Thinx* was the first to include a trans man in an advert for their 'boyshorts' back in 2016. Making menstruation more inclusive is partly about language, as well as safety and access.

In terms of emotional and physical wellbeing, Alexandra Pope and Sjanie Hugo Wurlitzer[19] have created various excellent if somewhat cis-centric resources, including the book *Wild Power*, about working with the menstrual cycle as a powerful tool for self-care.

Childbirth

A proactive approach to sexual health includes knowing the risks of childbirth to sexual functioning and thinking about how to decrease these. For example, the perineum (the area between the vagina and the anus) can be very sensitive to touch, pressure and vibration during arousal as it houses a dense body of blood vessels that engorge during sexual response. There is a risk of the perineum tearing during childbirth. Some say this is increased by the current tendency towards induction of labour, which speeds up the process and gives the perineum less time to stretch naturally. Just over 3% of UK vaginal births incur an Obstetric Anal Sphincter Injury (OASI) – a third- or fourth degree that involves the back of the vagina and the muscles of the perineum and extends partially or completely through the anal sphincter and into the rectum. Stitches are required and 20–40% of sufferers experience symptoms of incontinence or urgency 12 months after giving birth. In 20–25% of singleton vaginal births in the UK, an episiotomy will be performed in an attempt to avoid tearing.[20] This is a cut from the back of the vagina in a diagonal line. It cuts through the perineal sponge and the pubococcygeus (PC) muscles (part of the sexual organs) and can therefore sometimes decrease sensation. A comparative study[21] found that two years after giving birth, there is an increased incidence of dyspareunia (pain with intercourse) and vaginal dryness for those who were given an episiotomy. This can be a vicious cycle, as associations of intercourse with pain can cause the vagina to tighten or not lubricate, making intercourse more painful and so on in a vicious cycle. Although the NHS website says there is no evidence for the efficacy of perineal massage in the last trimester of pregnancy, the Royal College of Midwives 2008 practice guidelines[22] state: 'Antenatal perineal massage is an effective approach to increasing the chance of an intact perineum'.

Sex after childbirth can also be affected by hormonal changes when breast or chest feeding (increased prolactin can decrease sexual desire and vaginal lubrication). Interestingly, male-bodied parents experience a drop in testosterone when caring for new babies, and the more care they provide, the greater the drop. Finally, the new responsibilities, role shifts and sleep deprivation of caring for a baby can affect the sexual feelings of any parent and caregiver.

Menopause

The menopause is a huge transition. It is still quite a taboo subject and has many negative images associated with it. It is often portrayed as a decline (to be halted with HRT), rather than the transition that it is.

So what happens during menopause? No longer ovulating each month, the body does not need such high levels of oestrogen, so goes through a process of change to readjust to new levels of hormonal needs. This has biological, mental, emotional and existential effects. Perhaps the major biological change during the menopause is that the adrenal glands take over from the ovaries as the main endocrine (hormone-producing) glands, and androgens are changed into oestrogens. Also the production of progesterone comes to an end. This process can take years, during which time hormones can be fluctuating. The adrenal glands are where stress is processed, releasing adrenaline and then cortisol. This is fine in short bursts, when our survival systems of fight or flight are needed, but prolonged or on-going stress is hard on our bodies. High levels of adrenaline and cortisol weaken our immune system and our digestive processes; we absorb less nutrients and find it harder to eliminate waste. The cardiovascular and nervous systems are also activated. All of this can undermine our mental and emotional sense of well-being, and is a time when we really need to up our self-care.

One of the first biological changes is where FSH fluctuates; there are no ova left to trigger the fertility process, so at first higher levels of FSH are released but eventually this settles. This fluctuation can feel very unsettling, sometimes causing anxiety and mood shifts. Most of the 'symptoms' during the menopause come in waves and cycles, but eventually settle as the body readjusts to the changes.

There are great general resources available about the menopause now. We particularly like Lara Briden's *Hormone Repair Manual*[23], Karen Arthur's podcast *Menopause Whilst Black*[24] and the new book *Wise Power.*[25]

Some trans and non-binary people will obviously experience menopause, but are often excluded through very woman-centric language which can make accessing healthcare and support challenging. For a queerer, more inclusive and contemporary perspective, take a look at *What Fresh Hell Is This*[26] (2021), by Scarleteen founder Heather Corinna. Also the excellent *queermenopause* website[27] is full of resources and support.

Dr Christiane Northrup is an American physician, author and pioneer in women's health with an informed but very cis-gender perspective. In *The Secret Pleasures of Menopause,*[28] she educates that the menopause can be an exciting transition from mother/nurturer to crone/elder. It is a time to stop focusing so much on the needs of others and give time to one's own wants and desires. Northrup contends that during the menopause women revisit unfinished business from puberty/teenage years – and indeed Lara Briden calls menopause 'second puberty'. It is an opportunity for resolution and healing, for us to refresh ourselves. Because of distressing physical symptoms, this phase in our life can trigger feelings of fear, worry and anxiety. Menopause is also an existential phase; we are questioning who and what we are, what we value and what we want to change. This can feel very unsettling.

It is a common misconception that sexual desire and activity inevitably decrease at menopause. Although this is true for some, it certainly does not have to be for all. What we believe about sexuality at menopause has a lot to do with our sexual expectations and experience. Many of the following midlife changes in sexual function have been associated with normal peri-menopause (the period of time shortly before the menopause itself) and menopause:

- Increased or reduced sexual desire
- Change in sexual orientation
- Decreased sexual activity
- Vaginal dryness and loss of vaginal elasticity
- Pain or burning with intercourse
- Decreased or increased clitoral sensitivity
- Decreased or increased responsiveness
- Fewer orgasms, decreased depth of orgasm
- Increase in orgasms, sexual awakening.

This list shows that change itself, and not the nature of the change, is the common theme. It is important to remember that during the perimenopausal transition, with all of its changes, libido may go underground for a while as the person prioritises their life and how they use their energy. This is perfectly normal and can yield great dividends. But it is only temporary. There is no reason for diminished sex drive to become permanent after menopause. And, while some truly do notice a decline in libido at menopause, others experience heightened sexual desire and activity after menopause. We hope that some of the exercises in this book will be helpful in addressing any changes you are going through and giving you some ideas about what you may now prefer sexually.

Northrup identifies *three hormonal patterns during the menopause years*:

1   Oestrogen similar, progesterone low (PMT-type symptoms, sleeping problems)
2   Low oestrogen (hot flushes, night sweats, anxiety)
3   Low testosterone (affecting sexuality).

Table 5.1 addresses some of the difficulties and suggests self-help remedies to manage them. Fresh air and regular physical activity can boost feel-good endorphins and improve your body image. It can also help if you reduce your caffeine intake, have a good diet and stay hydrated. Geranium, rose or lavender essential oils may be used *with caution*; use two or three drops in a bath, an oil burner, a bowl of water on the radiator, a water spray bottle or directly on your pillow.

Top Tip: Anything that reduces stress for you mentally, emotionally and physically will help.

Professor Myra Hunter[29] was researching for women who could not take hormonal treatments for menopause difficulties due to health problems like cancer. She has developed brief cognitive behavioural (CBT) interventions for menopausal symptoms, hot flushes and night sweats, and has conducted successful clinical trials in this area.[30,31] Many of those attending discussion groups and learning to think differently about themselves, the menopause and its challenges, found a significant reduction in their physical symptoms.

The 'male menopause' (sometimes called the 'andropause') is an unhelpful term sometimes used in the media to explain the following symptoms in men:

• Depression
• Loss of sex drive
• Erectile dysfunction
• Hot flushes
• Mood swings
• Loss of muscle mass
• Fat redistribution, such as developing a large belly or 'man boobs' (gynaecomastia)

Table 5.1 Support with Menopause Challenges

Estrogen similar, progesterone low	
Breast tenderness	Gentle massage with essential oils (use with caution, check safety data). A supportive bra
Mood swings, irritability	Essential oils and/or flowers essences
Trouble sleeping	Camomile tea before bed. A warm (not hot) bath with lavender oil
Low estrogen	
Hot flushes	Lavender and Geranium Essential Oils in a spray bottle in your bag. Clary Sage Essential oil in bath. Rescue Remedy (Bach Flowers). Drink Sage Tea. Wear COTTON clothing, layers (cardigans easier to take off). Make a note of hot flushes and see over time if there are any common triggers. Avoid spicy foods, alcohol, caffeine. Address any feelings of anger
Night sweats	Lavender and Geranium Essential Oils in a spray bottle by your bed. Camomile tea before bed. A warm (not hot) bath with Clary Sage Essential Oil. Cotton bedding. Reduce caffeine and sugary foods. No caffeine after 6 pm
Vaginal dryness	Lubricants; see www.shwomenstore.com
Erratic cycles. Mood swings	Essential Oils and/or flowers essences
Mental confusion	Rosemary – essential oil or as herb in food
Urinary incontinence	Pelvic floor exercise to strengthen the pelvic floor muscles
Low testosterone	
Loss of sex drive	Sensualising exercises. Communicating with partner about accelerators and brakes
Decreased sexual response	Using a lubricant to help with arousal and ease vaginal dryness. Discover your Erotic Template (see The Erotic Mind by Jack Morin). Aphrodisiac foods. Kegel Exercises to tighten the pelvic muscles can work to enhance the sensations you feel during sex and help boost desire
Decreased sense of well-being and energy	Do some things that makes you feel good: like a dose of pampering, walking in a park, reading, listening to music, taking a nap … .

- Tiredness and a general lack of enthusiasm or energy
- Increased sweating
- Poor concentration and short-term memory
- Irritability.

The label is misleading because it suggests the symptoms are the result of a sudden drop in testosterone in middle age, similar to that which occurs in the female menopause. This is not true. Although testosterone levels fall as men age, the decline is steady – less than 2% a year from around the age of 30–40 – and this, in itself, is unlikely to cause any problems. In fact, many of these symptoms may well result from lifestyle or psychological problems (family, work, stress, anxiety). Having said that, male-bodied people may find that their spontaneous desire or preoccupation with sex slowly declines with age, and this is biologically normal.

Heart's Desire

Solo Exercise

If you are in a stage of your life where your sexuality is affected due to ageing, ill-health or social difficulties, can you identify one thing that soothes you; that brings you pleasure and some relief from your challenges?

Put your hand on your heart, take a breath and say, 'I want …' and listen to your very first thoughts. Can you somehow allow yourself the thing you answered?

Exercise with Partner/s

Tell each other your 'heart's desire'. See if you could assist each other in letting it/making it happen. If this is not possible, what might be the next best thing, given what is available.

The Senses

Our various senses are like a gateway, through which we experience the outside world, other people and our environment. We might see or hear something, which then passes through the sensory nerve pathways to the brain where the stimulus will be assessed via our memory centres and then responded to, all in seconds. Our sensuality includes the five senses of sight, smell, touch, taste, sound and is a precursor to sexuality. We can think about each of the senses in turn and contemplate what we do and do not enjoy. For example, if you think about the sense of smell, which aromas are pleasing to you, which turn you on and which turn you off, the same can be considered for each of the other senses – sight, touch, taste and sound. What is pleasurable is unique to each individual.

Of the five senses, touch is a vital aspect of our sexuality, both touching and being touched. It is through our skin that we experience touching and being touched, an activity which stimulates feel good hormones such as oxytocin.[32] Our skin is the largest body organ; it is what keeps all our organs and body systems inside our body, and it demarks a boundary between each of us as individual human beings and the outer world of our environment and other people. Our whole skin is an erogenous zone, with highly sensitive nerve endings; the amount and location of pleasure differs from person to person, perhaps including the breasts, chest, nipples, lips, ears, face, neck, buttocks, thighs, toes and fingers. The desire to kiss, to touch and make contact with an other's lips is an indicator of sexual arousal. Which areas are the most sensitive and pleasurable in your body?

Sensuality

Solo Exercise

Take your attention to your sense of SIGHT. Think about sights, visions, images that turn you ON, make you feel good. Now think about what turns you OFF. How does that make you feel? Notice what happens in your body to your breath, heartbeat and your muscles. Notice your thoughts.

Take your attention to your sense of SOUND. What sounds do you like, what turns you ON, makes you feel good? Now think about what turns you OFF. How does that make you feel? Notice what happens in your body, to your breath, heartbeat and muscles. Notice your thoughts.

Now think about your sense of SMELL. What smells turn you ON. Now think about what turns you OFF. How does that make you feel? Notice what happens in your body, to your breath, heartbeat and muscles. Notice your thoughts.

What about your sense of TASTE? What tastes do you like? What tastes turn you ON and which turn you OFF? How does that make you feel? Notice what happens in your body, to your breath, heartbeat and muscles. Notice your thoughts.

Now think about your sense of TOUCH. What things that you touch turn you ON. Now think about what turns you OFF. How does that make you feel? Notice what happens in your body, to your breath, heartbeat and muscles. Notice your thoughts.

Exercise with Partner/s

Share both what turns you off and what turns you on, when you are touching and being touched by each other.

Take twenty minutes apart, and then talk about what you were learning about each other.

Happy Hormones

During sexual arousal, all the body systems are involved in a network of communication between our bodies and our brains via the *endocrine* and the *nervous systems*. Neurochemicals are made in the brain and can be distributed throughout the whole body through the nervous system.

These chemicals can also be transformed into hormones and be directed to specific organs or areas of the body by the endocrine system. Hormones travel via the bloodstream.

The main endocrine gland is the pituitary which regulates the activities of this system. The other glands include the thyroid, which regulates growth and metabolism; the pancreas, which regulates digestion and insulin; the adrenal gland which produces hormones for survival such as fight and flight, and the ovaries and testes, which regulate reproduction.

When we take in the outside world through our senses, it stimulates the hypothalamus in the brain which activates the endocrine and nervous system. The release of hormones sets off a sort of chain of events, affecting many body systems. Hormones include endorphins and opiates, which are natural pain killers. They are our own, free, natural 'feel good' chemicals, which induce pleasurable emotions and sensations, with no come-downs or side-effects. The hormones involved in the sexual arousal process are, not surprisingly, similar to those involved in fertility and birthing.[33] One of them, oxytocin is known as the bonding hormone and sometimes called the 'love' drug; it pulses rhythmically through the body during sexual arousal and birthing. There is a surge and a peak at orgasm, as there also is at the moment of delivery. Table 5.2 shows the main sex hormones and their effects.

Your Delights and Pleasures

Solo Exercise

Think about something general that gives you pleasure. Notice how it feels inside your body; what physical sensations and emotions reactions are triggered. Notice what thoughts are generated.

Now think about something that pleases you sexually and again notice the sensations, emotions and thoughts. Spend more time considering your different senses (sights, sounds, smells, tastes, ways of touching and being touched) which arouse you, until you feel really familiar with what feeling pleasure feels like physically and emotionally.

Turn your attention to your imagination. Give yourself at least ten minutes; allow yourself to wander and dream; to see what images come into your mind triggered by you delighting in your senses. Which senses are most pleasurable to you; how do they make you feel physically and emotionally?

Exercise with Partner/s

Go back to the last paragraph of the solo exercise and tell each other what came up in your imagination when 'delighting in your senses'. Tell each other about your physical and emotional responses.

Table 5.2 Sex Hormones and Their Effects

Sex Hormones	Effects
DHEA (dehydroepiandrosterone)	Master sex hormone, increases desire, boosts energy and reduces stress
Androstenedione	Increases testosterone and oestrogen, enhances libido
Oestrogen and testosterone	Control fertility, motivate sexual interest, increase oxytocin
Adrenaline	Alertness, fires of energy, increases heartbeat
Prostaglandins	Contracts smooth muscle genitals, stimulates and sharpens senses
Acetylcholine	Relaxation, parasympathetic nervous system
Pheromones	Scents we secrete which excite us and attract others
Endorphins and opiates	Natural painkillers, relaxants, stimulated by play touch
Oxytocin	Relaxation, empathy, bonding and attachment, peaks at orgasm

The Nervous System

The sexual arousal charge moves through the parasympathetic branch of the autonomic nervous system to cause genital arousal and the sympathetic branch is activated for ejaculation and for orgasm. Sexual arousal may be triggered by an outside stimulus via the senses, or by an emotion or an internal body sensation. It can also be activated by the imagination or by a memory. All will feed back to the brain, which will activate the autonomic nervous system to react as described earlier. There are many nerve-rich areas in the human body. The most pronounced are the lips, the fingertips and the genitals.

The nervous system plays a central role in the sexual arousal process sending neurotransmitters (brain chemicals) throughout the body. See Figure 5.2. It has different elements: the *central nervous system* (CNS), which is the brain, spinal cord and the vagus nerve, and the *peripheral nervous system* (PNS). The PNS relays information to and from the body, and to and from the CNS. It has two aspects: the *sensory division* and the *motor division*. The sensory division also has two aspects. The *exteroceptive* includes our five sense: sight, sound, touch, taste and smell, which take the outside world in. The *interoceptive* includes the internal experience of our body organs, like pain and proprioception, the relationship of the body internally, of various body parts to others.

The motor division also has two parts: somatic and autonomic. *Somatic* nerves control conscious functions, like moving muscles and *autonomic* nerves control reflexes, the automatic reactions, such as breathing and heart rate. The autonomic nervous system also has two parts. Basically our bodies

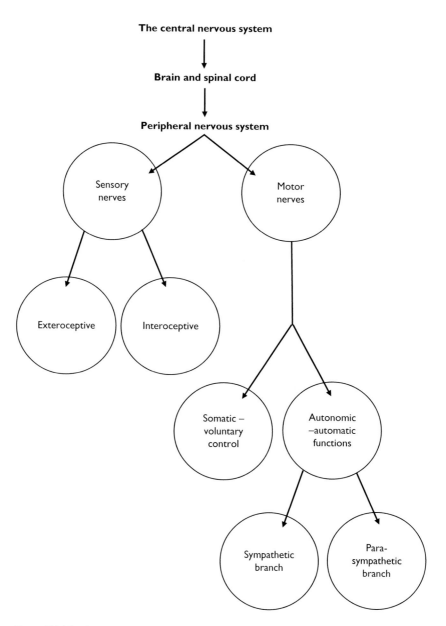

Figure 5.2 The Nervous System.

are either relaxed or activated into arousal. The *sympathetic* nervous system moves us into arousal and the *parasympathetic* takes us back into relaxation.

Another nerve worth mentioning is the vagus, which meanders through the body with branches connecting with the abdomen, heart, lungs, stomach and ears, among other body parts. It carries incoming information from the nervous system to the brain, providing information about what the body is doing. It also transmits outgoing information which governs a range of reflex responses, including our breathing, heartbeat and muscle control. There is further information on polyvagal theory in Chapter 6 and we also describe a polyvagal-informed approach when working with recovery in Chapter 7.

Research[34] has also shown four different nerve pathways, via the vagus nerve, which carry sensory signals from the vagina, cervix, clitoris and uterus, all potentially contributing to orgasm. It is believed that people with spinal cord injury are able to experience orgasm via the vagus nerve which travels outside the spinal cord and into the brain. It has also been found that people can have orgasms from imagery alone, without touching their body.[35]

Body and Breath Awareness

Solo Exercise

Take yourself to your Safe Space where you will have at least thirty minutes to not be disturbed. Get yourself into a really comfortable and warm sitting or lying position. Close your eyes and allow a few minutes to settle and begin to relax. Notice sounds around you, and just let them be, notice the thoughts you have and let them go.

Focus on your out-breath; imagine you are gently blowing out through a straw, then just allow the in-breath to follow. Do this for a while until you feel your body relaxing. Notice your thoughts and just allow them to pass.

Scan down your body and imagine any tensions leaving with the out-breath; from your forehead, your eyes and jaw; your neck muscles, shoulders, arms and hands; down your back, across your chest, your stomach and pelvis; your genitals and buttocks, legs, ankles and feet.

For a while, allow yourself to just sit or lie and focus on the rhythmic pattern of your breath coming in and leaving; just noticing and being aware of your body. If you get distracted do not worry, just take your attention back to your breathing.

Place one hand on your heart and one hand on your genitals and continue to focus on your out-breath then in-breath. Notice any changes afterwards. Just sit for a few minutes to get a sense of a connection between these two parts of your body.

When you are ready to complete this relaxation, first consciously deepen your breathing and become more mindful of where you are before you open your eyes. Stretch if you want and wiggle your fingers and toes.

Sit quietly for a few moments and reflect on your experience. You may want to write or draw a picture about it.

Exercise with Partner/s

Take the time to do this exercise together. You could each be quiet in your own space but in each other's company. Or one of you could read the solo exercise out and guide the other through it as a visualisation.

Getting Hot

Sexual desire can refer to a more abstract concept of our sexual drive or libido, where we might think about the strength or intensity of our desire. For the purpose of understanding, we are separating the impact of sexual desire on the mind, body, brain and emotions. In reality, a change in either the mind, body, brain or emotions causes reactions in the other aspects and also a response in all or any of them.

When we get 'turned on' sexual energy is set in motion, triggering actions and reactions. Sexual desire is controlled and affected by hormones and brain chemicals. It is impacted by physical stimuli such as sight, sound, touch, taste and smell and also psychological stimuli such as imagination and mood, as well as social and cultural factors. Sexual desire can trigger a yearning and longing for contact with another, especially to touch and be touched and an oral desire to kiss and be kissed. It can trigger physical sexual arousal, but not necessarily. Many feelings can be generated, including excitement and curiosity, anticipation and hope. There is often happiness and euphoria, feelings of wellbeing. There can also be the grief, fear and anger of frustrations and disappointments.

We can distinguish sexual desire – the activation of neurochemicals from the brain – from sexual arousal: the physiological impacts on the body. Brain activation will also include reactions from the memory centres. Desire also activates our minds and our imagination which feeds our arousal with sexual fantasy and anticipation of pleasure. Just imagining can turn us on. It will include input from our belief systems, preferences and choices. We can also become sexually aroused through physical stimulation. Physical arousal includes a heightened arousal of all our senses and the nervous system, which also can lead to agitation and disruption of body systems such as sleep and eating patterns. It impacts our breathing and heart rate and our temperature rises; vaginal lubrication is released from the Bartholin's glands and other erogenous zones are awakened.

When we get turned on, there is tension in the motor muscles of the body, and at the same time relaxation of the smooth muscle in the genitals, which together with an increase of blood flow to the pelvic area facilitates erection. In general, sexual activity is good for the body, regulating hormones, invigorating the circulatory and respiratory systems and toning organs, glands and muscles. It helps to protect against many conditions and illnesses caused by the dis-regulation of any of the above. Table 5.3 shows the impact of sexual desire within the homeodynamic quadrants.

Table 5.3 The Impact of Desire

Brain	Mind
Neurochemicals – dopamine, vasopressin, serotonin	Imagination – potentials and possibilities
Activation of memory centres, flashbacks to previous sexual arousals/ traumas	Preoccupation about choices and actions – ways to make it happen
	Social and cultural beliefs – promotion and prohibitions

Sexual Arousal	

Body	Emotion
Increase in heartbeat, body temperature and breathing	Yearning and longing for contact with 'other' – to touch and to kiss
Hormones – adrenaline and cortisol	Excitement and curiosity
Tightness in stomach	Anticipation and hope
Stirring in genitals	Happiness, feelings of euphoria and well being
Heightened arousal of senses and nervous system	Frustration and disappointments – fight, flight, panic, shame, shock
Agitation and disruption to body systems, food and sleep	

Sexual Touch

Solo Exercise

Make a time for yourself in your Safe Space. Make it warm.

Take your clothes off or just those covering your genitals, sit for a few moments and settle. Close your eyes and put your hands on your genitals. Spend a few minutes just breathing and noticing how you are feeling and what you are thinking.

At first keep your eyes closed and gently touch and explore your penis or vulva with your fingers. You might want to start with just hovering above the skin. Explore touching the outer and the inner vulva lips and inside the vagina, or the penis, including the foreskin (if you have one), the scrotum and the anus. You might well want to use some lubrication.

Explore the rest of your body, touching your skin all over. Notice where it feels sensuous and where it feels erotic. Experiment with touching your skin with your hands and fingers, also through clothing or other materials. As you touch yourself notice any sensations in your body and any feelings evoked. Notice what it feels like to touch yourself (the sensation to your fingers) and also what it feels like being touched (the sensations in your genitals).

Open your eyes or keep them closed while you experiment with your touch, paying attention to what you like, what feels good and also what you do not like. Play with touching yourself more firmly and more gently, making your touch faster or slower.

Notice what touch you like and consciously continue to touch, to pleasure yourself. Experiment with your breathing, deeper or shorter breaths to see which increase or reduce your pleasure. Notice what ideas, desires, thoughts and imaginations get triggered while you are doing this.

For this exercise you are invited to stop once your arousal is high; to not continue to orgasm, but to just sit and breathe and experience yourself in high arousal and be conscious about that. Notice what you feel in your body and what you are thinking about. Allow time for your arousal to subside as you no longer feed the charge. How easy or difficult is it for you to stop, and just be conscious of what is happening?

Take some time to reflect on and write about what you have experienced.

Exercise with Partner/s

Can you allow each other to explore your genitals sexually in the same way you did yourself? Can you bring a sense of awe and wonder to the uniqueness of each other's similarities and differences?

If not, would you prefer to explore yourself and let your partner/s watch and/or talk with you? Or maybe you would just prefer to tell each other about your solo experiences of this exercise.

Discuss what it was like to be sexually aroused but to choose to allow the arousal to diminish. How did it make you feel physically and emotionally?

Build the Charge

Once a sexual charge has been triggered it proceeds through various physical stages, as explained in Figure 5.3. This is based on the Masters and Johnson's (1966,[36] 1994)[37] model but expanded to show the distinction between orgasm and ejaculation. All the elements of sensuality, feelings and emotions will be building this charge. Any breaks to arousal, that is, any 'turn offs', can stop the charge from continuing. And equally, any 'turn ons'

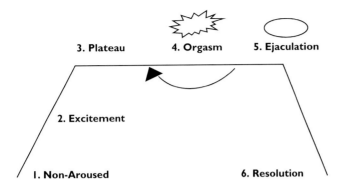

Figure 5.3 Six Stages of Sexual Arousal.

can be used to restore the charge and bring it back online. This is a generalised model, and you may wish to refer back to exercises on self-pleasuring to consider how your pattern of arousal may be similar or different.

1   Non-aroused is how we are before a stimulus triggers an arousal.
2   Excitement can last from a few minutes to several hours:

   •   We get 'turned on' and begin to build a charge of sexual energy
   •   Muscle tension increases
   •   Heart rate quickens and breathing is accelerated
   •   Skin may become flushed
   •   Nipples become hardened or erect
   •   Smooth muscle in the clitoris and penis relaxes, allowing erection
   •   Blood flow to the genitals increases, resulting in erection of the clitoris or penis
   •   Vaginal lubrication begins
   •   Breasts become fuller and vaginal walls begin to swell
   •   Testicles swell, the scrotum tightens and pre-ejaculate (a lubricating liquid) is released

3   Plateau extends to the brink of orgasm:

   •   Relaxing, letting go to enjoying a heightened state of sexual arousal
   •   The changes begun in the excitement phase are intensified
   •   The vagina continues to swell from increased blood flow, and the vaginal walls turn a dark purple
   •   The clitoris becomes highly sensitive and the glans retracts under the clitoral hood to avoid direct stimulation
   •   The testicles are withdrawn up into the scrotum

- Breathing, heart rate and blood pressure continue to increase
- Muscle spasms may begin in the feet, face and hands
- Muscle tension increases

4   Orgasm is the shortest of the phases:

- Blood pressure, heart rate and breathing are at their highest rates, with a rapid intake of oxygen
- A rash or 'sex flush' may appear over the entire body
- Involuntary muscle contractions begin, particularly in the pelvic floor
- The muscles of the vagina and base of the penis; the uterus and prostate gland undergo rhythmic contractions
- Surges of hormones and neurochemicals trigger a reflex action through the nervous system and the release of sexual tension throughout the whole body
- After orgasm, the body returns to its pre-orgasmic phase, and can experience multiple orgasms

5   Ejaculation can happen at the same time as orgasm or separately.

- Rhythmic contractions of the pelvic floor muscles result in the release of ejaculatory fluid from the prostate and seminal glands, or from the paraurethral glands.
- After ejaculation, the body returns to stage 1; non-aroused and needs a recovery time before it can become aroused again

6   Resolution

- During resolution, the body slowly returns to its normal level of functioning, and swollen and erect body parts return to their previous size and colour
- The duration of the refractory period varies and usually lengthens with advancing age
- This phase is marked by a general sense of well-being, enhanced intimacy and, often, fatigue.

Understanding the stages of arousal can be useful to clarify any difficulties we may be having. We first need to distinguish between desire: do we want to be sexual? and arousal: are we able to respond physically? If our attempt to be sexual is matching our desire but we are having difficulty with phys-iological arousal, knowing what stage of the arousal process this is hap-pening at can give us clues about how to encourage our body to respond. For example, if excitement is not building at all or increasing but then stopping, we may want to slow down and focus on what does build our sexual charge. Learning that our sexual charge can ebb and flow is useful;

also knowing that a subsiding erection does not necessarily mean 'it's all over', depending on our choices and attitudes.

The plateau stage is an important awareness in psychosexual health. We seem to believe the charge builds and builds until release, so when we reach plateau, it may be experienced as a decline. Often at this point we become more aware of our thoughts and feelings, as well as our sensory experiences which can feel disconcerting as we seem to believe we are supposed to be lost in it all. This also requires a consciousness about being sexual, and therefore a relative ease about being so. Sexual shame can get in the way of sexual self-esteem and will be discussed later.

Separating orgasm and ejaculation as differing stages allows us to think about our sexual behaviours in a new way also. Ejaculation, obviously correlated with our 'reproductive model of sex' thinking, brings the physiological process of sexual arousal to a conclusion, albeit temporarily. Orgasm, however, takes the process back to pre-orgasmic, allowing for the possibility of multiple orgasms.

The distinctions between arousal and desire can be more complex. It is known that both penile erection and vaginal lubrication can also occur in response to unwanted touch, for example, during sexual abuse. This can confuse people who believe there must have been some desire present. Such physiological responses are reflexes triggered through the autonomic nervous system purely by touch, which indicates we need to consider not just the ability to be aroused but the subjective experience of that: what a person feels about what is happening in their body. For more on unwanted arousal, see Emily Nagoski's Ted Talk.[38]

Research from the 1990s and 2000s about female desire can also help us nuance models of sexual arousal. Seeing that many women did not seem to confirm to the linear model of arousal described earlier, Whipple and Brash-McGreer (1997) proposed a circular sexual response pattern (Figure 5.4).

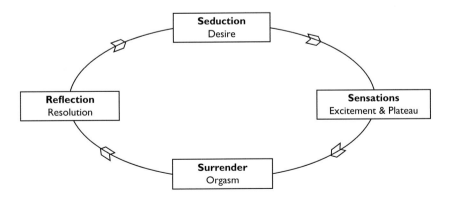

Figure 5.4 A Circular Sexual Response Pattern.

They suggest that pleasant and satisfying sexual experiences may have a reinforcing effect, leading to the seduction phase of the next sexual experience. If, during reflection, the sexual experience did not provide pleasure and satisfaction, there may not be a desire to repeat the experience.

Following from this, Basson (2000)[39] constructed a new model of female sexual response which acknowledges the importance of emotional intimacy, sexual stimuli, and relationship satisfaction. She believed that although women may experience spontaneous sexual desire and interest in some circumstances, many women, especially those in long-term relationships, are more likely to participate in sexual activity in response to a partner or through a desire for intimacy. Dr Karen Gurney has taken up this mantle in her excellent book *Mind the Gap: The Truth about Desire and How to Future Proof Your Sex Life* (2020). Gurney emphasises that in this respect there is a difference between male and female experience. She includes all women in this regardless of the gender they have been assigned at birth, while acknowledging that there are aspects of desire and sexuality that are specific to trans people that her book does not really address.

It is easy to see how without this understanding, women may be concerned if they are no longer experiencing spontaneous desire in a long-term relationship, and their partners may stop initiating because they are the only one who *is* initiating. If we understand, however, that many women may not spontaneously desire to have sex, but may start to feel like it either once they have experienced some arousing physical touch and/or some flirtatious emotional contact (responsive desire), couples who want to cultivate their sex life may find themselves able to approach sex in a different way. Gurney has made excellent short online courses on desire available through her workplace The Havelock Clinic,[40] and you can also watch her Ted Talk on responsive desire.[41]

The responsive desire model is particularly useful during the menopause and the ageing process. In later life we are not so driven sexually by our hormones and need to find a new way into our desire than how we have been used to. Northrup[42] explains how rather than the body becoming 'hormone deficient' at menopause, the high levels of oestrogen required for ovulation are no longer needed. In fact the whole endocrine system is transitioning, so that in time the adrenal system will change androgens into oestrogen to provide the levels now needed. The most important care during the perimenopause years, while this change is happening, is of the adrenal system: to reduce the stresses which over-activate it. Discovering more about the specific ways we feel turned on, emotionally and physically can help this process. Rather than feeling a lack of desire, many discover that the gateway to their desire has changed. Allowing for this and exploring new avenues into sexual activities often results in a renewed interest and fulfilling experiences of sex.

Nagoski (2015)[43] says that everyone has both accelerators and brakes to their sexual arousal. The accelerator notices all the sexy things in the environment and sends the signal that says, 'Turn on!' Brakes are things that turn us off. These can range from reminders of past trauma – perhaps particular smells, tastes, sights, words, types/places of touch – to 'to do lists', to kids next door or beliefs that being sexual is bad or shameful. Everyone has them. Getting to know both and eventually communicate about them can help us avoid or deal with brakes, and to enhance accelerators to increase our sexual fulfilment.

Sexual Fantasy

Solo Exercise

Take some time to think about what you have learnt about yourself physically and emotionally with regards to your sexuality. In order to further explore what accelerates your arousal, write a sexual fantasy in as much detail as you want. Imagine a scenario where you are receiving exactly what you want, for example, where you are and who with; what happens, in what order.

Notice if anything breaks your arousal, and explore for a moment what and why and then remind yourself of your accelerators.

When you have done this, compare your fantasy with your real-life experiences. Is this particular fantasy one you prefer to keep to the world of your imagination or would you like to share it, or part of it with a partner?

Exercise with Partner/s

Tell each other about your sexual fantasy if you wish, or share in detail what you have learnt about your accelerators and breaks.

All Together Now

We have explored our mind, our beliefs and thinking, the physiology of our body and our brain during sexual arousal. Let us now consider linking it all back together. The brain releases chemicals which trigger changes in the body, setting energy in motion, triggering thoughts, memories, triggering more chemicals and so on, a chain of events, a cycle of interaction. This cycle can also be seen as a circuit; it can get switched on and it can get switched off.

A trigger to arousal can start in any section but will activate the others. It may start from an external sensory stimulus like sight or touch, or an internal stimulus like a thought or a memory. Once triggered it causes an autonomic reaction in the body to arousal. We can turn off this arousal and cut the circuit if, for example, our thinking tells us it is not appropriate right now, or we do not want to follow the urge right now. It is important as humans that we can exercise some choices. As said before, we are constantly negotiating with our drives and urges. We may suppress; switch off, the desire to laugh, to shout or cry. We may feel a hunger that we put off until we can eat next. We can do the same sexually. Our mind-body-brain-emotion is always in dialogue (Figure 5.5).

If we feel sexual desire and sexual arousal in our body, we can choose to switch it off, which will break the circuit and stop further production of neurochemicals, which are triggering the physical changes; physical arousal will subside. We cannot change how we feel; what our reactions are, but we can choose how we react: whether we 'allow' a continuation of excitation to build through the stages of arousal, or whether we break the circuit. Knowing in greater detail what enhances our arousal and what breaks the circuit can help us to switch it back on if we want to.

Sometimes this switch off can happen more unconsciously. For example, if we are attempting to 'perform' but do not really want to be in this scenario; with this person or doing what we are doing, our body, our physiological arousal, can grind to a halt. Similarly, if our feelings or values are not in sync with our actions, our circuit of arousal can be broken. Again, understanding where in the circuit we are experiencing the rupture can help us to re-evaluate our behaviour and either repair the break or choose not to continue.

We rarely take time to contemplate all the different components to human behaviour mainly because the communication between our brain reactions, our body sensations, our emotions and our thoughts, all happen so quickly. The actions that we take: how we behave, are the consequence of the myriad issues we have addressed so far. Our history, our beliefs and our body responses will all be having an input into the decision making which pre-cedes action. It is important to acknowledge our capabilities and choices in relationship to our sexual urges and arousal. The model that we are mostly likely to see (on screen, for example, with some notable exceptions!) usually implies we have little control: that once we are turned on, we will be

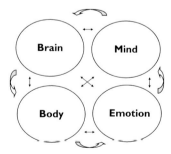

Figure 5.5 A Homeodynamic Circuit of Arousal.

overtaken until we have fulfilled that urge, by the physical act of sex. This is obviously not true; how much responsibility we take for ourselves sexually is a core tenet of this book.

Sexual Stimulation

Solo Exercise

Make a time for yourself in your Safe Space. Make it warm. This exercise is similar to that of sexual touch but develops in a different way.

Take your clothes off or just those covering your genitals, sit for a few moments and settle. Close your eyes and put your hands on your genitals. Spend a few minutes just breathing and noticing how you are feeling and what you are thinking.

At first keep your eyes closed and gently touch and explore your penis or vulva with your fingers. You will probably want to have lube to hand, and might want to start by hovering over your skin. Explore touching the outer and the inner vulva lips and inside the vagina, or the penis, including the foreskin (if you have one), the scrotum and the anus. Explore and play more with the other parts of your body that also create an erotic charge.

As you touch yourself notice any sensations in your body and any feelings evoked. Notice what it feels like to touch yourself (the sensation to your fingers) and also what it feels like being touched (the sensations in your genitals).

Open your eyes or keep them closed while you experiment with your touch, paying attention to what you like, what feels good and also what you do not like. Play with touching yourself more firmly and more gently; making your touch faster or slower. Play with touching and then stopping and just holding yourself and breathing, and then touching again.

Notice what touch you like and consciously continue to touch, to pleasure yourself. Experiment with your breathing, deeper or shorter breaths to see which increase or reduce your pleasure. Notice what ideas, desires, thoughts and imaginations get triggered while you are doing this.

For this exercise you are invited to continue your pleasuring to orgasm, and to remain mindful and conscious of what you are feeling in your body. Notice any thoughts that may arise. Notice your imagination; how are you feeling your desire?

Take some time to reflect on and write about what you have experienced. How easy was it for you to stay connected to what was happening in your body? How do you feel having done this and what do you think about it?

> ### *Exercise with Partner/s*
>
> *Can you allow each other to explore your body sexually in the same way you did yourself? Can you bring a sense of awe and wonder to the uniqueness of each other's similarities and differences?*
>
> *If not, would you prefer to explore yourself and let your partner/s watch and/or talk with you? Or maybe you would just prefer to tell each other about your solo experiences of this exercise.*
>
> *Discuss what it was like to be sexually aroused and to choose to allow the arousal to build to its own natural conclusion? How did it make you feel physically and emotionally?*
>
> *Consider if you have discovered other elements that you would like to add to your sexual life.*

Go with the Flow

Sexual arousal starts an energy charge which passes through the circuit as described earlier. If all aspects are in tune, it will continue the circuit and build the charge up through the stages of arousal of excitation and up to the plateau. Given the right factors, it is a natural reflex to orgasm and/or ejaculate in response to sexual arousal.

Each of the aspects of mind, brain, body and emotion is impacted by sexual arousal and each has needs too. Our sexual arousal circuit will flow at its easiest when these needs are met. We will be affected internally and also by our outside environment: where we are and who we are with. If our sexual activities and behaviour are acceptable to our thinking, memories and beliefs, then feel good chemicals will flow, if not we may produce adrenaline which could trigger fight or flight emotions and/or shut down physical arousal.

There can also be extraordinary and unusual responses to and during sexual arousal when considering a history of sexual violence. Due to the impacts on the limbic system there can be unwanted arousal to stimuli evocative of events. There can be confusing beliefs about and responses to the distinctions between pain and pleasure; what is in our best interest and what is not. Survival strategies can take over, triggering fear or rage and perhaps freeze or disassociation.

Imagination and fantasy are really important in sexuality too. Just imagining can turn us on. When our sensuality is being turned on, and not off, and we are receiving the quality and quantity of touch and specifically, genital stimulation that we enjoy; then orgasm/ejaculation will be reflexive responses. Some people can even orgasm from thought alone, without being touched by themselves or another. Unwelcome thoughts, feelings or emotions can also switch off the circuit, as can stress or illness; these issues will be addressed in more detail later.

The best environment to enhance our sexual pleasure is when all aspects of our body-mind-brain-emotions are being satisfied. Primarily sexuality is a relationship with ourselves. When we know what turns us on, sensually and sexually; what satisfies our beliefs and choices; what harmonises our emotions, then we allow the sexual charge to flow; getting to experience the pleasures of a sexual experience and be satiated through orgasmic release. The bio-neurochemical experience of sexual activity is great for our body, heart and soul.

Dr Karen Gurney[44] talks about similar processes in a slightly different way. When discussing conditions for good sex, she suggests that sexual fulfilment depends on high levels of our unique taste in three things:

- Physical touch
- Being in the moment
- Psychological arousal.

Each individual can explore what kinds of physical touch turn them on or off. Also, how they can bring themselves into the moment (for survivors this may relate a lot to being in a 'window of tolerance'). Finally, what turns them on or off psychologically, which can be to do with the connection with the other person, environment, closeness to what they might fantasise about, etc.

Mindfulness has become well known and widely practiced as an effective way of bringing ourselves into the present moment. The related concept of bodyfulness[45] is also helpful. We can think of four pillars of bodyfulness – breath, sound, movement and muscle tension. By becoming aware of and deepening our breath, allowing and even encouraging ourselves to make sound, amplifying the movement of our bodies and in particular our hips, and playing with tensing and releasing our pelvic muscles, we can become much more fully embodied, which will heighten sexual pleasure. Tantric practices can be useful with this – we would particularly recommend more gender-expansive neo-tantra practitioners such as Layla Martin[46] and Barbara Carrellas.[47]

Given the pain and struggles of human life, it is a wonderful gift to be able to experience sexual pleasure and physical satiation, with all its benefits. It can be blissful also, emotionally and existentially, to be able to connect with and be intimate with another; to play and share making love together. Sexual expression can take many forms, including dancing, masturbating or being sexual with someone else. How we express our sexuality and how we relate to others is influenced by all the things we have been discussing.

Drawing together all the issues and factors we have identified, we can see our drive towards being sexual includes the pleasure principle and the erotic principle. It is also about creativity, our fire energy and fuels our passions, including love and spirituality. Given our reactivity and our ability to reflect and choose, to some extent, how we will react: how do we want to behave sexually? Drawing together our sexual beliefs and preferences; our physical desire, brain and body: how do we want to meet and be sexual with another?

Having an in-depth understanding of our sexual physiology is a bit like understanding how our digestive system works: we do not need to know in order to be able to enjoy eating. Indeed, it is interesting how little we know about sexual as opposed to reproductive functioning. Equally people do not need to be told about how to have sex. This book is more a manual about sexual nutrition; what our body does, why it does it, with what consequences and why. We know innately how to be sexual; we are exploring why we think, respond and act as we do.

So we can see that as humans, we are constantly reacting and responding to stimuli from our outside world. These stimuli trigger a range of automatic, internal responses, most of which are happening so fast and so unconsciously that we do not even notice. As explained earlier, we are reacting with our brains, our beliefs, our bodies and our feelings; all affecting and being affected by each other.

There are many types of arousal. We may be activated to feel hungry, and notice an inner sensation of our belly grumbling or an outer awareness, like seeing or smelling food we like. It is noticed with food and drink that we often feel some satiation just knowing that we can fulfil this desire. For example, our thirst will diminish as we raise the liquid to our lips before the physiology of hydrating the body has occurred. This is not the case with sexual desire.

During sexual arousal, our whole body is activated with sensations and energy, specifically in our genitals. Feeling stimulated into a sexual charge is not that different than say, feeling hungry or the urge to shout or cry. There will be an automatic physical response, an energy charge in the body which we sometimes react unconsciously to, and others we make daily decisions and choices about. For example, even though we may feel angry and have an urge or a desire to shout at someone, we may decide it is inappropriate or not wise to do so. The point is that even though we feel something, we do not always act on that feeling. As described in Chapter 4, we humans are very capable of controlling or suppressing any feelings.

In Chapter 4, we explored our thoughts, beliefs and values about sex and sexuality. In this chapter, we have described in detail the anatomy and physiology of sexual arousal, separating our reproductive functioning and our sexual arousal process. We have discussed the biology of sex, including not just the genital changes but also how our respiratory system and musculature is affected. We can see how the changes are activated through the endocrine system transporting hormones and the nervous system relaying messages between our bodies and our brains.

We have seen the relationships between ourselves and others; our inner and outer worlds. The relational desire in the sexual urge to reach out, to touch an 'other', could inspire us to see sex as more than an act that someone does. We can begin to value our sexuality as something more complex and integrated, more subjective and experiential. In the next chapter, we will discuss another facet of our sexual experiences, the brain. We will explore the neurochemistry and stages of sexual arousal and the inter-relatedness between our thinking, our bodies and our brains.

Review of Chapter 5

Solo Exercise

Read back through the exercises for this section and what you have written in your journal. Take some time to reflect on your exploration and to evaluate your work. Which exercises did you like and which ones did you not like? Think about why.

What have you discovered about your body and your sensuality? Have any discoveries surprised you; if so, what and why? How do you feel about this?

What have you discovered about your sexual arousal? Does it differ if you do this exercise at different times and in difference places; if so, which do you prefer?

Are there any exercises that you would like to do again? If so, notice what is similar or different if you do them a second time.

Is there anything you want to change; if so, how could you do that?

Talk to someone, write or draw something about how you are thinking and feeling having worked on this chapter.

Exercise with Partner/s

Give yourselves an hour each and use the Conscious Communication dialogue to explore each other's reviews in detail.

Take your time to learn more about yourselves and your partner/s as you discover what has been important about the work on this aspect of your sexuality.

Discuss where you feel this leaves your relationship now and identify one aspect that needs your combined attention. Explore how you may want to do this.

Notes

1 SPOKZ. (2020). *Sex Aids*. Available at: https://www.spokz.co.uk/sex-aids.html (Accessed: 22 August 2022); The Outsiders Trust. (no date). *The Outsiders Club*. Available at: https://outsiders.org.uk/club/the-outsiders-club/ (Accessed: 22 August 2022); Kaufman, M., Odette, O., & Silverberg, C. (2005). *Ultimate Guide to Sex*

and Disability: For All of Us Who Live with Disabilities, Chronic Pain and Illness. San Francisco: Cleis Press.

2 Phillips, L. (2022). *Psychotherapy and Sex Therapy.* Available at: https://www. drleephillips.com/ (Accessed: 22 August 2022).

3 Fielding, L. (2021). *Trans Sex: Clinical Approaches to Trans Sexualities and Erotic Embodiments.* Routledge.

4 Gurney, K. (2020). *Mind the Gap.* Headline Publishing Group; TEDx Talks. (2022). *The Power of Orgasms to Address Gender Inequality: Karen.* Gurney at TEDxLondonWomen. 31 March. Available at: https://www.youtube.com/watch? v=4oy7UH9rNl4 (Accessed: 22 August 2022).

5 Garcia, M., & Zalizynak, M. (2020). 'Effects of Feminizing Hormone Treatment on Sexual Function of Transgender Women', *Journal of Urology,* 1 April, pp. 203–204.

6 Montañez, A. (2017). 'Beyond XX and XY: The Extraordinary Complexity of Sex Determination', *Scientific American,* 1 September.

7 Veale, D. et al. (2015). 'Am I Normal? A Systematic Review and Construction of Nomograms for Flaccid and Erect Penis Length and Circumference in Up to 15521 Men', *British Journal of Urology International (BJUI),* 115(6), pp. 978–986.

8 Dodsworth, L. (2017). *Manhood: The Bare Reality.* London: Pinter and Martin; Laura Dodsworth. (no date). *Bare Reality.* Available at: https://www. lauradodsworth.com/bare-reality-photography/ (Accessed: 22 August 2022).

9 Dodsworth, L. (2019). *'Womanhood: The Bare Reality'.* London: Pinter and Martin.

10 Lewis, R. et al. (2017). 'Heterosexual Practices Among Young People in Britain: Evidence from Three National Surveys of Sexual Attitudes and Lifestyles', *Journal of Adolescent Health,* 61(6), pp. 694–702.

11 Underwood, S. (2003). *Gay Men and Anal Eroticism.* Routledge.

12 Porn Hub. (2022). *2021 Year in Review.* Available at: https://www.pornhub.com/ insights/yir-2021#top-20-countries (Accessed: 22 August 2022).

13 The National Archives. (2022). *Prohibition of Female Circumcision Act.* Available at: https://www.legislation.gov.uk/ukpga/1985/38/contents (Accessed: 22 August 2022).

14 Alison Macfarlane and Efua Dorkenoo. (2017). *Prevalence of Female Genital Mutilation in England and Wales National and Local Estimates.* Available at: https://ukdataservice.ac.uk/case-study/prevalence-of-female-genital-mutilation-in-england-and-wales-national-and-local-estimates/ (Accessed: 22 August 2022).

15 Home Office. (2022). *Female Genital Mutilation Resource Pack.* Available at: https://www.gov.uk/government/publications/female-genital-mutilation-resource-pack/female-genital-mutilation-resource-pack (Accessed: 22 August 2022).

16 Federation of Feminist Women's Health Centres (FFWHC). (1995). *A New View of a Woman's Body.* Los Angeles, CA: Feminist Health Press.

17 Chalker, R. (2000). *The Clitoral Truth.* New York: Seven Stories.

18 Women's Environmental Network. (no date). *Seeing Red.* Available at: https:// www.yumpu.com/en/document/read/29560735/download-seeing-red-womens-environmental-network (Accessed: 22 August 2022).

19 RedSchool. (no date). *Women's Stories.* Available at: https://www.redschool.net/ categories/womens-stories (Accessed: 23 August 2022).

20 NMPA. (2022). National Maternity and Perinatal Audit: Clinical Report 2019. Based on births in NHS Maternity Services between 1 April 2016 and 31 March 2017. Available at: https://maternityaudit.org.uk/filesUploaded/NMPA%20Clinical %20Report%202019.pdf (Accessed: 11 September 2022).

21 Ejegård, H. et al. (2008). 'Sexuality after Delivery with Episiotomy: A Long-Term Follow-Up', *Gynecol Obstet Invest*, 66(1), pp. 1–7.

22 Royal College of Obstetricians and Gynaecologists, Working Party. (2008). *Standards for Maternity Care*. Available at: https://rcog.org.uk/media/wispcst3/wprmaternitystandards2008.pdf (Accessed: 22 August 2022).

23 Briden, L. (2021). *Hormone Repair Manual: Every Woman's Guide to Healthy Hormones After 40*. GreenPeak Publishing.

24 Arthur, K., & Karen Arthur. (2022). *Menopause Whilst Black*. Available at: https://www.thekarenarthur.com/menopausewhilstblack (Accessed: 10 September 2022).

25 Pope, A., & Hugo Wurlitzer, S. (2022). *Wise Power: Discover the Liberating Power of Menopause to Awaken Authority, Purpose and Belonging*. Hay House.

26 Corinna, H. (2021). *What Fresh Hell Is This? Perimenopause, Menopause, Other Indignities and You*. USA: Piatkus.

27 QMC. (no date). *Resources*. Available at: https://www.queermenopause.com/resources (Accessed: 23 August 2022).

28 Northrup, C. (2008). *The Secret Pleasures of Menopause*. UK: Hay House.

29 Hunter, M. (2019). 'Understanding Menopause with Professor Myra Hunter', *unmind*, 30 September. Available at: https://blog.unmind.com/menopause-with-professor-myra-hunter (Accessed: 10 September 2022).

30 Menopause Matters. (no date). *CBT for Menopausal Symptoms*. Available at: https://www.menopausematters.co.uk/cbt_for_menopause.php (Accessed: 10 September 2022).

31 Hunter, M., & Smith, M. (2021). *Living Well Through the Menopause: An Evidence-Based Cognitive Behavioural Guide*. Robinson.

32 Odent, M. (1999). *The Scientification of Love*. London: Free Association Books; Panksepp, J. (1998). *Affective Neuroscience*. New York: Oxford University Press.

33 Kitzinger, S. (1985). *Women's Experience of Sex*. New York: Penguin.

34 Komisaruk, B., Beyer-Flores, C., & Whipple, B. (2006). *The Science of Orgasm*. Baltimore, MD: John Hopkins University Press.

35 WebMD. (2022). *Hands Free Orgasm: What It Is*. Available at: https://www.webmd.com/sex/hands-free-orgasm (Accessed: 23 August 2022).

36 Masters, W.H., & Johnson, V.E. (1966). *Human Sexual Responses*. New York: Little Brown.

37 Masters, W.H., & Johnson, V.E. (1994). *Heterosexuality*. Thorsons.

38 TEDx Talks. (2018). *The Truth about Unwanted Arousal: Emily Nagoski at TEDxVancouver*. 4 June. Available at: https://www.youtube.com/watch?v=L-q-tSHo9Ho (Accessed: 10 September 2022).

39 Basson, R. (2000). 'The Female Sexual Response: A Different Model', *Journal of Sex and Marital Therapy*, 26(1), pp. 51-65.

40 The Havelock Clinic. (2022). *Courses*. Available at: https://havelockonlineworkshops.teachable.com/courses (Accessed: 10 September 2022).

41 TEDx Talks. (2020). *The Surprising Truth about Desire Everyone Needs to Know: Karen Gurney at TEDxRoyalTunbridgeWells*. 17 July. Available at: https://www.youtube.com/watch?v=krA8-_iXptE (Accessed: 10 September 2022).

42 Northrup, C. (1995). *Women's Bodies, Women's Wisdom*. London: Piatkus; Northrup, C. (2003). *The Wisdom of the Menopause*. New York: Bantam.

43 Nagoski, E. (2015). *Come as You Are: The Surprising New Science That Will Transform Your Sex Life*. Simon Schuster.

44 Gurney, K. (2020). *Mind the Gap: The Truth about Desire and How to Futureproof Your Sex Life*. UK: Headline; The Havelock Clinic. (no date). *Conditions*

for Good Sex.pdf. Available at: https://drive.google.com/file/d/1oFcK755Ne-0hcIOuQ5futwDgruxgnkyt/view (Accessed: 23 August 2022).

45 Allyn, R. (2021). *The Pleasure Is All Yours: Reclaim Your Body's Bliss and Reignite Your Passion for Life.* Shambhala.
46 Available at: https://laylamartin.com (Accessed: 12 September 2022).
47 Carrellas, B. (2017). *Urban Tantra: Sacred Sex for the Twenty-First Century.* Ten Speed Press.

Chapter 6

Brain

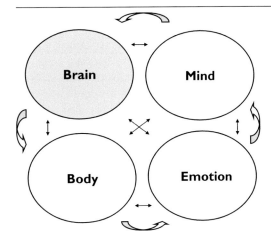

Frisson

In this section, we will explore the brain in more detail with regard to sexuality and sexual functioning. It is often said we cannot help who we fancy, which has some truth in it. Research about sexual attraction is inconclusive except that when an attraction happens, it will be registered within seconds. Day by day, we are having instant reactions, which we are constantly evaluating and choosing to act on, or not.

By describing in more detail what happens physiologically in the brain, we can gain a deeper understanding of why we experience our sexuality as we do. We can also begin to comprehend how our brain interacts with our minds and our bodies as described in the previous chapters, giving us a clearer idea of why we react as we do and why we choose to behave in some ways and not in others. We see how trauma affects the brain and how this can bring our past experiences very much into the present. Sexual arousal neurochemicals are triggered in the inner regions of the brain and our memory centres are activated. In our mind, our frontal lobes, we can become preoccupied with thoughts and choices about how we could make

DOI: 10.4324/9781003322405-7

things happen. Our imagination can begin to run wild with potential and possibilities. We will also be aware of our social and cultural beliefs which may encourage our desires or present prohibitions. There can be many changes in the body including an increase in heartbeat, body temperature and breathing rate; a tightness in the stomach; and a stirring in the genitals. There will be a heightened arousal of all our senses and the nervous system. Many feelings and emotions will be stirring, and this is all in the first five minutes. An interactive chain of events has been initiated in our inner world by a stimulus of something or someone in our internal world or from the outer world. The sexual arousal circuit has been activated, has been turned on.

Morin[1] has provided much insight into our relationship with the erotic mind through his research. He suggests that by reviewing our 'peak erotic experiences' and discovering exactly what made them so, we can discover our 'core erotic theme': our internal blueprint for arousal. He offers a sexual excitement survey and suggests ways to explore your unique erotic fingerprint. This can be useful where there are difficulties with low sexual desire, or to enhance your relationship to your erotic desire. A related but different approach is offered by Jaiya, who has created a typography of 'erotic blueprints'. These – called sensual, kinky, energetic, sexual and shapeshifter – describe different ways into eros. The idea is that people have more of a propensity to one or two blueprints, and that if there is a mismatch between sexual partners then sexual connection and satisfaction can be challenging. Jaiya's website[2] offers a quiz to establish your unique erotic blueprint pie chart, with suggestions as to how to enhance your erotic experience and to connect with partners with different blueprints.

Desire

Solo Exercise

Think about your desire. Write about what this word means for you. How does desire differ from 'want' or 'need'?

Write a list of your desires, generally. Write a list of your sexual desires.

Take some time to review what you have written and notice what you think and feel about what you have written. Do your desires sit comfortably with your beliefs and values; if not, do you wish to re-evaluate your desires, and/or your beliefs and values?

Exercise with Partner/s

Share your lists of sexual desires. Where do they overlap? Where they are different, are there caveats which would make them agreeable to all?

Draw up a list of mutual sexual desires that are compatible with your beliefs and values.

The Busy Brain

Historically, most research on the brain was conducted on people with injury; our knowledge about brain functioning was extrapolated from how damage to certain areas was seen to affect behaviours. With the advent of technology to see inside our brains, there has been a revolution in neuroscience. We now know that certain areas are activated and 'light up' during different activities. We understand more about sexual neurochemistry and the role of our brain in sexual functioning.

Neuroscientist, psychologist and author, Lisa Feldman Barrett[3] describes the brain as a prisoner within the skull. It receives its only information from the outside world through interoception (via the senses) and also constantly monitors the inner world (heart rate, breathing, the immune system, etc) in order to respond, react and regulate.

We also know more these days about the distinctions and relationship between the frontal 'thinking' lobes and the deeper, more primitive reflexive areas. The *brain stem* is one of the most primal aspects of the brain and includes the medulla oblongata which regulates reflexes such as heart rate, blood flow and breathing, all affected during sexual arousal. The brain is continually evaluating triggers from the outside world and the inner body and is continually responding to these stimuli. In nanoseconds, decisions are being made with us being in a state of constant interaction or homeodynamic function, as described earlier.

The cerebellum controls and coordinates movement and the cerebrum receives the messages from our senses like sight and sound. Other areas in the brain are primary centres for speech and learning, and the frontal lobes are considered to oversee personality and intelligence. The more we learn about the brain the more we realise how complex, interactive and interrelational all elements are. Deep within the brain sits a cluster of cells and systems referred to as the *limbic system*, a crucial element in sexual functioning. Illustration 6.1 shows the brain stem, the limbic system and the prefrontal cortex.

Emotional Awareness I

Solo Exercise

Take some time to sit and relax. Allow your body, your breath and your heartbeat to settle. Remember a time when you felt sad. Notice your body; where do you feel sadness? Notice any muscle tension or discomfort. Now notice your thoughts and what sort of memories come to mind. What is your internal dialogue about these memories? Spend a few moments with your experiences about sadness then take some deep breaths and allow your thoughts and feelings to pass.

Now take your attention to the emotion of fear. Again, notice first what happens in your body; where do you feel fear somatically? What is happening to your breath and your heartbeat? Notice your memories and your thoughts; and what you are thinking about what you are experiencing. Allow some time to be with what is happening and then imagine just letting it go. You may want to imagine breathing out through a straw; long, slow breaths.

Repeat this exercise thinking about anger, noticing your body and becoming familiar with the sensations, thoughts and beliefs you have when experiencing the emotion of anger.

Now turn your attention to feelings of joy and happiness, and what sensations happen in your body. How is your breathing and heartbeat now? What memories are evoked, and what sort of mind talk is happening? Stay with these feelings longer than with the others, and revel in feeling joy.

Write or reflect on the similarities and differences of how you experience each of these emotions in your body and what impact they have on your breathing and your heart rate. Notice what you were thinking about each of them. Which emotions do you feel comfortable with or not?

How were emotions dealt with in your family; were certain feelings encouraged and were others disallowed? Reflect on what you have written about your relationships to your emotions now and how this may correlate with your childhood experiences.

Exercise with Partner/s

Share your experiences of the solo exercise. Tell each other about your most uncomfortable and most comfortable emotions. Explore where this may come from in your childhoods and discuss how this impacts your relationship now.

Consider ways in which you could support each other with your emotional awareness.

The Limbic System

The limbic system is the name given to a group of brain structures including the hypothalamus, the thalamus, the two hippocampi and the two amygdalae (Illustration 6.2). The hypothalamus regulates our urges and appetites, acting as a bridge between our brain and our body. It directs the thalamus as to which neurochemicals it should release, in which quantities and when. The amygdala and hippocampus systems (commonly referred to in the singular) are part of our memory centre. All internal and external stimuli are evaluated primarily by our memory centres; it is our first port of call: do I know this,

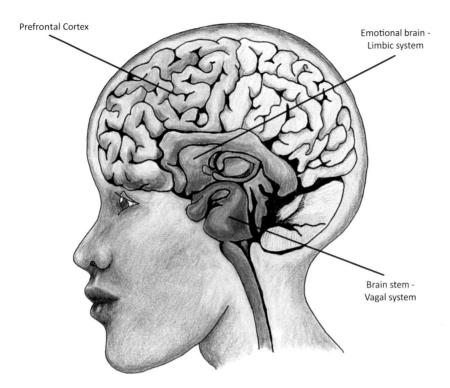

Prefrontal Cortex

Emotional brain - Limbic system

Brain stem - Vagal system

Illustration 6.1 The Brain.

have I experienced this before? As infants we learn through memory; we store experiences in our memory centres to draw on as we need, continually building our story of the world and how it works.

The hippocampus also connects with an area called the PAG (periaqueductal gray) which registers our experiences of pain and pleasure. The amygdala stores the raw experience and the hippocampus orders the time sequence of events. The amygdala can be seen to act as an alarm system, alerting us to the need for fight or flight. For example, if we suddenly hear a loud noise, we will be activated into fight or flight. However, if the sound is stored in our memory as say, a car backfiring, we register that we know what it is, and can then respond appropriately or ignore it. If we do not know what it is, we may look to see; again we may remember what this is and again, react or ignore. However, if we have a similar noise stored in our hippocampus memory as a gunshot that we experienced in the past, putting us into mortal danger, we may freeze or drop to the floor, or start running, or yelling. It has been well known for a while that the amygdala registers

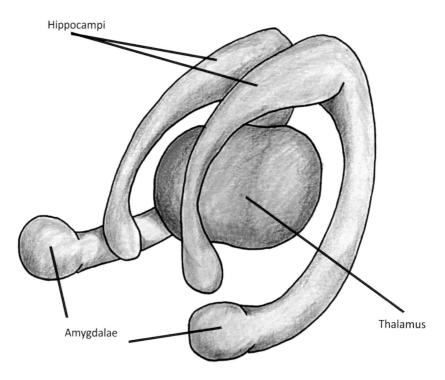

Hippocampi

Amygdalae

Thalamus

Illustration 6.2 The Limbic System.

fight or flight. It is now understood that the PAG also registers intense pleasurable experiences.[4]

Recent research has taught us much about how trauma impacts the limbic system in particular. Our emotional centre can become overwhelmed in response to certain stimuli; we literally get flooded with neurochemicals as the amygdala triggers an alert. Survival circuits become activated; there may be horrific images and incidences, experiences stored in the memory centres. We may go into rage, disassociation or a state of freeze, like a rabbit in headlights. If our brain circuits have been over activated in childhood, neural pathways can become 'hard wired' leading to a heightened reactivity to and propensity for fear or rage.

However, a recent study[5] by Professor of Psychology and Neuroscience, Wen Li, published in March 2022, found that the human sensory cortex, not the amygdala, is responsible for storing our memories of frightening events from the past. This reminds us how our knowledge is constantly evolving.

Studies into post-traumatic stress disorder have shown damage to the hippocampus. It seems that when people suffer flashbacks for example, feelings, sensations and memories are experienced as if they are happening now, rather than as events from the past; as if the time sequencing has gone askew. It is uncertain whether the traumatic event may have caused the damage, or whether the person suffered post-trauma because their hippocampus was already faulty.

Trauma is an important consideration concerning sexual issues because many people have experienced sexual violence as children and/or as adults. This can affect our brains, bodies, hearts and minds and will be discussed in a wider context in the next chapter. Herman (1993)[6] widened our understanding of trauma, to include all forms of emotional, sexual and physical violence – specifically within a powerless environment. She also believed that recovery needs to occur within a healing and safe relationship.

Touch and sensory experiences are central to our sexuality and they can also trigger traumatic memory. Our bodies hold memories (as do our emotions). Pert (1998)[7] has shown there to be neurotransmitter receptor sites, not just in the brain but throughout the body, indicating the physiology of the brain-body feedback loops. Therapists such as Levine (1997)[8] and Rothschild (2000)[9] have contributed great understanding to the theory and treatment of post-traumatic stress, combining our knowledge from neuroscience and body psychotherapy. Recovery is focused on soothing the arousal circuits in the brain, body, emotions and thinking processes.

We can also be reactive to many things that we would not necessarily consider to be traumatic; they could be issues or incidents that did have an impact on our limbic system in our past and still activate us now. Some people get hot under the collar about things that other people seem to take in their stride for example, injustice or being disbelieved; they may feel furious if people cancel appointments or are late, or they might hate being ignored. We could use this information to understand ourselves better and to realise that where there is heat, there is history. If we find ourselves over-reacting to something, we could explore why that is and what might lie beneath it.

Triggers

Solo Exercise

Take some time to think about what sort of events or situations you know you are reactive to in comparison to how you see others react. Choose one to explore in more depth.

Write in detail about an incident that happened recently and include how you felt. Notice your body sensations as well as emotions and thoughts. See if you can identify exactly what it was that upset you. If you find this difficult, imagine what you would have liked to have happened differently.

Think back to your childhood and see if you can remember whether this was something that used to happen to you then. Write about how you felt then and consider how familiar your feelings were then to how they are now.

Explore whether there are other feelings behind the ones you usually feel or express. Consider what it would be like to express these feelings instead.

Exercise with Partner/s

Use the Conscious Communication dialogue for this exercise. Allow at least 30 minutes each. Tell each other about ways in which you are reactive to each other.

Ask each other for support in helping you become more aware of your triggers and what would help to reduce your reactivity.

When you have finished, practice the exercise by Pat Ogden, where first you shake, and then stretch, and then rock or sway. This helps to re-regulate your nervous system. She says having a conscious awareness of this experience **sends messages back to the brain** *helping to re-run and strengthen neural pathways.*

The Vagus Nerve

The vagus nerve is unique in several ways. It is not contained within the spinal cord, like other peripheral nerves but is seen to meander down through the body with branches connecting with the abdomen, heart, lungs and stomach, as well as the genital area. It not only has a pathway down from the brain stem but also pathways up into the facial muscles,[10] especially the ears, eyes and mouth. These develop into *myelinated* nerves, that is, these nerve pathways run faster. The vagus nerve carries incoming information from the nervous system to the brain, providing information about what the body is doing. It also transmits outgoing information which governs a range of reflex responses, including our breathing, heartbeat and muscle control.

Polyvagal theory was introduced in 1994 by Stephen Porges[11] to describe the effect of the vagus nerve on human experience. This has greatly contributed to trauma-informed therapy and been used to create the 'traffic light system' we have previously referenced. Porges says humans have three principal defence strategies: fight, flight and freeze.

Freeze (stuckness, collapse, dissociation, depression, immobilisation) is the oldest survival system. The vagus nerve shuts us down like a mouse playing dead when there is no safe escape (red).

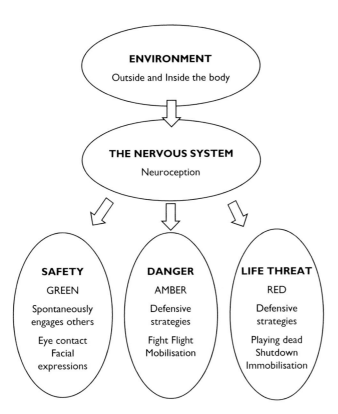

Figure 6.1 Social Engagement System.

Fight (irritability, anger, aggression, moving towards) and flight (anxiety, fear, panic, avoiding, 'what if …?') are where we feel safe enough to act in response to danger, via the limbic system: our sympathetic nervous system mobilises us (amber).

The social engagement system (Figure 6.1) is our newest evolutionary development, in operation when we can rely on feeling safe in relationship and our environment, and our nervous system is calm (green). The social engagement system is about facial expressions, eye contact, sounds and tone of voice – all vagal pathway nerves, building attachment on a neurochemical level. Face-to-face contact, eye gazing, seeing and being seen, witnessed, validated. In our early experiences of infant-carer bonding, we develop a relationship blueprint, creating a template or prototype for what to expect of future relationships and experiences of being in connection. It is important to know that this relationship-prototype is, to some extent, elastic and that positive relational experiences, such as in therapy or healthy adult

Figure 6.2 Four Trauma Patterns.

relationships, can help to heal difficult early templates of neglect or abuse. The early prototype might still rear its head in times of stress, but more connected and healthy templates or 'operating systems' can be 'installed', and the more they are used the more automatic they become.

Apart from fight, flight and freeze, there is also a fourth trauma response: fawn (Figure 6.2). This is where, as a survival strategy we go along with someone or something; are seen to be in agreement with what is happening, as a way to ultimately come out alive. This can develop into avoiding conflict, prioritising other's needs, people pleasing and difficulties saying no. We will discuss trauma and survival patterns more in Chapter 7, where we address sexual violence. The fawning response is important to understand around sex, as many survivors will – from a place of trauma – focus on just 'getting through' a situation they do not want, rather than risk conflict. This makes a trauma-informed understanding of consent all the more important.

The fawning trauma pattern can also be seen in what is called *Code-Switching,* which 'involves the suppression of multiple aspects of one's cultural identity', such as clothing, hairstyles and language, in the hope of reducing racism. Kyaien O. Conner[12] explains in more depth what Code-Switching is and how it affects Black, Indigenous and People of Colour (BIPOC) communities. Code-Switching is also one way of understanding the 'masking' – covering/altering the authentic self – that neurodivergent people often become skilled at in order to get by in a neurotypical world. It is easy to see how these types of suppression have detrimental impacts on the well-being and self-esteem of the people involved.

Multigenerational trauma can affect us genetically, biologically and psychologically.

Dr Avril Gabriel[13] explains more about how this may hinder our abilities to look after our physical and emotional well-being. Dr Joy DeGruy[14] coined the term Post-Traumatic Slave Syndrome (PTSS), as 'a theory that explains the aetiology of many of the adaptive survival behaviors in African American communities throughout the United States and the Diaspora'.

Trauma Patterns

Solo Exercise

Can you identify which, if any, of the four trauma patterns is most familiar to you. Can you bring compassion to this part of yourself? What would support you most in these moments?

Exercise with Partner/s

Can you identify any of the trauma patterns in each other? What signs do you pick up –body posture, tone of voice, (lack of) eye contact, etc?
Check with your partner whether your perceptions are correct.
Discuss what would help each other the most to re-regulate when these patterns get triggered.

Neuroception

Neuroception supports the brain to distinguish safe from dangerous contexts at a most primal level. We are constantly seeking and utilising sensory information from our environment to evaluate risk. We do this by combining our internal bodily states and the biological movements, tonal quality of voice, facial expression, movements of head and hands, and touch with others.

It can be helpful to see this as a traffic light system (albeit upside down to what we are used to) where green is the social engagement system working.

Green	Ventral Vagal	I am connected to others
Amber	Sympathetic NS	I am in danger and need to run or fight
Red	Dorsal Vagal	I am overwhelmed and frozen

Deb Dana (2018)[15] says the autonomic nervous system is shaped and regulated through interactions with others. If the social engagement system fails to create a sense of safety for us (green), we can utilise fight or flight (amber), and if that fails the freeze/disassociation response (red) can be triggered.

The vagus nerve helps us to get back into a calm and social place after stress. We need what is called good 'vagal tone' to do this. This means the vagus nerve has a good ability to regulate our system – like putting the brakes on a bike. Our exercise *Applying the Brakes* is a way of developing vagal tone. Primarily we develop good vagal tone through relationships which are co-regulating: listening to music, humming, rhythmic movement, practising and experiencing empathy.

Traffic Lights

Solo Exercise

Choose one recent issue where you became triggered. Did you go into fight or flight (amber) –or go numb or shut down (red)?

Ask yourself what you needed to come back into the green zone, to reconnect with yourself and with others.

Exercise with Partner/s

Each chooses a recent incident where you were triggered by each other. Use the Conscious Communication dialogue to share what happened.

Ask each other for support for the future. For example, what things might escalate difficulties and what would help to reduce them?

Brain Chemicals

There are many brain chemicals (called neurotransmitters) that impact human sexuality. They are released from the inner regions of the brain, the limbic system, to the central nervous system, and then flood through the body via the peripheral nervous system. As nerves pass these chemical messages to each other, links and pathways become created which run quicker and quicker the more they are used. Like learning to play an instrument, the more we practise the easier it becomes. We become conditioned, which is partly how we learn.

Neurochemicals can also be transformed via the hypothalamus to become hormones, which are then sent through the bloodstream, usually to a specific place in the body, whereas neurotransmitters pass through the nervous system to many areas. These substances are made in the brain and affected by our diet. A healthy diet will ensure a good supply of those needed for emotional well-being in the same way a diet balanced in proteins, carbohydrates, vitamins and minerals will support our physical health. Equally, a diet deplete in nutrients such as vitamins and minerals will undermine our mental health and ability to deal with the everyday stresses in life.

The following are the main brain chemicals involved in the sexual arousal process:

- **Dopamine** motivation, curiosity, intensifies pleasure
- **Serotonin** arousal, joy, excitement
- **Vasopressin** stimulates genital erection
- **Noradrenaline** increases sexual arousal and stimulation
- **Endorphins and Opiates** natural pain killers, relaxants, stimulated by play and touch
- **Acetylcholine** stabilised by comfort and soothing, impacts the autonomic nervous system
- **Oxytocin** relaxation, empathy, bonding and attachment, peaks at orgasm, triggered by touch
- **PEA** (phenyl ethylamine) – the euphoria of 'falling in love', effects digestion and the heart (Crenshaw 1997)[16]

We are familiar with some of these neurochemicals from what we know about recreational drugs. The most common neurochemical is the 'excitatory' glutamate.[17] Its counterbalance, GABA, regulates anxiety levels and is activated by alcohol. Ecstasy or MDMA increases serotonin (which heightens arousal, attention and excitement) and dopamine, which triggers motivation and initiating action. Noradrenaline pathways are stimulated by ritalin, cocaine, speed and amphetamines. Some of these chemicals can have varying impacts, e.g. separation distress triggers high levels of acetylcholine in the brain, whereas in the body it can have a calming effect, activating the parasympathetic nervous system. Interestingly, we also have cannabinoid receptor sites,[18] implying we can naturally produce cannabinoids, which are known to soothe pain.

Sexual activity triggers many of these feel-good chemicals, which is what makes it so good for us. Under certain conditions – usually a desire to get away from painful emotions – seeking these 'neurochemical hits' can lead to compulsive behaviours. This is explored further in the next chapter. In 2010 David Kessler,[19] ex head of the American Food and Drug Administration, described how some in the food industry are cynically using our knowledge of the body's reward system to create an optimum sugar, fat and salt combination which triggers dopamine and makes us want to eat more. Whether some trends in porn and dating are equivalent to a type of sexual 'fast food', with its own range of health concerns, is a question addressed further in the next chapter.

Feel Good

Solo Exercise

Think about a recent time when you felt really happy and joyous. Spend time recalling where you were; who you were with and what was being said or done; what was happening. Go over the details and revel in remembering your experience.

> *Take your attention to your body. Where are you feeling your happiness, which parts of your body and in what way? Try to imagine the feel-good hormones being pumped from your brain through your body, into your nervous system, your muscles and organs. Notice your breathing and your heartbeat. Become really aware of what it feels like physically to feel happy.*
>
> *Notice your thoughts. Are other memories of similar scenarios being evoked? There may be some sadness, about the fact that people or times in your history are no longer with you. If so, leave this aside for the moment, and focus back into your joy. How easy is it for you to do this?*
>
> *Notice what sort of dialogue you have with yourself while you are happy; what types of words, what tone and pitch of voice? How does this differ from when you feel sad, scared or angry?*
>
> *Take some time to write about what you have experienced and then to reflect on what you have written.*
>
> ### Exercise with Partner/s
>
> *Share with each other your explorations about feeling good, in as much detail as possible.*
>
> *Tell each other about a recent experience of feeling good together. Again, share in detail how it made you feel emotionally, in your body and what your thoughts were.*

Human Universals

We have been discussing our reactivity and instinctual reactions in order to understand what they are, and how much conscious control we can exert over them. We have discussed our physiological responses to the directives of neurotransmitters and hormones from the brain, in response to triggers. We have acknowledged the role of our frontal lobes; our thinking capacity to make choices in nanoseconds. We are all making thousands of different decisions every day, influenced by our different histories, where we are on the globe, our cultures and customs. So what is universal, innate to all of us?

In the 1970s, Ekman's[20] anthropological study of peoples who had previously been socially isolated, found they could recognise six human facial expressions. This led to the view that they were universal, regardless of culture or geography. However, in 2009, Callaway's[21] study asking East Asians and Caucasians to interpret a standardised set of facial expressions about fear and disgust, indicated that these interpretations may not be universally applicable but culturally nuanced. Still working in this area in 2018,[22] Ekman has provided much research on micro-expressions and also confirms the understanding that there are cultural differences in beliefs about the outward expression of emotions.

Tomkins expanded on the notion of primary feelings and the six universally recognised facial expressions. He described what he called 'Affects' – feelings,

Table 6.1 Six Human Facial Expressions

Anger	Tells us something is not okay; we need to take action – fight	Brows lowered, lips pressed firmly together, eyes bulging
Fear	Tells us something is not okay; we need to withdraw – flight	Brows raised, eyes open, mouth opens slightly
Sadness	Sorrow, our experience of grief, sadness and loss, separation distress – panic	Lowering of mouth corners, raised in portion of brows
Happiness	Joy, things are okay	Raising and lowering of mouth corners
Surprise	Shock, may trigger the fight, flight or freeze response	Brows arch, eyes open wide, jaw drops slightly in
Disgust	A socially learnt concept of repulsion, rejection and shame	Upper lip is raised, nose bridge is wrinkled, cheeks are raised

triggered by something or someone, that impact on our body causing physical sensations and are visibly recognisable by specific body postures and facial expressions.[23] Tomkins' Affects can be experienced from low intensity to high intensity; whether they are valued as positive, neutral or negative is cultural.

Table 6.1 shows the facial expressions in column 1, the emotions in column 2 and the Affects in column 3.

Four of these six facial expressions are our primary emotions of anger, fear, sadness and joy; the other two are shock and disgust. All play a crucial part in human sexuality. This is a vital link in human connectedness and emotionality that we can instantaneously feel an emotion, a reaction in response to another and can trigger the same in others too; recognising and comprehending all these non-verbal communications. More complex emotions include contempt, embarrassment, guilt, shame and the more positive feelings of amusement, contentment, pride in achievement, relief, sensory pleasure and satisfaction.

Emotional Awareness 2

Solo Exercise

Think about your awareness of and reactions to other people's emotions. Can you identify the facial expressions, body postures, tone and pitch of voice in others that alert you to which emotions they are expressing? Think about the primary emotions of anger, fear, sadness and joy; and then also other expressions of emotion like disappointment or confusion. Consider the following:

When I see someone else crying, I feel … and I think … .
When I see someone else looking frightened, I feel … and I think … .
When I see someone else being angry, I feel … and I think … .
When I see someone else being happy, I feel … and I think … .

Notice which of these emotions in others you find easier or more difficult to respond or relate too. How does this relate to how you experience your own emotions? Is there a similar pattern or are you able to tolerate expressions in others that you do not allow for yourself? Again, how does this mirror your childhood experiences?

Reflect on what you have written and identify one thing you would like to change and consider how you could do that.

Exercise with Partner/s

Take it in turns to share with each other:

> *When I see you crying, I feel … and I think … .*
> *When I see you looking frightened, I feel … and I think … .*
> *When I see you being angry, I feel … and I think … .*
> *When I see you being happy, I feel … and I think … .*

Discuss what you have heard each other say and how it may relate to your childhoods.

Could you help each other feel more comfortable with the other's emotions?

Seven Human Imperatives

Invaluable work has been done by Panksepp (1998)[24] and Sunderland (2007)[25] in integrating knowledge from neuroscience with psychotherapeutic understanding. Building on their work, we can review our understanding of human sexuality by looking beyond the sexual drive as a reproductive urge. Panksepp identifies seven brain circuits which will trigger predictable behaviours when certain areas of the brain are stimulated. The first four – seeker, lust, caring and joy – all induce feel good chemicals such as dopamine, endorphins, oxytocin and prolactin and activate the basal forebrain. The others distress us and our limbic system.

• **Seeker**	Ecstasy, happiness exploration
• **Lust**	Consummatory behaviour, hunger and the procreative urge
• **Care**	Love, nurturing and social bonding
• **Joy**	The need for touch, to rough and tumble play
• **Rage**	Anger, frustration, thwarted drive
• **Fear**	Terror, fear, anxiety
• **Panic**	Utter misery, grief/loss. Separation anxiety, abandonment

Recent studies in neuroscience have taught us a lot about human functioning. Most previous research regarding sexuality had been derived from studying animal reproductive patterns, which were then applied to humans, resulting in a focus on the reproductive model of sex as discussed earlier. We can, however, explore sexuality in a wider sense when we include other reasons for humans being sexual. By reviewing current research we can consider the socialising and relational issues involved in sexual attraction and sexual functioning. If we remove lust, as the reproductive imperative, out of the equation for a moment, we can consider what role the others may play in human sexuality and our sexual appetites. We could see fight (rage), flight (fear) and panic (sadness) as survival reactions that move us *away from* or against others (Table 6.2), and caring, curiosity (seeker) and joy as drives with a socialising function, which move us *towards* others (Table 6.3).

Rage and fear are the fight and flight responses, both of which activate the amygdala and hippocampus in the limbic system; quickly triggering the release of adrenaline for urgent action, and more slowly, cortisol for stamina. These hormones disrupt links to the frontal lobes, impairing our thinking. We need to be able to get on with it, not think about how we feel. The fight response can be experienced mildly, as irritation, through to rage when levels are high. Fear can be mild or be terrifying; we may be able to withdraw or may become frozen, like a rabbit in headlights. Disassociation and out of body experiences may be triggered. Panic activates the hypothalamus which triggers a sudden drop in oxytocin, the bonding hormone. Panksepp identifies panic as a state of separation anxiety due to loss of attachment (perhaps often seen as sadness). This is an important differentiation as we often relate to panic as anxiety, as a fear emotion. Reframing this experience in connection to attachment, as a relational experience, could alter our thinking and treatment strategies for panic attacks.

Table 6.2 The Survival Brain Circuits

Survival	Reactions against Other
Fight	danger, need to take action
Flight	need to get away, withdraw
Panic	abandonment, loss, separation distress

Table 6.3 The Socialising Brain Circuits

Socialising	Move Us Towards Other
Caring	our capacity to have empathy and look after other people
Curiosity	our interest in others and the world around us
Play and physical contact	our need for touch and fun with others

The relational or socialising drives are vital for us as humans. Our caring circuit moderates our empathy skills, the desire to nurture and soothe that is crucial to our survival. Because infants and children are so physically and emotionally dependent on adults to stay alive, let alone thrive, we humans need more than a good live birth rate to maintain our species. Empathy is a vital human attribute for a healthy society; it is important that we can and do feel compassion for others, so we can help the more vulnerable, and ensure survival. The issue of empathy and its opposite, lack of compassion and objectification, are important issues in our social structure, specifically so in the arena of sexuality. A lack of empathy allows humans to hurt others without regard to how it may feel; to hurt without care.

Our incessant inquisitiveness as humans may seem to get us into trouble at times but we probably would not do much without it. It is the curiosity circuit that encourages an infant to reach out or motivates its desire to move; first to crawl and later, to walk. As children, our curiosity is rampant and can be a source of exasperation to many parents, teachers, carers and siblings, who often do not know the answers to a child's 'why, how and what' questions. It is our curiosity, motivated by the brain chemical dopamine, which gets us to explore and to consider 'what if?' Many things we use in our modern world were invented because of someone's curiosity and imagination. Somebody thought, 'what if we could move around in a vehicle or fly through the sky or have a device like a mobile phone?'

An urge for play and touch has been identified in the young of many mammals and is probably central to human sexual urges too. Infants explore their environment firstly through their senses: sight, sound, taste, smell and touch. Anything felt in their hands will primarily be moved to the mouth to be tasted and smelled. Physical contact is of vital importance to children who often seek touch and physical connection with their carers. Research on children in orphanages in Romania in the 1980s showed that despite being fed and clothed (their physical needs cared for), a lack of touch and physical contact with carers in the first few years of life had led to brain damage.[26] Frontal lobes (necessary for thinking and choosing) had not grown sufficiently and neural pathways linking to the limbic system were not developed either. Such damage has also been seen in brain scans of children in Britain whose emotional needs have not been met.[27]

Towards and Away

Solo Exercise

Think about some recent incidents where you definitely felt attracted towards someone or something that was happening, or where you felt repelled. Choose one of each and consider each in more detail to identify more about why you were attracted or not.

> *Now think about yourself sexually. What types of experiences and encounters with others attract you (turn you on) and which repel you (turn you off)? Think about this with regard to your physical body and sensations, your emotions and feelings, and your belief system and preferences.*
>
> *Reflect on what you have written and consider if there are things you would like to change, and if so, how you could do so.*
>
> ### Exercise with Partner/s
>
> *Share your experiences of what attracts you sexually to your partner/s, and what turns you off.*
>
> *Discuss how you could incorporate your knowledge of yourselves and each other into your shared sexual life.*

Attachment and Relationships

Let us now consider relational and intimacy issues. If our sexual desire is often triggered by an 'other', creating a want to reach out, to kiss or touch them, what are our relational needs from sex and our sexuality? These are important issues to consider given our attitude that sex is something we do; that we make love *to* someone, rather than *with* them. Relational issues also question our cultural objectification of sexuality; that we should look attractive *to* someone rather than *feel* sexual, and our increasing normalisation of depersonalised sex.

To explore the relational and relational field of our sexuality, let us go back and consider the fundamental relational needs of humans and the vital developmental stages in our formative years. Hendrix[28] outlines a Psychosocial Journey of the Self from birth to teenage, with six identifiable stages, each with a primary behaviour. Table 6.4 shows how we build these psychosocial skills which lead to an integrated sense of responsibility to self and to society.

Table 6.4 The Hendrix Psychosocial Stages of Development

Age	Developmental Task	Developmental Behaviour	Psychosocial Skills
Birth–18 months	Attachment	Reaching	Emotional security
18 months–3 years	Exploration	Exploring	Differentiation and intact curiosity
3–4 years	Identity	Asserting	Secure sense of self
4–7 years	Competence	Competing	Sense of personal power to achieve
7–13 years	Concern	Sympathising	Concern for others
13–19 years	Intimacy	Integrating	Intact sexuality and ability to love

Hendrix believes that when a child is allowed and supported through each stage successfully, it will lead to a specific developmental achievement. Transition through all stages will allow a development of responsibility to self and to society; an acceptance of our needs, a fundamental belief in our right to have these needs and our trust that they can, and mostly will, be met (also known as secure attachment). When our needs are not met, we may essentially believe somehow we should not have these needs and feel shame in relation to them. If this is the case, what impact may this have on how we feel about ourselves sexually?

We would like to build on Hendrix's model to look beyond the family of origin when considering child development. Quinn (2020)[29] develops understanding about Adverse Childhood Experiences (ACEs) – well known to have serious long-term physical and emotional health impacts – to also include Environment and Community, as shown in Figure 6.3. We can ask ourselves, how do all these factors impact on our relational development, and how can we build resilience in response?

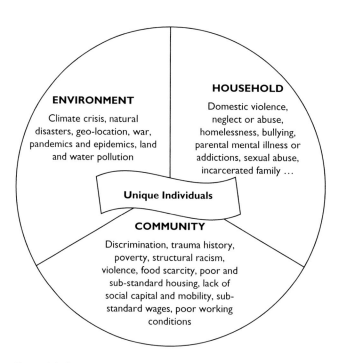

Figure 6.3 Social Dimensions of Diversity and Culture(s).

Attachment Pattern

Solo Exercise

Think about a recent time when you felt upset about something. Were you inclined to reach out to a friend or loved one for comfort or support? Or perhaps you are familiar with not expecting this and believing that your difficulties are for you to deal with alone.

Look back at the exercises on Emotional Awareness and see how you responded to your own feelings and emotions and how you respond to them in others. What can this tell you about your own attachment pattern?

See if there are any changes you would like to make and consider how you could do so.

Exercise with Partner/s

Discuss the solo exercise above and consider how this plays out in your relationship/s now. Are you inclined to turn towards each other if you are in emotional distress? If you notice you turn away, how do you do this? Do you become silent or withdrawn? Do you start a fight as a way of distancing?

Talk about the attachment patterns in your relationship/s and how you feel about how you respond and how your partner/s react. Are there any patterns you would like to change? If so, discuss how you could support each other to do so.

Developmental Tasks

Much has been written about our early attachment relationships and their effects on future choices of partners and abilities to sustain sexual relationships as adults. Putting together the stages of development by Hendrix,[30] discussed earlier, with Kaufman and Raphael's[31] outline of Basic Interpersonal Needs (shown in bold) allows us to consider the development of sexual self-esteem.

Need for touching and holding
ATTACHMENT, leading to emotional security

Our need for relationships with other people is significant in the first stage, which Hendrix calls attachment. We reach out for touching and holding. As infants we need someone to feed us and nurture us or we will die. We reach first with our mouths for food, then as we can grasp, we move whatever we touch to our mouths, where we taste, and given our nose is so near, probably smell too. Attachment is the beginning of our social bonding, where the sense of sight is also vital, the importance of seeing and being seen.

When the infant's gaze is met with a smile (the facial expression of joy) from the primary care giver, it is soothed and will experience emotional security. If it is met with anger or indifference, it will feel distress and react through one of the survival circuits of fight, flight or panic. Very basically, each interaction will induce either our reward system or our survival circuits. The feelings of pleasure will activate the reward system and release feel-good neurochemicals like serotonin or oxytocin. Or our distress will induce feelings of pain and activate our survival system, prompting the release of adrenaline and cortisol. Gerhardt[32] describes in detail how brain development is impacted by our early experiences and why indeed, love matters so much. She also explains the harm that can be done physically, to our neurochemical patterning and nervous system; psychologically, to our emotional well-being, and therefore socially; impacting our expectations and capacities in adult relationships.

If in the first year and a half of our lives, our attachment needs are adequately met, we will have a biochemical pattern of feeling pleasure, and therefore expect to receive pleasure when we reach out to someone to be in relationship with them; to be touched and held. We will have achieved an internal sense of emotional security, leading to a fundamental belief in our right to exist; in our desires to reach out and a trust in other people that they will respond positively. During the attachment phase, the infant decides through its experiences with parents and carers, whether relationships are trustworthy or not. If our needs are not met, our biochemical pattern is one of stress hormones and the need for survival reactions, leading to emotional insecurity. Perhaps here we learn a sense of shame about our need for others.

Within the arena of sexuality our wants and needs for attachment, for touching and holding are not valued in our society. The fact that we desire another, who we want to kiss and feel, is rarely acknowledged. We do not seem to teach or encourage these needs as primary; rather we focus on sexual acts and sexual positions. Hite[33] noted that when researching what people liked about being sexual, there was one activity that many people mentioned that we have no quick phrase or word to describe: lying alongside their lover, naked, kissing, holding each other and feeling their whole bodies touching, while they looked into each other's eyes.

Identification – Need to belong, feel at 'one' with others
Differentiation – Need to be different and separate
EXPLORATION – leading to differentiation and intact curiosity

The second phase is exploration, between eighteen months and three years old. The child can now move independently and explore the world around them. Encouragement to discover their world (along with guidelines about obvious dangers) will promote an intact curiosity and a sense of differentiation. During the exploration phase, the child is developing autonomy and self-worth or a sense of shame; of low self-esteem which can lead to self-doubt and a feeling of not being able to rely on anything or anyone.

Another way we are often shamed sexually is through adults' response to children touching their genitals. There is a natural inclination for children to do this; it is a form of self-soothing. Parents often discourage their children from doing this, especially in public, telling them it is bad or dirty. Depending on the degree of shaming that continues as the child grows, this can lead to shame about masturbation and other forms of self-pleasuring as an adult.

This exploration phase is activated during sexual attraction where we become curious about someone and want to get to know them or more about them. Feeling shame about our curiosity having been discouraged about 'wanting to know' or ridiculed for asking questions will dampen our sense of inquisitiveness. It may discourage us as adults from acting on our attractions or desires.

We also have a need at this stage for identification; to belong and feel 'at one' with others but also to be different and separate. How much we have been encouraged and allowed to do this as children will influence our capacity to accept ourselves and to tolerate differences in others.

Need for power in our relationships and in our lives
IDENTITY – leading to secure sense of self

The third phase is identity. Aged between 3 and 4, the child begins to assert these differences. If they are accepted and kept in attachment, i.e. not rejected for these differences, they will feel supported to have a unique sense of identity and develop a secure sense of self. For example, are they allowed to show personal preferences for food or clothing? We have a need for power in our relationships and in our lives. Not meaning power over others, but a sense of personal power, like the right to choose, to want something different or feel something different from others.

This is important for a sense of sexual self-esteem. This is particularly important for people of minority sexual identities and sexual preferences, as their ability to fend off homophobia, internally and external, may be strengthened or weakened by how strongly their sense of self has been allowed to develop around this age. This phase can also impact on our ability to feel individuated in relationship, which can lead to power struggles and conflict in friendships and work relationships, as well as with sexual partners.

Affirmation – Need to feel worthwhile; valued and admired
COMPETENCE – leading to sense of personal power to achieve

The fourth phase is competence, where the four-to seven years old focuses on competing. If affirmed, valued, admired and made to feel worthwhile, the child will experience a sense of personal power in their right and ability to succeed and achieve. We are learning to master our world; reading and writing, developing physical skills like sports or playing an instrument or learning to be in relationships; learning to share and to negotiate and accommodate between what we want and what others want or need. The more we receive support and empathy from others; our carers, parents and peers, about our struggles and difficulties in developing these skills, the more sympathetic and less critical we will be of ourselves and of others.

This stage is intrinsic to a sense of self-worth, of being seen and valued as a unique human being. Difficulties in this phase can undermine a growing sense of being OK; of valuing your own uniqueness, your own body shape and attributes. Current cultural body shaming and desire for cosmetic surgery would indicate that many people have not been allowed to develop successfully through this stage.

Need to nurture; care for and help others
CONCERN – leading to concern for others

Between seven and thirteen years old, we learn to sympathise, to feel concern for others. As a species, we have a need to nurture; to care for and help others. Our abilities to empathise are vital for successful social and sexual relationships. Seven is also seen as the age at which we begin to develop a consciousness; an awareness about what is happening around us. We become more aware of what people say and do and how this makes us, and others, feel.

The ability to empathise, to be able to step into another's world and imagine what it is like from their perspective is vital for good relationships. The ability to empathise with ourselves and our human imperfections is vital too. Difficulties through this stage can lead to the development of a strong critical stance towards the self, and therefore usually also towards others. This can lead to perfectionist traits which, due to the impossibility of achieving perfection, can leave someone with a sense of failure or of never being good enough; and nothing and no one is ever good enough for them. Again, this is evident in our culture, with our media encouraging us to always look for more, for bigger, for better. A lack of feeling that ourselves, our relationships or our things are 'good enough', can lead to a general sense of discontentment; a lack of satiation and ultimately a compulsion to try to be perfect.

Need for relationships with other people
INTIMACY – leading to intact sexuality, ability to Love

In the final phase of Hendrix's model, between thirteen and nineteen years old, we are developing our needs for intimacy and our developmental behaviour is integrating. Successful transition through this stage will, in Hendrix' opinion, lead to an intact sexuality and an ability to love. At this stage of sexual development, how our carers, parents and peers respond will be vital in developing a sense of sexual self-esteem.

This must be confusing to young people given our cultural ambivalence to sexuality. On the one hand, they live in an environment with a highly sexualised media, with sex being used to sell just about everything. On the other hand, there is little celebration about sexuality; what an amazing gift it is to be able to experience free, sexual pleasure in our bodies or through sharing sexually with another. If adults do not feel comfortable about their own sexuality, they will find it difficult to openly discuss and support or promote and celebrate their children's emerging sexuality.

This stage brings together all the other developmental phases. Successful transitions through the phases will motivate the reward system, the feel-good neurochemicals such as dopamine and serotonin. We will feel accepting of our basic needs and confident that generally they will be received and accepted by others. Difficulties through these stages can lead to a preponderance of stress hormones as the survival brain circuits are more often activated. This in turn can lead to a reduction in our frontal lobe development, impacting our ability to think things through, evaluate and make choices. We may feel intrinsically ashamed about our basic needs, and being human, we develop coping strategies to get our needs met. As adults these strategies can, and do, become outmoded and can undermine our ability to have successful social relationships. Difficulties in social relating obviously impacts our abilities to have sustaining and fulfilling sexual relationships.

A main principle of this book is relationships; the internal interplay between our reactive brain and/or reflective mind, and the dialogue between these and our body and our feelings. Another facet that humans like about sexuality is sexual love and having sexual relationships. They may start from a sexual attraction that leads to a sexual encounter that develops into a sexual relationship, which may then lead onto marriage, civil partnership or living together; being flatmates, companions, friends and perhaps co-parenting. Or they may start from a friendship or work relationship that develops into a sexual relationship. Love is a subject that fascinates us and is a wonderful part of being human. What exactly love is, has been a question for debate for centuries. Love takes many forms that are non-sexual like loving our family, children, friends or animals. It makes us feel good and can bring great joy and delight. When things go wrong in our love relationships, it can also bring deep distress and heartache.

Some people want and deeply enjoy the intimacy that develops through having sex with the same person again and again. Others prefer sexual encounters with different people, who they are in relationships with or with strangers. Some want relationships that are not sexual but deeply loving. At different stages or times in our lives we may want either, neither or all. We may have dilemmas about wanting to experience the intimacy of one emotionally deep sexual partnership, while also desiring variety in our sexual encounters. Whatever we choose, we can still be in good relationship with ourselves; we can be embodied and conscious. Becoming clearer about our sexual beliefs and values, our tastes and our desires for sexual relationships, encourages us to be more selective, to choose the type of sexual encounters or relationships that we want and value; the types of sexual expression that will nurture our bodies, hearts and souls.

Developmental Tasks

Solo Exercise

Think about the stages outlined earlier. Write a few words about how they were supported or undermined during your childhood.

Attachment - Touch and holding Exploration - Belonging, being different
Identity - The right to choose
Competence - Affirmation of being worthy Concern - Care for others
Intimacy - Relationship with others

Reflect on how this has impacted on you as an adult. During which phases were you encouraged and supported through or hampered? How has this affected how you feel towards yourself and towards others?

Exercise with Partner/s

Tell each other about you most difficult developmental stage and how you feel it might be affecting your relationship now.

Identify what feels helpful from your partner/s when you get triggered around this material, and explain more to them about why and how their behaviour or attitudes help you.

Us and Them

Building on the work by his father John Bowlby (1988),[34] Richard Bowlby (2004)[35] has shown that although children seek 'rough and tumble' play with others, the quality of this contact is vital. A primary attachment figure is often the mother but not necessarily so; it is the main carer, 'the person who most often attends the child's calls of physical and emotional distress'. When this is experienced as secure, consistent and reliable, the child gets soothed by the interventions of the adult; gradually learning to self soothe and develop an inner sense of the world as a safe place. When soothing is not offered, the rage, fear and panic circuits become more activated and more entrenched. This hyper-arousal together with damage to the frontal lobes can be disastrous for a growing child, causing long-term difficulties with self-esteem and relationships as adults.

Richard Bowlby's work, a twenty-one-year study on attachment, showed the equal importance of a secondary attachment figure, often but not necessarily the father. This person would be more likely to engage in rough and tumble play with the child, which can develop their sense of confidence in the outside world; of being in the public realm. However, he found that a bullying or critical attitude from this adult role would produce the opposite; a lack of public confidence, again bringing problems for adults' social, sexual and work lives. As humans we are constantly responding to our outside environment with self-preserving, hardwired brain reflexes. We are also social beings, interested in and seeking out others to interact with. These socialising drives are modulated mainly around pleasure or pain, which can be either physical or emotional, usually both.

Pain and pleasure are both experienced in an area called the PAG, which connects with the hippocampus in the limbic system. Neurochemicals such as dopamine and serotonin are seen as part of a 'reward or punishment' system. Dopamine is triggered by acts of short-term pleasure, and touches five brain receptors, perhaps leaving us wanting more. Serotonin is triggered by acts of long-term satisfaction, and touches fourteen brain receptors, leading to a greater sense of satiation. Basically, when our encounters result in pleasure, we continue, we move towards. When they result in pain, one of the survival modes of fight, flight or panic will come into play, we react against and move away.

So what about sex and sexuality? The three socialising drives for caring, curiosity and play and physical touch seem very pertinent to how and why humans express their sexuality and the sexual behaviours they display. Sexual behaviours could be seen as a playground where adults get their 'rough and tumble' play; how much rough and how much play is surely a question for consideration, given Bowlby's findings. If the fight or flight circuits get activated, the system gets flooded with adrenaline, perhaps alongside the pleasure chemicals, serotonin and dopamine. Can our fundamental ability to distinguish pain (i.e. move away from) and pleasure (move towards) become confused?

Our curiosity circuit is clearly triggered in sexual attraction, sexual desire and sexual arousal. We become interested and intrigued; we want to know more, see more and feel more. We often want to care for, protect and tend to our lovers; perhaps to cook for them, take them out, bring pleasure and make them happy. These aspects speak much more to the relationship and intimacy needs of our sexuality than the biology of reproduction that tends to be focussed on. It implies much wider needs than a sexual act.

Sexual arousal in humans often triggers a desire for other, to reach out and touch, both literally and metaphorically, to make contact, connection. Our circuits of curiosity, care and joy are activated, and move us towards socialisation. They trigger feel good hormones, the reward system of the body. Touching skin and being touched and held, cuddled, releases oxytocin, the love and bonding hormone. Oxytocin, which floods the body during sexual arousal and peaks at orgasm, is seen as an evolutionary mutation of vasopressin, which triggers reproductive behaviour in mammals (Panksepp 1998). The next strand of our story – the next chapter – will be exploring the feelings and emotions evoked by our sexual energy charge, neurochemistry and body changes.

Review of Chapter 6

Solo Exercise

Read back through the exercises for this chapter and what you have written in your journal. Take some time to reflect on your exploration and to evaluate your work. Which exercises did you like and which ones did you not like? Think about why.

What have you discovered about your instinctual drives? What have you discovered about your emotional intelligence, and what upsets you in relationships and what makes you feel good?

What have you discovered about your desire in terms of what you think; how you like to be touched and what fires your imagination?

Is there anything you want to change; if so, how could you do that?

Are there any exercises that you would like to do again? If so, notice what is similar or different if you do them a second time.

Talk to someone, write or draw something about how you are thinking and feeling having worked on this section.

Exercise with Partner/s

Give yourselves an hour each and use the Conscious Communication dialogue to explore each other's reviews in detail.

Take your time to learn more about yourselves and your partner/s as you discover what has been important about the work on this aspect of your sexuality.

Discuss where you feel this leaves your relationship now and identify one aspect that needs your combined attention. Explore how you may want to do this.

Notes

1 Morin, J. (1996). *The Erotic Mind.* New York: Harper Collins.
2 Erotic Blueprint Breakthrough. (2022). *About.* Available at: https://missjaiya.com/about/ (Accessed: 11 September 2022).
3 Barrett, L. F. (2021). 'Your Brain Predicts (Almost) Everything You Do'. Available at: https://www.mindful.org/your-brain-predicts-almost-everything-you-do/ (Accessed: 23 August 2022); Lisa Feldman Barrett. (2022). *Seven and a Half Lessons About the Brain.* Available at: https://lisafeldmanbarrett.com/ (Accessed: 23 August 2022).
4 Tonegawa, S. (2017). 'Brain Circuit That Drives Pleasure Inducing Behavior Identified', *Neuroscience News.* Available at: https://neurosciencenews.com/pleasure-amygdala-neuroscience-6286/ (Accessed: 23 August 2022).
5 Li, W. (2022). *Current Biology.* Available at: https://neurosciencenews.com/fear-sensory-cortex-20250/ (Accessed: 7 August 2022).
6 Herman, J. (1993). *Trauma and Recovery.* New York: Basic Books.
7 Pert, C. (1998). *Molecules of Emotion.* New York: Simon and Schuster.
8 Levine, P. (1997). *Waking the Tiger.* Berkeley, CA: North Atlantic Books.
9 Rothschild, B. (2000). *The Body Remembers.* New York: Norton.
10 Porges, S. (2007). 'The Polyvagal Perspective', *Biological Psychology*, 74, pp. 116–143; Active Pause. (no date). *Scientific Evidence for the Polyvagal Theory.* Available at: https://activepause.com/polyvagal-theory-evidence/ (Accessed: 23 August 2022).
11 Porges, S. (2017). *The Pocket Guide to the Polyvagal Theory: The Transformative Power of Feeling Safe.* New York: W.W. Norton; Stephen W. Porges. (2022). *Polyvagal Theory.* Available at: https://www.stephenporges.com/ (Accessed: 23 August 2022).
12 O. Conner, K. (2020). 'What Is Code-Switching?', *Psychology Today,* 3 December. Available at: https://www.psychologytoday.com/us/blog/achieving-health-equity/202012/what-is-code-switching (Accessed: 29 August 2022).
13 Gabriel, A. (2021). 'Trauma: How It Gets Passed on and Breaking the Cycle', *Counselling Directory*, 26 October. Available at: https://www.counselling-directory.org.uk/memberarticles/trauma-how-it-gets-passed-on-and-breaking-the-cycle. (Accessed: 29 August 2022).
14 DeGruy, J. *Post Traumatic Slave Syndrome (P.T.S.S.).* Available at: https://www.joydegruy.com/ (Accessed: 29 August 2022).
15 Dana, D. (2018). *The Polyvagal Theory in Therapy: Engaging the Rhythm of Regulation.* New York: W.W. Norton.
16 Crenshaw, T. (1997). *The Alchemy of Love and Lust.* New York: Pocket Books.
17 Frothingham, S. (2018). 'Excitatory Neurotransmitters', *Healthline*, 12 December. Available at: https://www.healthline.com/health/excitatory-neurotransmitters#excitatory-neurotransmitters (Accessed: 11 September 2022).
18 Gibb, B. J. (2015). 'A Quick Guide to Drugs, the Brain and Brain Chemistry', *Welcome Collection,* 1 November. Available at: https://wellcomecollection.org/articles/W9hIBBAAAHAb74ma (Accessed: 11 September 2022).
19 Kessler, D. (2010). 'Obesity: The Killer Combination of Salt, Fat and Sugar', *The Guardian*, 13 March. Available at: https://www.theguardian.com/lifeandstyle/2010/mar/13/obesity-salt-fat-sugar-kessler (Accessed: 23 August 2022).
20 Ekman, P., & Paul Ekman Group. (no date). *Are Facial Expressions Universal or Culturally Specific?* Available at: https://www.paulekman.com/blog/facial-expressions-universal-culturally-specific/ (Accessed: 25 August 2022).
21 Callaway, E. (2010). 'Human Facial Expressions Aren't Universal', *New Scientist,* 19 March. Available at: www.newscientist.com/article/dn17605-human-facial-expressions-arent-universal.html (Accessed: 23 August 2022).

22 Ekman, P., & Paul Ekman Group. (no date). *About*. Available at: https://www.paulekman.com/about/paul-ekman/ (Accessed: 27 August 2022).
23 Kaufman, G., & Raphael, L. (1996). *Coming Out of Shame*. New York: Doubleday.
24 Panksepp, J. (1998). *Affective Neuroscience*. New York: Oxford University Press.
25 Sunderland, M. (2007). *What Every Parent Needs to Know*. London: Dorling Kindersley.
26 Boyd, C. (2020). 'Children Who Lived in Deprived Orphanages in Romania Have Brains That Are Almost 10% SMALLER Than English Adoptees', *Times of Naukri*, 7 January. Available at: https://ukraine.timesofnews.com/health-care/children-who-lived-in-deprived-orphanages-in-romania-have-brains-10-smaller-than-english-adoptees.html (Accessed: 25 August 2022).
27 Batmanghelidjh, C. (2007). *Shattered Lives*. London: Jessica Kingsley.
28 Hendrix, H. (1993). *Getting the Love You Want: a Guide for Couples*. London: Pocket Books; Hendrix, H. (1995). *Keeping the Love You Find*. London: Pocket Books.
29 Quinn, J. (2020). '3 Realms of ACEs – Updated!', *PACEs Connection*, 7 October. Available at: https://www.pacesconnection.com/g/hutchinson-ks-aces-connection/blog/3-realms-of-aces-updated (Accessed: 5 August 2022).
30 Hendrix, H. (1995). *Keeping the Love You Find*. London: Pocket Books.
31 Kaufman, G., & Raphael, L. (1996). *Coming Out of Shame*. New York: Doubleday.
32 Gerhardt, S. (2004). *Why Love Matters*. Hove, Brighton, UK: Brunner-Routledge.
33 Hite, S. (1994). *The Hite Report on the Family*. London: Bloomsbury.
34 Bowlby, J. (1988). *A Secure Base*. Abingdon, Oxon: Routledge.
35 Bowlby, R. (2004). *Fifty Years of Attachment Theory*. London: Karnac.

Chapter 7

Emotion

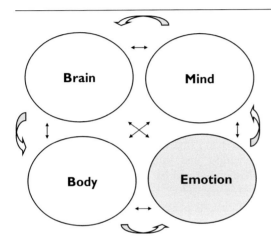

Dark Side of the Moon

In Chapter 4, we explored current social and cultural beliefs and values about sexuality. These included use of language, attitudes to sexuality and pleasure and concepts such as the reproductive model of sex. We discussed options and choices for sexual nourishment and sexual self-esteem.

Chapter 5 described our sexual anatomy in detail, not just the genitals but other vital body systems such as the endocrine and nervous systems. It also explained the various stages of the sexual arousal process and outlined our physiological sexual potential.

Chapter 6 described the neurochemistry of sexual arousal and the role of the brain in sexuality and sexual functioning. Reframing neuroscientific information about brain circuits gives us a deeper understanding of human sexuality; seeing our sex urge as much more than a vital human imperative to reproduce.

In this chapter, we shall discuss emotions and how they relate to love and sex. Why do we have sex, on an emotional level? What influence does culture have on our emotions around sex? What kind of emotions are stimulated in

DOI: 10.4324/9781003322405-8

sexual situations? What are emotions, anyway? We will delineate four basic emotions, and some more complex ones, and then give special attention to the experience of (sexual) shame. How do our emotions develop? How are they impacted by our early experiences with our caregivers? And then as adults, how does culture, and specific aspects of it, like porn and social media, affect our sexual self-esteem? What are the links between emotions and sexual compulsivity? How does sexual violence impact us emotionally? And then what about relationships? How can we develop our ability to hold on to ourselves and express ourselves well in intimate relationships? And how might this effect our chances of creating a fulfilling sexual relationship over the long term? Finally, what about our spiritual life? Are we interested in exploring more sacred forms of sexuality?

So, on an emotional level, why do we have sex? Remember neuroscientist Panksepp[1] and the survival and socialising brain circuits? Well, the socialising brain circuits (caring, curiosity and play) are highly relevant to our sexuality. We might want to express love, care or affection for another person. We might be curious as to what sensations we can evoke in ourselves and each other. And we can think of sex as an adult form of play, of rough and tumble – a way to express and enjoy our bodies together and often to connect emotionally. The survival circuits (fight, flight and panic) are also clearly relevant to sexual relationships: just think about arguments, insecurities and the experience of being dumped by a partner you still love. The reason we have devoted a whole section to sexual shame is that it's a common response to these survival circuits being stimulated.

How is it to consider the emotional aspects of sex in this way? Imagine if sex education included this. How might our sexual attitudes and behaviour be different if this understanding was central to our culture?

Your Dark Side

Solo Exercise

Write about how you feel good about yourself sexually and how you don't feel good. Explore in depth what you don't feel good about. Is it your beliefs, your body, your behaviours or your experiences?

When you have done this, reflect on what you have written and consider the context for your words in terms of your upbringing. How have your beliefs and experiences been influenced by what you were taught or learned as a child or young person?

Exercise with Partner/s

Each share one thing you feel good about and one thing you don't.

> *Tell each other what you understand about how your childhood experiences may have influenced how you feel.*
>
> *Use the Conscious Communication dialogue to help each other explore and understand more.*

Truths and Lies

It can feel difficult to imagine sexual self-esteem, both as individuals and as a culture, when we do not have a cultural sex-positive attitude. What would it be like to value diverse expressions of sexuality, to foreground consent and pleasure, to honour our emotional and relational needs?

Children pick up our embarrassment, even from the language we use about their bodies. Parents and relatives might delight in an infant's discovery of their toes and fingers but not of their genitals, often responding with embarrassment, or even anger. For example, one of the authors witnessed a scene where a two-year-old was asking her mother a question about her genitals. After much giggling, the embarrassed mother referred to her daughter's vulva as your 'not a willy'. Shere Hite[2] raised the question of what impact it must have on girls' experience of themselves sexually, when they can see that they have external organs but these are not named and often ignored. When toddlers ask about the differences between boys and girls that they can see, they are often answered with descriptions of penises (outside the body) and vaginas (inside the body) and in time, told about males and females 'making babies' through intercourse.

That females have a clitoris is not mentioned much and, even if it is, often misrepresented in size and function. The external genitals, the vulva, is rarely referred to. It is common for the word 'vagina' to confusingly be used to describe both the vulva and the vagina itself. In addition, the potential discrepancy between biological sex (genitals, hormones, secondary sex characteristics), gender identity (inner sense of gender) and gender expression (clothing, way of moving, interests, etc.) is rarely mentioned to younger children, although hopefully this is changing.

The adult world of sexuality must also seem confusing to children, with its many mixed messages and paradoxes. Sexy clothing is widely advertised and revered on celebrities, pop stars, etc., yet also slut-shamed. Sex is used to sell many things, but at the same time many adults are too embarrassed to talk about it. Breasts are emphasised in a lot of clothing and advertising, yet we are expected to be discreet, if not hidden, when breastfeeding an infant.

Then, as teenagers, the focus seems to be on looking hot and acting sexy, rather than feeling sexual and experiencing pleasure. It can be more about how you perform than how you feel inside. To make matters worse, because adults are often so awkward, or old-fashioned, when talking about sex, many teenagers prefer to get their sex education from their peer group (unreliable) and porn (often objectifying and non-relational, portraying sexual acts rather than emotions or intimacy). It's not all doom and gloom, however, as there are many inclusive, holistic, sex-positive media sources available to teenagers now, from the Netflix series *Sex Education*[3] to websites like bishuk,[4] sex-positive families[5] and Scarleteen,[6] and books like Heather Corinna's *S.E.X: The All-You-Need-To-Know Sexuality Guide to Get You Through Your Teens and Twenties*[7] and School of Sexuality Education's *Sex Ed: An Inclusive Teenage Guide to Sex and Relationships.*[8]

Starting with ourselves, within a Homeodynamic Model, we can more consciously create the sort of sexual life we want. We can learn about our brain reactions and our body's sexual potential. We can use our emotions as basic information; as an immediate response about whether we like what's happening, or not. By also becoming explicit about our thinking (our beliefs and values), we can create a framework to further inform how we may want to act; how we want to behave sexually.

Your Truths

Solo Exercise

Write two lists, one about the things you think are true and one about the things you think are lies, about what you see and hear about sexuality, in the media or from family, friends or peers.

Of the things you think are lies, consider why such things may be said and believed by others. Clarify for yourself your list of truths; add any more that you think are missed by us culturally and think out for yourself why you think they are truths.

Exercise with Partner/s

Share your lists of truths and lies. If you have things that you initially disagree on, discuss with an attitude of curiosity. For example you may ask: 'Can you tell me more about why you think … is true/is not true?'

Create a shared list of what you each believe to be true about sexuality.

Full of Feelings

We use the word 'feelings' to mean many things, like an emotion, a sensation, a thought or a hunch. It can be useful to separate them out within the Homeodynamic Model for health. Talking about 'feeling sexual', for example, can mean several things. Having a feeling and choosing whether to act on it or not is a central tenet of this book. Figure 7.1 shows a Homeodynamic Model of feelings.

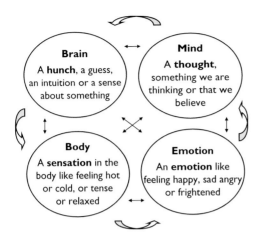

Figure 7.1 A Homeodynamic Model of Feelings.

Whenever a reaction is triggered in us, our neurochemistry responds, causing physiological effects, moving energy through the body, generating thoughts about all this, and immediately more reactions, responses and so on. We are exploring a complex interwoven web of 'being human'. The brain relies on outer sensory information and internal monitoring to make executive decisions. Based on neuroception, it prioritises physical safety, on a survival level, over the quality or pleasure of consequent outcomes.

Understanding these different aspects or strands of our 'feelings' can help simplify them and provide problem-solving tools. This is especially so with sexuality. To separate out 'feeling sexual' into components of a physical urge, an emotional desire and/or a thought, can inform us in more detail about what we really want. One strand may mean we feel turned on and want to be sexual, with ourselves or with someone else; another may mean we want some emotional closeness or intimacy, or we may want both. Such distinctions can help guide us to getting our deeper needs met.

To explore the emotional aspect of sexuality in more depth, it is useful to go back to some basics; to understand the building blocks behind our more complex emotions. There are four primary emotions expressed in the extreme by human infants and, most often, more moderately by adults. We have four basic emotions:

Ecstasy	>	Joy
Rage	>	Anger
Terror	>	Fear
Misery	>	Sorrow

They are called primary emotions because they can be experienced by us all and we can recognise them in others. They are reflexes, triggered in response to something or someone. They are processed first through the memory centres of the limbic system in the brain, reacting with a flood of neuro-chemicals, activating the autonomic nervous system and causing physio-logical effects.

Let us take a moment to consider how we know which emotion we are feeling. Usually there is a combination of physical sensations and reactions and specific thoughts. It is useful to notice and accept the somatic experi-ences of each emotion and to separate out our thoughts. Anger will increase our heart rate and trigger muscle tension causing a firmer body stance. Joy and happiness are often welcome feelings, producing waves of pleasure in the body, excitement and anticipation. Fear may induce a desire to retreat, a tensing of the stomach and legs, a thumping heart, and thinking about what to do. Sorrow may produce a pain in the heart, the release of tears, feelings of sadness and thoughts of being rejected and abandoned.

The survival circuits are necessary for our well-being. As we described in the brain section, fight tells us we are in danger and need to act. When we show anger and someone takes us seriously, and perhaps offers acts of correction, we feel cared about. Fear indicates a need to get away and requires actions to re-establish safety. If we appear frightened and someone takes action to increase our sense of security, we feel looked after. Panic is an expression of sorrow and loss of attachment to others. If we express our sadness and are met with acts of compassion by another, like empathy or a cuddle, we can feel soothed. The socialising brain circuits introduced in Chapter 6 (caring, curiosity and play) often elicit feelings of joy, vitality and expressions of pleasure. When we show our joy and another responds by smiling at us, we feel seen and witnessed.

Because emotions are processed through the memory centres, our experience of them and what we think consequently will be related to our unique histories. We learn through experience after experience, gradually building up a picture or story of how the world operates. This will also develop according to how our emotions as children are responded to by our caregivers. If our emotions, desires and frustrations were responded to kindly we will more comfortably accept our own emotionality and that of others. For example, some people may feel comfortable being sexual or showing this aspect of themselves in front of someone else, others may feel deeply ashamed.

We may have been taught, and still think or believe, that certain emotions are signs of 'weakness' and inappropriate to show. Cultural stereotyping dictates that women may show tears but not rage; that men may show anger but not fear. Certain emotions are criticised or encouraged in different cultural environments, too. Which emotions were encouraged or accepted, and which squashed or judged, when you were young? Our thoughts about our feelings, and resulting judgements of our behaviour, are often more distressing than our actual emotions. We could utilise our emotional response as a baseline reaction: we are either feeling happy with what's happening, or not. Either we are OK, or we are sad, angry or frightened. Our emotions, rather than being problematic for us, can become an easy, clear indicator if we consider their purpose. Their universality could be seen as a non-verbal method of communication within and between humans; their expression is an attempt to elicit a specific empathic response in others. Understanding the purpose of different emotions helps us to be clearer about our own responses, and what we may want. It also helps us to understand what others may want from us in response to their expressions of emotion, which is vital for good relationships.

Here, we want to acknowledge that both authors are neurotypical, and as such our conceptions of emotions may not ring true for neurodivergent people. We also want to call out the widespread misconception that autistic people lack feelings or are unemotional. Of course, autistic and other neurodivergent people are hugely diverse in their (emotional) experiences. However, we contend that it is not a lack of emotionality but a different kind of emotionality, and a different way of expressing it, that sometimes causes difficulties in inter-neurotype relationships. For example on the NeuroClastic website ('the autism spectrum according to autistic people'), founder Terra Vance[9] writes about their 'very grand emotions' of justice, fairness and truth, and contends that these rather than feelings such as sadness or happiness are the most fundamental (to them). Vance goes on to write about the difficulties this can cause in inter-neurotype relationships: 'Our direct, blunt, and sometimes brutal honesty is offensive to neurotypicals; and in turn, their roundabout, indirect, suggestive language reads as confusing, manipulative, and patronising to us'. As therapists and as sexual partners, awareness and curiosity is crucial to effective communication in inter-neurotype relationships.

Going back to the four basic emotions, we can understand them as an instinctive reflex from the brain, causing identifiable physical expressions including facial responses, body postures, tone and pitch of voice. The frontal lobes then reflect and assess and decide how to react. This sounds simplistic, but on one level it is simple. By becoming more conscious about how we think about our emotions and how we use them, we can acknowledge that how we think has the biggest impact on how we behave. As discussed in Chapter 4, what and how we think is also correlated to our past experiences, as well as our social and cultural beliefs. We can consciously evaluate and update our values and belief system and so change and adapt our thinking. By accepting our basic reactivity and understanding and having compassion for our own personal history, we can more consciously take responsibility for how we behave now as adults.

There are also more complex emotions such as confusion, frustration, disappointment, jealousy, envy, pride, embarrassment, sympathy and gratitude. Frustration may be a combination of anger and sadness; confusion, wanting to do one thing and thinking we should do something else. Complex emotions are connected to our perceptions of our emotions; to us as social beings and what others may expect of us or think about us. Our feelings and emotions about sexuality are deeply affected by cultural messages we received about sexuality and sexual shame.

In *The Erotic Mind:* Jack Morin[10] suggests that as well as the more obvious emotional experiences connected with peak sexual experiences – for example exuberance, satisfaction and closeness – more 'negative' emotions can also play an important part, particularly anxiety, guilt and anger. Consider the thrill of having sex outside, or of having an affair. Does this ring true for you?

The more clearly we can identify the different aspects of our experiences of sexual arousal and desire – reactive reactions from the back brain, somatic responses in the body, thoughts and beliefs, and now, the specifics of our emotions – the more we can understand and consciously choose how we want to act in response. Within this model, all are happening, and all are affecting and being affected by others. It may be useful to consider which of these aspects are most easily identifiable and which you struggle more to comprehend.

Your Feelings

Solo Exercise

How do you relate to your feelings? Consider the primary emotions of anger, fear, sadness and joy. Think about each one in turn. How do you experience each emotion in your body and what thoughts are generated? How comfortable or uncomfortable do you feel experiencing each emotion?

Think about the more complex emotions of disappointment or frustration, for example. How easy or difficult is it for you to manage these feelings?

Consider which feelings and emotions were easily expressed and allowed during your childhood or not allowed and discouraged. How have your early life experiences impacted on how you are as an adult? Identify any ways of responding to your feelings that you would like to change and think about how you could do that.

Think about your feelings and experiences of joy, happiness and excitement. How were these treated during your early life? Consider how this may have impacted on how you feel about your sexuality now?

Exercise with Partner/s

Share with each other how you manage more complex emotions like disappointment and frustration.

> *Discuss what helps and what makes things worse in how you each respond to the other, when one of you is feeling disappointed or frustrated.*
> *Talk about how you could bring more joy, happiness and excitement to your relationship.*

Shame and Sexuality

In Britain we have a culture of shame around our emotions. Being emotional is often seen as a weakness and being 'rational', a strength. If we have feelings, we are encouraged to suppress and hide our somatic reactions; displays of emotion are often criticised as a sign of immaturity. Bradshaw's work on shame[11] identifies different levels of shame from mild to toxic and how this plays out within family systems. Within the Homeodynamic Model, experience of ourselves and of others is a combination of a reaction in the back brain, a series of somatic experiences and emotions, and a capacity to reflect on all of these and make some choices about how we will behave in response. To believe some feelings or aspects of our humanity are more important or valuable is to deny a large part of being human. This general shaming around emotions contributes to our experience of our sexuality as shaming, as being sexual includes displaying our emotions, feeling sensations in our body, thinking sexual thoughts and often, behaving in sexual ways.

Nathanson[12] says one reason we have a social shaming of sexuality is because there is no other human activity which so exposes what is normally private (our bodies). We are therefore made capable of embarrassment by nearly everything associated with sexual performance. When we are being sexual with others, we give up our social rules to modulate displays of emotion, and this can leave us feeling very exposed.

Kaufman and Raphael[13] see our current gender ideology as heteronormative,[14] with unspoken rules about power and control in male/female relationships: that men should exercise power and dominate over women; that women should not exercise power and should submit to men. They consider that one reason for the shaming of sexual minorities is because they challenge these cultural rules about expressions of emotions and of power. And of course, social and cultural homophobia contributes to internalised homophobia – shame about one's gayness.

In Tomkins' work on *Affects,*[15] (which means both the experience of an emotion and the set of physiological responses that goes with it), he goes into some detail about the so-called negative emotions of disgust and shame. He adds *Dismell*, a reaction to aromas or odours, where the upper lip and the cheeks become raised, and the nose bridge wrinkled. Smell is a powerful sense for humans, probably because there is only one synaptic jump from the olfactory bulb in the nose to the limbic system. It is known to quickly trigger strong memories. We have a cultural *Dismell* to our natural smells especially in relation to ourselves sexually, with many products aimed at disguising or hiding them. This is strange as pheromones – smell aromas that we release and respond to – are part of our human sexual responses.

Disgust is described as ranging from contemptuous: scornful, disrespectful or sarcastic to disgusted: revolted, repelled or put off by, where the lower lip becomes lowered and protruded. Shame includes feeling exposed, embarrassed and self-conscious or more intensely, feeling humiliated: mortified, alienated and disgraced; expressed with the head lowered, downcast eyes and a vasodilation of the face and skin resulting in blushing.

Shame can be seen as the principal source of our conscience; that something is not OK between us and another person. Shame is often perceived as information about the self but Lee (2008)[16] says it is information about what is happening in the relational field, that is, between an individual and someone else. He says shame is an attempt to protect ourselves when we know, or imagine, that there is not enough support in the relational field for us to be accepted. It is about the quality or lack of reception in the relationship (being accepted; acceptable). Shame helps us to keep the problem (of not being received) hidden and therefore not show our vulnerability or distress.

Shame can be seen as a necessary survival regulator; it protects us against rejection (not being received/welcomed). Humans need relationships; as infants we would die if not 'in relationship' with someone who cares for us. Kaufman and Raphael (1996) say that without the experience of shame there would be nothing to alert us to ruptures in our relationships. So on an evolutionary level, shame provides protection and safety; we hide and withdraw, brush down and get space to collect ourselves. Then, we can go out again and try to be received by someone else – this keeps our desire and curiosity intact and honours our human need to stay in relationship.

Carolyn Spring[17] sees shame as part of the Freeze Trauma response. She says that we learn to feel shame as toddlers, at a time when independence is happening due to the freedom of physical movement, and the limbic system is beginning to come online. She suggests shame is a protective mechanism, which can shut down any potential outbursts of emotion, particularly anger, that may risk physical or emotional harm to the child.

Where there is shame there is yearning or desire. We are only capable of experiencing shame if we care about the connection; what we want and/or who we want it with. We cannot feel shame if there's nothing to lose. Equally, the greater the importance, the more intense the experience of shame will be. When we are not received in relationship this undermines our confidence and sense of self; we become unsure of what's going on 'between' us. This can lead to self-shaming where instead of seeing that the other person is not the one to meet our yearning, and seeking someone else who may do so, we believe we should not have wanted it in the first place.

We may have internalised negative beliefs about our rights to have needs and desires, and our rights to have these needs met in relationship. We may close down these needs and hide physically and emotionally from ourselves as well as others. Healing shame requires us to go back to the original yearning: what is it we wanted, and to feel and process the pain and disappointment of not having that yearning met. We can then reclaim or moderate our desire, and then again, ask for that yearning to be met.

We can have many reactions to shame. We may become fearful, distressed or become enraged; all act to shield the exposed self. Nathanson (1994) suggests we have four main counter-shaming strategies: withdrawal, avoidance, attack self or attack other. He says all are an avoidance of intimacy, of eye contact, avoiding the gaze of others (see Figure 7.2).

If shame is an indication of a rupture in the relational field, what might this mean for us with regards to sexual shame? Our sexual feelings can be triggered by a sensory experience of someone else (a sight, sound or smell) or a memory of a sexual encounter. However, when our arousal is triggered, it often results in a desire to be sexual with an 'other'. Whether that desire is to touch and be touched, to cuddle or to kiss, to penetrate or be penetrated, it is often something we want to do to or with someone else. Even when we are being sexual with ourselves, we are being in a relationship of sorts: we are responding physically to a feeling: a desire, a sensation with a choice to behave sexually.

Withdrawal
Distress, Fear
(submission)
Abstinence
Impotence
Casual sex

Attack Other
Rage, Contempt
(dominance)
Objectifying
others
Sadism
Blaming
Abusive relationships

**Defences
Against
Shame**

Attack Self
Disgust
Masochism
Perfectionism (body)
Abusive relationships

Avoidance
Denial of self/imperfection
False self
Humour
Machismo/ narcissism
Striving for power/ controlling

Figure 7.2 Defences against Shame.

One way of counteracting sexual shame is to engage in sexual self-care and celebration. For example, giving yourself time and space to be sexual, alone; to explore what you enjoy the most, celebrating your sexiness in the mirror, allowing yourself to flirt, noticing and taking pride in small steps you take to becoming more sexually expressive and assertive.

Sexual Shame

Solo Exercise

Most of us probably experience some degree of shame about our sexuality, given our cultures. Think about your beliefs about the different aspects listed below and indicate whether they make you feel proud or ashamed.

Beliefs about	*Proud*	*Ashamed*
Sex		
Sexuality		
Sensuality		
Your childhood sexual history		
Your teenage sexual history		
Your body		
Your body image		
Your sexual identity		
Your relationship to sexuality now		
Your current sexual behaviour		
Your sexual relationships		
Your sexual fantasies		
Your creativity and passion		

Review your list. Overall do you predominately feel proud or ashamed of your sexuality? Choose one issue you feel ashamed about. Consider whether you want to reclaim a sense of self-esteem about your choices or preferences or whether your shame is an indicator that you may want to change your beliefs or behaviour in some way.

Exercise with Partner/s

Share your lists with each other and notice what is similar and different. Discuss how you feel about the similarities and differences.

Tell each other about the issue you chose in the solo exercise that you feel ashamed about, and if and how you might want to change that.

Use the Conscious Communication dialogue to help each other explore and understand more.

Self-Worth

Our emotional attitude to ourselves – otherwise known as our sense of self-worth – has a strong impact on our experience of sexual pleasure. Dr Karen Gurney (2020)[18] talks about the three conditions for good sex. For her, good sex is a combination of being in the present moment, being psychologically aroused and receiving quality physical touch. Stress, shame and self-criticism can really get in the way of being in the moment, as we struggle to let go of our to-do list, or give ourselves a hard time for the way we look, how long we are taking to orgasm, what we said to so and so, how we're failing as a parent/partner/friend, etc. How can we foster gentleness towards ourselves, an attitude of loving-kindness, to use the words of Buddhist nun Pema Chodron?[19]

Taking time each day to savour sensations in your body, to meditate, be in nature, or simply sit on the sofa staring out the window, all help us develop a comfort with ourselves, an acceptance of things as they are. This can have a radical impact on our ability to enjoy and get the most out of sex. With busy lives, it can feel challenging to make this kind of space for ourselves, but giving yourself even 1% of what you need can make a difference – especially if you celebrate these little wins and allow yourself to feel a sense of pride and satisfaction.

What media we consume can also have a big impact, either positive or negative. One of the challenges of being LGBTQIA+, or not white, or older, or fat, or having disabilities or being in any other way marginalised, is that we will see far fewer positive representations of ourselves as desirable on screen and in social media. This matters – it can be hard to think of yourself as a sexual person when that's not what you see. So, consider curating your social media and selecting what you watch and read, to help you feel good about yourself as a sexual person.

This also applies to porn. If you watch porn, is there anyone you can relate to in what you are watching? Do you see people like you, depicted as subjective selves, authentically enjoying sex, rather than fetishised or treated as sex objects? For example, a lot of so-called lesbian porn is actually girl-on-girl action made for men, rather than anything actual lesbians can relate to. There are alternatives: to give a few examples, the directors Erika Lust[20] and Candida Royalle[21] produce ethical porn, centring the female gaze; *crashpad*[22] is an ethical queer porn series; Dipsea is an audio erotica app.[23] Does what you are consuming make you feel good about yourself, or somehow inadequate or not enough? We would suggest that these are good criteria by which to evaluate your consumption of media of any kind – how does it make you feel about yourself?

A note on porn: There are powerful arguments for and against porn. It is vastly popular, with estimates that up to 98% of men and 80% of

students of all genders have watched porn in their lifetime, with about 10%
of men watching daily. There is also a very polarised debate around the
impact – at one extreme the popular 'nofap'[24] movement, which argues
that masturbating to porn saps male energy, and advocates total abstinence. The other side says this is sex-shaming and there is no evidence
masturbation or porn consumption harms sexual performance, and that
it may even help people have more creative sexual encounters. In 2010 –
and things have obviously moved on since then – Feona Attwood's edited
book[25] found that experiences of porn and its effects are so varied that it is
hard to draw any firm conclusions. Atwood did find a gender difference –
she doesn't mention any studies of trans and gender-expansive porn
consumers, sadly – with men showing more positive impacts on both
sexual self-esteem and sexual satisfaction from watching porn, and this
being less so for women. There also seems to be some correlation between
watching porn and being more aggressive in sexual situations. In *The Porn
Report,* Australian authors Mckee et al. (2008)[26] surveyed over a thousand
consumers of pornography about their perceived negative and positive
effects of using pornography and found:

•   59% of respondents thought pornography had had a very positive or a
     positive effect on their attitudes towards sexuality;
•   35% felt it had had no effect;
•   7% thought it had a negative effect or a large negative effect.

The main positive effects, in order of reporting, were making consumers less
repressed about sex; making them more open-minded about sex; increasing
tolerance of other people's sexualities; giving pleasure to consumers; providing educational insights; sustaining sexual interest in long-term relationships; making consumers more attentive to a partner's sexual desires;
helping consumers find an identity or community; and helping them to talk
to their partners about sex. The most common negative effects cited in
this study were that pornography led consumers to objectify people, caused
them to have unrealistic sexual expectations, caused relationship problems,
caused loss of interest in sex and led to addiction. The idea of porn or sex
addiction is a controversial one, discussed in more detail below in the section
on compulsivity.

   From a purely sexual point of view, as we have already described, there
is still a lot of shame around masturbation. On average people discover
this form of self-soothing around eight years old (Hite 1994)[27] and most
have felt or experienced shame about it. This can lead to a sense that it
should be done in secret and fast. Using pornography to induce orgasm as
quickly as possible avoids the plateau phase of the arousal process: the
phase which necessitates a consciousness about being highly aroused.
Many people find that when masturbating to porn they use the same type

of grip, movement and/or position each time and derive arousal from the visual and psychological effect of what they are watching, more than from touch. Returning to Dr Karen Gurney's *Conditions for Good Sex* (psychological arousal, quality of touch, being in the moment), it is clear that partnered sex demands more ease with being in the moment, and being able to be aroused by a variety of touch from one's partner. Legendary sex columnist Dan Savage[28] coined the term 'death grip' to describe the use of a very tight firm pressure when masturbating. Some people of all genders find that this then makes it harder to experience satisfaction or orgasm from the gentler friction experienced from a vulva, vagina, mouth or anus. The good news is that this isn't terminal – you can't do any permanent damage to your penis or clitoris with the death grip! By mixing up your masturbation, taking a break from porn and zoning in – being mindful to the sensations in your body – you can definitely regain sensitivity, pleasure and satisfaction in partnered sex.

Some interesting points are raised by Maltz (2010),[29] who describes what happens in the body when masturbating to porn. She says pornography acts like a designer drug, aimed at hitting the reward system; offering novelty, excitement, escape and then relaxation through orgasm. It is ingested through the eyes and ears, not through touching or being touched by another. This can lead to a loss of sensuality and less oxytocin during the process of arousal, leaving it more adrenalised, more likely to activate the survival circuits of the brain; the primary emotions of anger, fear and sadness (less so when pornography is used as part of sex play with another). Pornography activates plenty of adrenaline to fuel the arousal; dopamine (which triggers the curiosity circuit) and endorphins which reduce feelings of pain. At climax there are surges of serotonin and prolactin, which make us feel good; and of oxytocin, which promotes feelings of love and bonding. However, what about the socialising circuits? With regards to play, if there is no real person to touch and play with, could an attachment become formed with the pornography itself? And what about the caring brain circuit?

McGilchrist (2009)[30] argues that objectification and the consumerism of sex utilise left brain activity. He says the right brain is embodied, in touch with ourselves and the reality of interaction with others. The left brain decontextualises our experiences, turning us away, in his opinion, from what most defines us as human beings: our capacity for caring, or empathy. It could certainly be said that mainstream pornography promotes a lack of empathy about the reality of the experience for the performers.

An indicator of sexual self-esteem is that we feel comfortable with and proud of our sexual arousal and sexual experiences. Perhaps, the question is not whether pornography is good or bad but rather whether the quality of what we are consuming makes us feel ashamed and bad about ourselves or enhances our sexual self-esteem.

Passionate Play

Solo Exercise

Explore your relationship to sexual play. Do you like to play sexually, if so, how do you do this? Do you like how you play or is there something you would like to change? If you don't like how you play, or how often you play, how could you change this? For example, do you make enough time and space in your life to play; are you playing in the way that you really want to?

Research online or go and visit a sex shop. You may want to go with a friend or a lover. There are some for heterosexuals, some aimed at gay men and some for women only. Explore what sort of toys are out there for sex play and see what you think and feel about them. Make some choices about what you like and what you don't.

Notice your first reactions, especially any strong reactions. Is there some attraction along with any repulsion? Explore whether there is shame about what you 'should or shouldn't' want and consider whether you want to challenge these first reactions. Discuss with a friend or therapist what you think and why.

Exercise with Partner/s

Think about each of the questions in the solo exercise with regards to your shared sexual play.

Agree on a time and space you would like to share some sexual play in the next week and discuss in detail what sort of sexual play you would like.

Do some shared research into topics that interest you.

Sexual Compulsivity

There has been a great deal of debate in recent years about whether sex addiction is a real thing. Those in favour (Patrick Carnes,[31] Paula Hall[32] for example) say that because sex can be a 'mood-altering experience' and people can engage in compulsive sexual behaviour that follows a detrimental cycle, with the behaviours often escalating, it qualifies as an addiction. Others say that addiction is an invalid term, as it implies the 'addict' cannot be held responsible for their behaviour and can attribute it to a disease (as in Harvey Weinstein checking into a 'sex addiction clinic'). Also, these critics (Silva Neves[33] for example) say there is no evidence that compulsive behaviours lead the person towards illegal and harmful acts.

However we want to phrase it, it remains true that some people engage in compulsive behaviours around porn, dating and/or sex, that occupy large amounts of their time and/or money, and about which they feel powerless and ashamed. We can see these behaviours as a coping mechanism, a way to regulate emotion and cope with unbearable feelings. However, they only abate these feelings temporarily rather than make them go away; the sexual behaviour is not satiating and the person soon wants to repeat the cycle. If this is you, you may want to work with a therapist on the emotions from which you are trying to escape, and find alternate ways to sit with and work through them. Sex is a vibrant, beautiful part of human life, and while you may need to limit your compulsive behaviours temporarily as you work through the underlying pain and shame, we do not believe that 'sexual sobriety' is something to aim for on a more permanent basis. Hopefully, the more you can liberate yourself from sexual shame the more you will be able to have sexual experiences you feel wholeheartedly good about.

In *Treating Out of Control Sexual Behaviour: Rethinking Sex Addiction,*[34] Braun-Harvey and Vigorito have set out six principles of sexual health which provide a framework for considering sexual behaviour and compulsivity in a non-pathologising, sex-positive way. Silva Neves expands on this thinking about sexual compulsivity, offering an excellent guide for clinicians and other interested readers.

As children we learn through repetition, by doing things again and again. As adults, we may do the same if learning to do something new. For example, we need to practice, repeat again and again, when learning a new language, developing a sports activity or playing an instrument. Where is the line between 'healthy' compulsivity (practicing, persistence) and not-so-healthy compulsivity? Is it about whether the consequences of our behaviour are beneficial to us or not, and how do we determine that?

Kaufman and Raphael use the word 'addiction' but actually support the view that shame is central to sexual acting out, with their suggestion being that we can become addicted to excitement itself. The chemicals released in the body during the high of sexual acting out include internal mood enhancers such as adrenalin and dopamine. As said in Chapter 6, dopamine is less satiating to us than serotonin. Kaufman and Raphael believe substances are less likely to be addictive when they are used to enhance positive effects, and more likely to be addictive when they are used to reduce or sedate negative effects. In their opinion addiction is most likely:

- when the substance is transformed into an end in itself;
- when an absence of the substance leads to panic;
- where the substance becomes the only relief from panic.

'Panic' within the homeodynamic model is about loss of attachment, sadness and grief – about loss of relationship. Gerhardt (2004)[35] suggests that emotional deprivation in early childhood alters dopamine pathways, particularly in the limbic system, increasing 'greedy' or compulsive behaviours. It is easy to see how unresolved attachment and developmental issues play a role in addictions and compulsivity: the urge to reach out; to be held and touched, to have physical and emotional needs satiated. Using sex as an activity to fulfil attachment needs will only work if there is an attachment. That doesn't mean that we should only have sex in 'relationships' but it helps if we are 'in relationship' with ourselves, by being embodied and consciously embarking on our sexual activities. Using the exercises in this book can help to highlight what relationship we want with our sexuality and encourage us to make more conscious choices about our sexual beliefs and sexual behaviour that we can feel proud about.

Food is a useful analogy here. Martin-Sperry (2003)[36] likens compulsive sexual acting out to the eating disorder bulimia, with a repetitive pattern of sexual binging and guilt, searching for comfort and relief. Do we want to condemn clients to a life of highly restricted, controlled eating, or help them move into a place where they can taste and savour from the delicious smorgasbord of sexual pleasures, be consciously, proudly sexual, and know when they are satiated?

Challenging Compulsion

Solo Exercise

Write a list of any compulsive behaviours that you have. Choose one that you would like to change or at least explore in more depth.

Sit for a while in your safe space and take some time to relax. Think more about what you like and don't like about this particular behaviour. Consider whether the compulsivity is connected to the behaviour not satiating your needs or whether it has become a habit. Try not to censor what is evoked for you but allow any thoughts, body sensations, memories and feelings and notice what they are.

Write something about each of the following and then reflect on what you have written:

> *My thoughts about this behaviour are … .*
> *Thinking about this behaviour evokes the following body sensations ….*
> *The memories that are triggered include … .*
> *How I am feeling is ….*

Now think back to the last time you acted out the behaviour you are exploring and take your attention to the hours and minutes just beforehand. What were you thinking and feeling then?

Can you identify exactly what outcome you wanted to happen; what need did you want met? Did you get that need met so you felt completely satiated? If not, what aspect did not get met?

Do you feel any shame about what you wanted? If so, think about why. Is this need something you were discouraged from wanting as a child? Is there something about what you are doing or how you are trying to get this need met that is not working for you? Try to identify what exactly is not working for you.

Now think about something that you do that leaves you feeling satiated. Describe in detail what it feels like to feel satiated, how does that feel in your body, your thoughts and your emotions?

Think about how you could change any aspect of the behaviour you have explored in this exercise so you could alter your relationship to it.

Exercise with Partner/s

Share with each other the topic of sexual compulsivity that you chose in the solo exercise, and what you learnt about it through doing the exercise.

Tell each other about a recent time when you felt satiated after a shared activity. It may have been sexual, or for example, a shared meal, outing or activity.

Describe in detail to each other what it is like physically and emotionally to feel satiated.

Sexual Violence

If you are someone who has experienced sexual violence as an adult or childhood sexual abuse, you may find reading this section evokes feelings of anger or distress. Please go back to the beginning of the book, re-read the exercise *'Applying the Brakes'* in Chapter 2 and consider whether you are in the right time and space to continue. You may want to skip this section and come back to it another time. Be kind to yourself.

Sexual violence is still a huge problem for many people, with estimates that one in four women have experienced rape or sexual assault[37] with young women being those most at risk. More than four-fifths of young women in the UK have been subjected to sexual harassment, according to a survey for UN Women UK.[38] Safeline[39] operate a national male helpline and SurvivorsUK[40] acknowledge, support and advocate for men and non-binary people who have been affected by rape or sexual abuse.

Added complications for male survivors include sexual stereotyping, they are supposed to be strong and able to take care of themselves, and myths that only gay men are raped. Male victims of sexual abuse may develop confusion over their gender and sexual identities; they may have a sense of being inadequate as a man and/or have a sense of lost power, control and confidence in their manhood. They may also be left doubting their sexuality, fearing sex, and may have difficulty forming relationships. Almost half of all transgender people have been sexually assaulted at some point in their lives (the figure is even higher for trans people of colour[41]), and accessing support comes with additional challenges, such as not all services being open to trans people, and fears about discrimination.

Sadly, despite the public profile of the #MeToo movement from Autumn 2017, there has not been a decrease in sexual violence. Reports of rape have hit a record high with the number of sexual offences recorded by the police showing a 12% increase in 2021 (CSEW).[42] The number of rape offences in the year ending September 2021 was the highest recorded annual figure to date (63,136 offences). Alongside this record high, rape prosecutions have dropped by a quarter in the last year marking a new record low.[43] Perhaps this is connected to public opinions, such as the 2018 YouGov survey[44] which found that:

- A third of men think if a woman has flirted on a date, it generally would not count as rape, even if she has not explicitly consented to sex (compared with 21% of women)
- A third of men also believe a woman can't change her mind after sex has started
- Almost a quarter (24%) think that sex without consent in long-term relationships is usually not rape
- 'Stealthing': 40% think it is never or usually not rape to remove a condom without a partner's consent

These attitudes have unfortunately not changed much since Amnesty International's report on attitudes to sexual violence in 2005.[45]

The impact of sexual violence and sexual abuse is devastating. It affects not only victims but also their families, communities and the wider society. Experiencing sexual violence and abuse is a risk factor for post-traumatic stress disorder (PTSD), clinical depression, generalised anxiety disorder and separation anxiety disorder. Many survivors attempt suicide or turn to substance abuse. Other long-term problems include guilt and self-blame, low self-esteem and negative self-image, problems with intimacy, compulsions or sexual difficulties. Sexual violence is an assault against the body and the mind, and it invades a person's integrity. It sullies an aspect of them: their

Table 7.1 Impact of Sexual Violence

Brain	Mind
• Post-traumatic stress activating the vagal nerve and limbic system	• Beliefs about blame and shame
• Dis-regulated neurochemicals	• Attitudes to male/female sexuality
• Agitation to the nervous system	• Low self-esteem
• Fusion or confusion between the reward and punishment circuits	• Control issues – angry or critical towards self and/or others
• Unwanted or inappropriate arousal	• Unwanted or inappropriate fantasies
• Flashbacks	• Compulsions or addictions
• Nightmares	• Suicidal plans

Violation of INTEGRITY OF SELF

Body	Emotion
• Physical damage from assault	• Overwhelming emotions and feelings
• Hyper or low arousal	• Anxieties and fears about safety
• Body tension, armouring. Pain-fear-tension triangle	• Terror or panic
• Disassociation	• Depression
• Negative body image	• Self-disgust, shame or humiliation
• Avoidance or indulgence (sexual or food bulimia or anorexia)	• Intimacy and trust issues
• Somatic illnesses (including sexual and gynaecological issues)	• Anger and communication difficulties
	• Isolation and feeling misunderstood
	• Despair and despondency
	• Suicidal feelings

sexuality, which is supposed to be associated with freedom and pleasure, not with pain, fear or confusion. Work by Herman (1993), Levine (1997) and Rothschild (2000)[46] has contributed hugely to our understanding of post-traumatic stress, its physical and psychological impacts and the reasons for different levels of trauma. This has also enhanced our knowledge and understanding of the recovery process.

Table 7.1 shows the range of impacts of sexual violence, using the homeodynamic model. Many of the topics could easily be placed in more than one section as they may have a physical and a psychological component, and as discussed earlier, all aspects may trigger or be triggered by other issues. This list is not exhaustive.

Our cultural and social inconsistencies with regards to sexual violence add to a misunderstanding of the scope and scale of this phenomenon. This plays a large part in the difficulties people face in recovering from assaults. For example, we still largely have a notion that sexual assault and childhood sexual abuse is committed by strangers, whereas the opposite is true. Most rapists of women are ex-husbands and partners or acquaintances and most abusers of children are known to them. Fifteen per cent of women reported being assaulted by a stranger, whereas this was true for almost half of male victims (43%). One-third of rapes of women take place in the woman's home and 26% in the perpetrator's home.[47] Perhaps the idea behind our 'stranger-danger' thinking allows us to believe that sexual violence is something that happens to other people, people who weren't clever or savvy enough to avoid it.

Sexual assault is a traumatic event. When we are in life-threatening or potential life-threatening situations our survival circuits come online. A flood of neurochemicals from the limbic system activates our fight or flight instinct and short-circuits the link to our frontal lobes: we don't get to register what we think or feel about the situation; the priority is 'to stay alive'. Sometimes the fight and flight circuits become overwhelmed, leading to disassociation or freeze, like a rabbit in headlights. We can become numb and go onto some sort of automatic pilot. In situations like rape, going along with something maybe a survival attempt, to at least 'only be raped', rather than being raped and mutilated, or raped and murdered. Untangling this web can be a very difficult phase for people in recovery.

As humans, we have to deal with many trials and tribulations throughout our lives such as tragedy and death. We have a natural capacity to recover from traumas by going through a series of reactions, usually starting with shock. This can take many forms including disassociation or denial. There will probably be phases of grief, sadness and anger. The important phase, which gets complicated in recovery from sexual violence, is the 'What if?' phase where we blame ourselves for 'allowing' the situation to have occurred. For example, people say, what if I had not got into the car that crashed, or what if I had not had the argument with my friend or lover the morning they were killed? Part of recovery is that we work through this phase, to realise that had we known beforehand that the traumatic event was going to happen, we probably would have behaved differently. This is about coming to terms with our powerlessness and the ensuing feelings that this brings: usually more grief and anger. Eventually, we are usually able to find some way of accepting or living with what has happened. This 'What if?' phase is interrupted for survivors of sexual assault because culturally, we do blame them. This leads to a much higher incidence of post-traumatic stress as people find it difficult to forgive themselves.

The support a victim receives after sexual violence can make a huge difference to the amount of lasting harm experienced. Being a victim of sexual violence or abuse is a risk factor for the development of serious mental health difficulties and therefore, the cultural context around sexual violence is extremely important.

If you have been sexually assaulted, raped or abused, please get support from a therapist, other mental health professional, friend or family member who believes you and does not in any way make you responsible for the attack. Sexual assault is committed by the perpetrator. Full stop. The harm caused by victim-blaming makes the decision to report to the police a complex one. Many feel that reliving the trauma through the courts is too much; many that they will be disbelieved, or they blame themselves anyway. While of course we believe sexual perpetrators should be held to account, we are also aware that a victim-blaming culture can cause significant additional distress to the victim. Each person's decision is personal and should be supported.

Childhood sexual abuse is an even more complex issue as a betrayal of trust is most often an additional factor in recovery. We now understand much more about 'grooming' and how an adult can manipulate a child's innocence and relative powerlessness, exploit their physical or emotional needs and trick them into complying with demands. Recovery from childhood sexual abuse requires an individualised approach. Not only are there factors like the duration and extent of the abuse, levels of physical or psychological damage or who the abuser was in relation to the child; but also consideration needs to be given to the very subjective experience of any of the above. It is beyond the scope of this book to address recovery from childhood sexual abuse or sexual violence as an adult, in the depth needed for recovery. However, some excellent books have been written by Bass and Davis (1990),[48] Haines (1999),[49] Lew (2004)[50] and Kelly and Maxted (2005)[51] which provide programmes to do so, focusing on regaining a sense of integrity of the self, acceptance and self-care. In 2015, Wendy Maltz[52] released her free sexual healing and intimacy videos, for individuals and those in relationships.

Nearly 30 years ago, Herman (1993)[53] identified the importance of doing recovery work within the context of a safe relationship (with a therapist, within a 'survivors' group or with a trusted friend), because it was within a 'relationship' that the abuse occurred. Working through the exercises in this book can aid recovery by helping to re-assert beliefs and values, and to gain a deeper understanding of how our sexual processes work, and how trauma can interrupt our otherwise natural reactions.

As this model is homeodynamic, it is believed that working in any area can also positively impact others. For example, reviewing our beliefs so we no longer feel self-blame can reduce emotions of anger towards the self, thereby reducing adrenaline in the body, reactivity in the nervous system and muscle tension. Replacing our most negative thoughts with positive affirmations can run new neural pathways and alter our physiology of stress. This in turn allows greater relaxation and more feel-good neuro-chemicals like serotonin, which impact our emotional states. Equally, taking greater care of our bodies can make us feel more loving towards ourselves and reduce any critical mind-talk. This can include exercise, good food and sleep habits. Spiritual practices like meditation can also help calm the mind and the body. A spiritual belief system or philosophical outlook on life can often help us to come to terms with many of the powerless experiences we have as humans by reminding us of our vulnerabilities. Can we strive for the courage to change what we can, the humility to accept what we can't and the wisdom to know the difference? Knowing more explicitly what we like sensually and sexually enables us to make more conscious choices about what type of sexual encounters we want and who with. Understanding and having compassion for our history and our ensuing reactivity can encourage us to reflect and think before we act; to become more conscious about our sexual behaviour. This, in turn, can make us more confident and trusting about our ability to look after ourselves, and also more trusting of others. Table 7.2 shows some ideas of recovery within the Homeodynamic Model.

Table 7.3 describes the Window of Tolerance, created by Pat Ogden,[54] with inclusion of the Traffic Light System as described in Chapter 6. It provides some ideas about how to widen our optimal green arousal zone. We can see how to get back to green if we move into an amber zone. We also see that to get back to green from a red zone, we need first to move back into amber.

Table 7.2 Recovery from Sexual Violence

Brain	Mind
• Running new neutral pathways	• Reviewing beliefs and values
• Positive affirmations	• Managing feelings/behaviour
• EMDR, EFT, TRE and other trauma recovery programmes	• Making choices
• Craniosacral therapy	• Being less critical – deciding what's good enough
• Humming, singing, being out in nature	• Practising loving kindness
• Attachment focused therapies	• Talking with friends and partners
	• Keeping a journal

REGAINING INTEGRITY OF SELF
Acceptance and self-care

Body	Emotion
• Relaxation and breath awareness	• Counselling or therapy
• Exercise	• Meditation
• Good food and sleep habits	• Some form of spirituality
• Sensualising exercises	• Getting out in nature
• Singing, dancing	• Healing relationships
• Gardening	• Aromatherapy
• Bodywork treatments	• Bach Flower Remedies

Table 7.3 Window of Tolerance

	Navigating the Traffic Lights
Hyper – Arousal Fight or Flight	AMBER Need to stop, take some breaths, allow body to calm down, to be able to move back into GREEN
Window of Tolerance	GREEN In the Social Engagement System. Feeling, calm, relaxed, content To widen optimal arousal zone: Do more of the things that bring you joy Spend more time with people who bring you joy Dance, sing, hum, spend time in nature Revel in your enjoyment, embed your experiences of pleasure
Hypo – Arousal Overwhelmed Numb, collapsed	RED Need to motivate body to move, take some action. We need to go through AMBER, to be able to move back into GREEN

Healing Trauma

Solo Exercise

If you are aware that you have experienced significant trauma in your history, please re-read the exercise 'Applying the Brakes' at the beginning of this book before you explore further.

Think about one issue that you consider still impacts in your sexual life now. Do not think about any details about the trauma but focus instead, on the here and now. Think about the circuit of arousal and see if you can identify where it gets interrupted. Explore in turn how you are affected now in your brain, your mind, your body and your emotions. Are any aspects more affected than others?

If you discover that your brain reflexes are still impacted, that you suffer from post-traumatic stress symptoms like flashbacks or nightmares, investigate treatments which may help to alleviate symptoms like EMDR (Eye Movement Desensitisation and Reprocessing) or Rewind Therapy.

If you find that your thoughts, beliefs and values are influenced still by past events, see if you can identify how you may change them. Explore whether your thinking is based on old or cultural beliefs and evaluate whether they serve you now. Seek out other opinions and beliefs to support any changes you want to make.

If you feel your body is still suffering, consider having some gentle bodywork therapy like massage, craniosacral therapy or Feldenkrais, for example. Ask friends or explore via the internet until you find a therapy that suits you. You may wish to treat yourself by having sensuous baths with relaxing essential oils, preparing nutritious food for yourself and making time to rest and relax more.

If you think your emotional life and relationships are still affected, consider some counselling or therapy to work through what impact the trauma may still be having on you. Again, shop around to find the style of therapy that suits you best.

Think about reclaiming your right to sexual pleasure. Go back to the exercises about sensuality and sexual pleasure to remind yourself about the specific things that turn you on. Remember you can use these to switch your arousal circuit back on if you want to.

Evaluate for yourself the achievements you have made in recovering from this trauma already and outline any further challenges you may have. Enlist the help of friends or professionals to support you.

Exercise with Partner/s

Healing from sexual trauma within a sexually intimate relationship takes time. We need to go slow enough until our bodies have a somatic experience of being safe. We need to be able to speak out our 'No', and have it heard and acted upon.

Go back to the sensualising exercises in Chapter 5 to re-experience the somatic responses. Use the body maps again to indicate Yes/Green, No/Red and Maybe/Amber.

Discuss beforehand what exactly you are going to do together. Use a time limit to help containment. Allow yourself to stop – as soon as you want to.

Use the Conscious Communication dialogue to help each other explore and understand more.

Relationships

We have many types of relationships, with family, friends, colleagues and neighbours. They vary in the time and the importance that we give to them. We also have many types of sexual relationships. Some people choose committed long-term relationships with one person, others prefer one-off or casual sexual encounters with different people, some may be polyamorous or consensually non-monogamous (involved in open, honest relationships with more than one person at a time), some may choose not to be sexual with other people at all, some may have secret affairs as well as their main, public relationship and others, a combination of these at different times of their lives.

During a lifetime, many adults will go through stages of wanting to create the types of sexual relationships they desire and can encounter difficulties or frustrations with this. Others may be in a state of heartache through being unable to have a relationship with someone they desire, for a variety of reasons including rejection, break-up, divorce or bereavement. There are also those trying to maintain and sustain long-term relationships, dealing with difficult life stages, conflict or loss of desire. We think and talk about our sexual relationships a lot; often involving much disappointment, confusion and grief. They preoccupy much of our time and energy. Sexual relationships can also bring great pleasure and joy, fulfil our desires for bonding, allowing us to love and feel loved. They can allow us to relax and to fulfil all the socialising circuits of the brain (caring, curiosity, play and physical contact).

For those seeking a relationship, how to meet someone can sometimes seem like a merry dance. The internet may appear to offer easier opportunities, but it can also demand a high degree of confidence and self-esteem. For many, the whole topic can feel like an emotional rollercoaster and difficult to navigate. There is often a need to believe that 'someone special' is out there and to trust in the potential possibility of meeting them.

The initial stage of meeting people is often one of getting excited and hoping it will work out between you. Sometimes it does or may do for a while, but then it may flounder. There may be disappointment with all the ensuing feelings or worry about not being good enough. Eventually, people regain their confidence to go out and try again, and again and again. Many question their expectations; am I asking too much, should I settle for less? Sometimes they may despair of ever meeting someone.

Cross-cultural couples can encounter added difficulties even after they have met. They may have acted outside of the perceived norm or expectation of their culture of origin, which can be experienced through national identity, race, colour, ethnicity, religion, class, education or sexual orientation. They may have experienced racism, oppression, discrimination and/or prejudice, from family of origin, wider community, and society, both as individuals and as a couple. They may need to negotiate issues regarding parenting, sexual beliefs, attitudes and behaviours, gender roles and traditions, and expression of emotion and conflict management. It should be noted that not all cultural differences cause difficulty or distress in a couple, and that not all problems intercultural couples encounter are culturally based.

Those in same-sex and/or trans, non-binary and intersex relationships may have to deal with homo/transphobia, prejudice, discrimination and potential violence from their families of origin, local communities and the wider society. There may be struggles related to 'coming out', a lack of role models and community, a lack of legal protection, and/or additional challenges regarding parenting and reproduction. Some find that a lack of supportive traditional and social rituals can add to the stresses of being in a relationship, although they may also find that their chosen queer family or community provide a great deal of support and belonging.

People exploring open, ethically/consensually non-monogamous (ENM/CNM) or polyamorous relationships may be interested in creating a broader spread of intimacy in their lives, or exploring what happens when we consider love and desire from an abundance rather than scarcity model – that if we fall in love with a second, or third person, this does not decrease the love we can give to another, but rather fills our lives with more love, making more to go around. CNM relationships might be short or long-term, involve children, living together, casual sex, porous or fixed boundaries. There are as many permutations as you can probably imagine. Participants will very likely need to delve into feelings of jealousy, challenges to self-worth, the need for assertive communication, how to tackle things like New Relationship Energy (NRE) in the context of existing relationships, sexual health agreements and how to create – and renegotiate! – boundaries and agreements that work for everyone. There are more and more supportive online resources available, as well as great books, by for example Martha Kauppi,[55] Jessica Fern[56] and Dossie Easton and Janet Hardy.[57]

Throughout this book we have been exploring a relationship with our own sexuality. Some analysis of the psychology of relationships can help to raise awareness of our unconscious (reactive) desires and attractions. This in turn allows us to become more conscious and think (reflect) about what type of sexual relationships we want, and with what type of person/people. Work in psychotherapy and neuroscience shows that humans are hardwired for relationships and connections. As discussed earlier, an infant is dependent on the attachment relationship with its primary carer to develop its brain functioning; its ability to soothe and manage its feelings are so vital for mental health and emotional well-being. Many believe our early attachment patterns inform our unconscious choices of relationships as adults.

Kaufman and Raphael (1996) say we have a predominant *Affect,* developed through our childhood experiences, which leads to patterns in adult relationships. For example, when enjoyment is our predominant mode, our relationship pattern will be for continuity and commitment, and when it's excitement, it will lead to desires for novelty and new lovers. When fear and excitement are linked, we are likely to pursue danger, and when fear and shame are linked, we are more likely to abandon relationships. They believe that shame as a primary affect leads to hiding, avoidance, and entering abusive relationships; and contempt leads to distancing others, superiority and creating abusive relationships.

Lack of sexual desire and managing conflict within a relationship are the two main difficulties that present in relationship therapy, and they are linked. Both are about our fire energy, our passion: how we experience it and how we express it too. Some people find themselves to be creative and spontaneous, they want to use their passion to make something wonderful and joyous. Others struggle with this aspect of themselves. Their creativity and free expression of their passions may have been quashed as a child. They may have been discouraged to 'be' themselves or may have grown up around arguing, fighting and conflict.

Healthy differentiation is vital to keeping passion alive in relationships, as are good communication skills. Bader and Pearson[58] describe differentiation as first, the ability to know what you think, feel and desire; second, the ability to put that across to your partner/partners; and third, the ability to accept your partner(s) as different from yourself, and be curious about their experience. It is important to pay attention to the language we use in communication. When we make 'I' statements, like 'I think' or 'I feel' rather than 'we', 'one' or 'you', we take ownership of our comments and make it clear that we are talking about ourselves rather than other people. Making distinctions about what we don't want to do rather than what we are unable or can't do, also helps to clarify a situation; as does using the word 'could' when appropriate, rather than 'should'. Using generalisations like 'you always' or 'you never' are often experienced as merely criticism, whereas being specific gives information and direction about what could be changed. For example: when you did (whatever it was), I felt (whatever you felt) and I would prefer it if in future you would (make suggestions).

Bader and Pearson have created a developmental model of relationships. When seen alongside the Hendrix developmental model of childhood development, it shows the developmental stages relationships go through, the challenges of those stages, and also ideas for how to address these challenges, see Table 7.4. It is worth noting that the Bader and Pearson model does not correspond to the literal time phases of Hendrix's model, but more stages or phases we may go through as a relationship progresses. If we see ourselves getting stuck at a certain phase of our relationship/s, it can be helpful to see the corresponding age in the Hendrix model, and the childhood developmental issue we may need to give some attention to.

The Conflict Resolution Network (2012)[59] has devised some guidelines for fair fighting:

- Do I want to resolve the conflict? Be willing to fix the problem.
- Can I see the whole picture, not just my own point of view? Broaden your outlook.
- What are the needs and anxieties of everyone involved? Write them down.
- How can we make this fair? Negotiate.
- What are the possibilities? Think up as many solutions as you can. Pick the one that gives everyone more of what they want.

Table 7.4 Bader and Pearson's Developmental Model of Relationships

Hendrix: Psychosocial Model	Bader Pearson: Developmental Model	
	Adult Relationship Stages	*Challenges for couples*
Attachment Birth – 18 months Existing Emotional security	"Being madly in love", merging, intense bonding, forming attachment. Nurturing freely given and received	Insecure attachment patterns will begin to emerge, making transition to the next phase difficult
Exploration 18 months – 3 years Becoming Differentiation and Intact Curiosity	Symbiosis If attachment foundation strong, couple able to move to differentiation	May get stuck in **Enmeshment** - avoid conflict and minimise difference or **Hostile Dependence** - stuck in anger and conflict
Identity 3 – 4 years Asserting Secure sense of Self	Differentiation: Re-establish boundaries, more aware of differences as well as similarities. This is challenging and exciting	If couple have not successfully negotiated Symbiosis, this may bring disillusionment
Competence 4 – 7 years Competing Sense of Personal Power to Achieve	Individuation Individuals engaging outside of the relationship; possible decrease in empathy and increase in self- centeredness	Issues of self-esteem, individual power and worthiness come to the fore. Conflicts may intensify, requiring good problem-solving skills. Partners may feel very separate
Concern 7 – 13 years Sympathising Caring Concern for Others	Well defined individual identities allows for more intimacy and emotional nurturance	
Intimacy 13 – 19 years Integrating Intact Sexuality Ability to Love	Mutual interdependence A relationship based on a foundation of growth rather than need	Vulnerabilities re-emerge; alternating times of intimacy and independence. Less fear of 'engulfment'; more trust in a strong self of 'us'

- Can we work it out together? Treat each other as equals.
- What am I feeling? Am I too emotional? Could I get more facts, take time out to calm down, tell them how I feel?
- What do I want to change? Be clear. Attack the problem, not the person.
- What opportunity can this bring? Work on the positives, not the negatives.
- What is it like to be in their shoes? Do they know I understand them?

- Do we need a neutral third person? Could this help us to understand each other and create our own solutions?
- How can we both win? Work towards solutions where everyone's needs are respected.

Bedroom politics include issues of power. In many countries and cultures a patriarchal view of marriage still exists. Many who try to develop a more egalitarian way of being in long-term relationships (with regards to housework and childrearing for example) are not sure how this equates with their sexual life. We need a degree of conflict, of frisson within a relationship for it to stay passionate. There needs to be a sense of other, of difference for there to be attraction – to create a spark. Perel (2007)[60] says we may confuse merger with love, which is a bad omen for sex. In her view, love needs the two pillars of surrender and autonomy; and eroticism thrives in the space between the self and the other. Sex is an arena where we can leave aside our cultural niceties and get on with being our raw, spontaneous selves, and follow our desires in the moment. Perel believes that the interest displayed in kink/BDSM often has far less to do with pain or wanting to hurt but with wanting to play with power. She sees this as a subversion of cultural abuses of power where those in authority dictate to those they wield power over. In bondage and dominance play, people get to dialogue and agree, exactly what, how and for how long. Many people experience a sense of powerlessness in their lives at times; so to be able to play sexually with having power can feel fun and liberating. Equally, many have demanding jobs or lives caring for others; whereas surrendering, letting someone else make all the decisions, can feel a relief and be relaxing.

Schnarch (1998, 2002)[61] also believes it is not a lack of closeness which may undermine a couple's sex life, but too much. His work on resurrecting sex and the place of passion in long-term relationships include a relationship with your own sexuality primarily, your own desires and preferences. Also an ability to accept the differences in a partner; and both being willing to talk, to tussle, to negotiate or dominate or surrender, at different times on that edge; and in the space in-between. He suggests a range of ways to reignite passion in relationships that are faltering. Love and Robinson (1995)[62] also discuss the desire that many people have for passionate intimate lovemaking within a long-term relationship. Their work provides a sexual-style survey which individuals complete and map, then share with their partner to identify areas of strength and issues of challenge. They also suggest ways of overcoming difficulties. Many exercises in this book will have helped your self-awareness; you may want to choose to do some with a partner, either together or separately and then compare.

Your Relationships

Solo Exercise

Explore your patterns in relationships. How do you relate to yourself: do you feel connected to your body and your emotions; is your internal dialogue kind or critical?

Think about how you are in relationships with family, friends and colleagues. Do you generally find them easy or difficult? Do you find it easy to negotiate and get your needs met or are you often left feeling disappointed? Do you find them easy to navigate or conflictual, frustrating? Is it easier with people you are very close with or with people you know less well? Can you see a pattern in how you relate? Is it similar to how you relate to yourself?

Now think about your sexual relationships. How are they similar or different to the patterns outlined above? Identify one thing you would like to change in how you relate and consider how you could do that.

Exercise with Partner/s

Share with each other your similarities and differences in your current relationship and how you are in other friendships or work relationships.

Identify for yourself one aspect you would like to change in how you relate to yourself, and one in how you relate to your partner/s.

Discuss how you could support each other with this.

Sacred Sexuality

Although many religious teachings seek to diminish the pleasure principle, all the major religions also have traditions of sacred sexuality. These take a very different approach, one in which the role of sexual pleasure is seen as vital, as a joyous aspect to being human where intimacy and conscious connectedness are at the heart, and relationships valued and respected. Sadly, this is usually seen as only being appropriate within heterosexual marriage.

In mainstream culture, talk of Tantric sex is somewhat ridiculed and laughed off as some sort of weird gymnastics. Lightwoman (2012)[63] explains Tantra as an embodied experience; being truly present to your somatic body and breath awareness and learning to ride waves of energy. A tantric encounter may start with 'eye gazing'; two people spending some time just looking at each other, seeing and being seen by each other, a crucial element to coming out of shame (intimacy can be sounded out as in-to-me-see). This is about consciously experiencing touching another's body and being touched, kissing and being kissed; deeply experiencing being in a sexual encounter and the impact this is having on your body, mind and heart. This 'bodyfulness' or embodiment is also part of what we teach in the popular psychosexual therapy intervention 'sensate focus', where one partner mindfully touches the other, each focusing on their sensations in the moment rather than on intentionally creating arousal. There can also be an overlap with BDSM in the emphasis on being in the present moment, entering an altered state and fully experiencing sensation.

Barbara Carellas' book *Urban Tantra* (first published 2007)[64] is a major contribution to applying the principles of sacred sexuality to relationships of all genders, orientations and durations. Carellas moves away from concepts of men and women or masculinity and femininity to focus on the energy of sex. She discusses concepts like bliss and ecstasy and how they differ from the adrenalised states we are encouraged to confuse them with. Adrenaline is part of the biochemical mix of sexual arousal, but it also creates a release of cortisol, which takes us into survival patterns and has longer-term deleterious effects on our bodies, including clouding our thinking and slowing down our digestive system.

Carellas suggest the simple path to ecstasy includes continually staying in the present moment; not trying too hard, dropping expectations and judgements, and learning to be more conscious in sexual encounters, whilst surrendering to being in the present moment. She also advocates consciously moving sexual energy around the body, for example in the Firebreath orgasm technique. This uses the chakra system as the basis for a guided visualisation, using conscious breath, sounding and hip rocking to raise sexual energy. Participants of any gender are encouraged to start by focussing attention on the first or 'base' chakra which is located on the perineum between the anus and the genitals, related to grounding and survival. The focus then moves up to the second chakra in the belly, the centre of relationships, sexuality and creativity; then up to the solar plexus, the place of will; of self-esteem, courage and trust. The intention can be to focus on breathing and imagining drawing the energy up from the genitals through the energy centres. The next chakra is the heart, the centre of compassion and love; and the next, the throat chakra, the place for communication, creative expression and choice. The sixth chakra, called the third eye, is located at the forehead between the eyebrows, and is seen as the centre for intuition and wisdom. The crown chakra, at the top of the head, is related to bliss, higher love and a connection to spirituality.

Taking time to pay attention to breathing; to draw the sexual energy up through these energy centres can invigorate the body and result in orgasms that are experienced through the whole body rather than just focused in the genital area.

Gerhardt (2003)[65] says that secure emotional attachments as children are developed through the experience of relationships, where we can learn to self-regulate, to co-operate and develop empathy. It is through touch and human connection that serotonin and dopamine pathways are nourished, which then reduce stress through the production of oxytocin. Sexual behaviour which relies on adrenaline activates the survival circuits, with potentially detrimental consequences to our health. Sexual experiences that are relational trigger the socialising circuits instead. As discussed earlier, being seen and accepted by an 'other' is an important aspect of coming out of shame. Relatedness can be seen as the bridge between our existential need for uniqueness and our desires for connection. It is a two-way flow between giving and receiving, and between strength and vulnerability. It is this relational aspect of our sexuality that we need to address. This isn't to imply that such experiences can only happen in committed long-term relationships; this is about a relationship with the self; about presence. Being conscious and present can bring sexual delights through self-pleasuring or in an encounter with someone you have met for the first time.

Brene Brown (2010)[66] conducted some research into why some people are happier than others and have a good sense of self-worth, while others do not. She believes it is shame that undermines our sense of self-esteem. To feel a good sense of self-esteem we need to feel worthy of being loved, feel accepted and acceptable in connection, and feel a right to belong. To find this, we need to be willing and able to show our vulnerabilities; to allow ourselves to be imperfect and to learn from the mistakes we may make. We need courage and compassion to overcome our fears about not being good enough; and we should strive for authenticity and uniqueness and welcome this in others. Empathy is crucial for good social relationships whereas anonymity makes it easier for us to exploit. Aims for perfectionism move us back into shame, and low self-worth.

Macy and Young Brown (1998)[67] explain 'holonic systems' (similar to the Homeodynamic Model) which honour the uniqueness and importance of each different part of the whole. The system self-generates from spontaneously adaptive co-operation between the parts, in benefit of the whole. We need a diversity of organs, cells, neurochemicals, etc., to be just what they are and to do their job, and to be in a feedback loop with other parts of the system. For example, it would not be good if the heart tried to become a lung, as each is equally important. For a healthy sexual society we need a diversity of tastes, preferences and sexual orientations too. Perhaps the most powerful way to set yourself up for a delicious and delightful sex life is to know and accept yourself just as you are – and be willing to share that!

Review of Chapter 7

Solo Exercise

Read back through the exercises for this chapter and what you have written in your journal. Take some time to reflect on your exploration and to evaluate your work. Which exercises did you like and which ones did you not like? Think about why.

What have you discovered about yourself emotionally and how comfortable you are with your feelings?

What have you discovered about your relationship to shame, does it impact you and if so, how? Think about what changes you could make to feel more proud.

What have you discovered about your relationship to sexual play, do you have as much fun as you would like to?

If you have been hurt around your sexuality, are there any ways in which you continue to re-enact that hurt? Can you identify any things you could do to help to heal yourself?

What have you discovered about yourself in relationships? Do you have the relationships you would like, if not what are the things that get in the way? Is there anything you want to change; if so, how could you do that?

What is your relationship to your sexuality now, is it kind and loving, are you good friends?

Are there any exercises that you would like to do again? If so, notice what is similar or different if you do them a second time.

Read your reviews from each of the other sections as well. Write some things for yourself about your sexual preferences and tastes. Remind yourself about what turns you on, and what turns you off, sensually and sexually. Consider your sexual beliefs, along with the sexual behaviours that you value for yourself. Decide what type of sexual relationships you want to have and what would be a satiating, nutritious sexual diet for you.

Talk to someone, write or draw something about how you are thinking and feeling having done this work.

Exercise with Partner/s

Give yourselves an hour each and use the Conscious Communication dialogue to explore each other's reviews in detail.

Take your time to learn more about yourself and your partner/s as you discover what has been important about the work on this aspect of your sexuality.

> *Discuss where you feel this leaves your relationship now and identify one aspect that needs your combined attention. Explore how you may want to do this.*

Notes

1 Panksepp, J. (1998). *Affective Neuroscience.* New York: Oxford University Press.
2 Hite, S. (1994). *The Hite Report on the Family.* London: Bloomsbury.
3 NETFLIX (2022). *Sex Education* (2019). Available at: https://www.netflix.com/gb/title/80197526 (Accessed: 22 August 2022).
4 BISH (2022). *A Guide to Sex, Love and You.* Available at https://www.bishuk.com/ (Accessed: 21 August 2022).
5 Sex-Positive Families. Available at: https://sexpositivefamilies.com (Accessed: 22 August 2022).
6 Scarleteen (no date) sex ed for the real world. Available at: https://www.scarleteen.com (Accessed: 22 August 2022).
7 Corinna, H. (2016). *S.E.X: The All-You-Need-To-Know Sexuality Guide to Get You Through Your Teens and Twenties.* Available at: https://uk.bookshop.org/books/s-e-x-second-edition-the-all-you-need-to-know-sexuality-guide-to-get-you-through-your-teens-and-twenties/9780738218847 (Accessed: 22 August 2022).
8 School of Sexuality Education (2021). *Sex Ed: An Inclusive Teenage Guide to Sex and Relationships.* Available at: https://uk.bookshop.org/books/sex-ed-an-inclusive-teenage-guide-to-sex-and-relationships/9781406399080 (Accessed: 22 August 2022).
9 Vance, T. (2019). *Very Grand Emotions: How Autistics and Neurotypicals Experience Emotions Differently.* Available at: https://neuroclastic.com/very-grand-emotions/ (Accessed: 23 August 2022).
10 Morin, J. (1996). *The Erotic Mind.* New York: Harper Collins.
11 Bradshaw, J. (2006). *Healing the Shame That Binds You.* Health Communications Inc.
12 Nathanson, J. (1994). *Shame and Pride: Affect, Sex, and the Birth of the Self.* W. W. Norton.
13 Kaufman, G and Rafael, L. (1996). *Coming Out of Shame: Transforming Gay and Lesbian* Lives Doubleday.
14 Morgenroth, T., Pliskin, R., & van der Toorn, J. (2020). 'Not quite over the rainbow: the unrelenting and insidious nature of heteronormative ideology'. *Current Opinion in Behavioural Sciences* (34), pp. 160–165. Available at: https://www.sciencedirect.com/science/article/pii/S2352154620300383 (Accessed: 23: August 2022).
15 Tomkins, S. (1962). *Affect Imagery Consciousness. Vol I: The Positive Affects.* New York: Springer; Tomkins, S. (1963). *Affect Imagery Consciousness. Vol II: The Negative Affects.* New York: Springer; Tomkins, S. (1991). *Affect Imagery Consciousness. Vol III: The Negative Affects: Anger and Fear.* New York: Springer; Tomkins, S. (1992). *Affect Imagery Consciousness. Vol IV: Cognition: Duplication and Transformation of Information.* New York: Springer; The Tomkins Institute (2022). *Affect Imagery Consciousness (Vol I-IV).* Available at: https://www.tomkins.org/what-tomkins-said/books-and-articles/affect-imagery-consciousness-vol-i-iv/ (Accessed: 23: August 2022).
16 Lee, R. G. (2008). *The Secret Language of Intimacy.* Gestalt Press.

17 Spring, C. (2021). *Shame Is the Handbrake on Anger*. Available at: https://www.carolynspring.com/blog/shame-is-the-handbrake-on-anger/ (Accessed: 29 August 2022).

18 Gurney, K. (2020). *Mind the Gap: The Truth about Desire and How to Futureproof Your Sex Life*. UK: Headline; The Havelock Clinic (no date) *Conditions for Good Sex.pdf*. Available at: https://drive.google.com/file/d/1oFcK755Ne-0hcIOuQ5futw Dgruxgnkyt/view (Accessed: 23 August 2022).

19 Chodron, P.; The Pema Chödrön Foundation (2022). Available at: https://pemachodronfoundation.org/ (Accessed: 23 August 2022).

20 ErikaLust (2022). Available at: https://erikalust.com (Accessed: 23 August 2022).

21 Candida Royalle (2022). *Feminist Porn*. Available at: http://candidaroyalle.com/feminist-porn/ (Accessed: 23 August 2022).

22 CrashPadSeries (2022). Available at: https://crashpadseries.com (Accessed: 23 August 2022).

23 Dipsea (2022). *Let Us Tell You a Sexy Story*. Available at: https://www.dipseastories.com (Accessed: 23 August 2022).

24 NoFap (2022). *Get a New Grip on Life*. Available at: https://nofap.com (Accessed: 23 August 2022).

25 Attwood, F. (Ed.) (2010) *Porn.com: Making Sense of Online Pornography*. New York; Oxford: Peter Lang.

26 McKee, A., Albury, K., & Lumby, C. (2008). *The Porn Report*. Melbourne, Australia: Melbourne University Press.

27 Hite, S. (1994). *The Hite Report on the Family*. London: Bloomsbury.

28 Savage, D. (2021). *Savage Love from A to Z: Advice on Sex and Relationships, Dating and Mating, Exes and Extras: Straight Talk on Love, Sex, and Intimacy*. Sasquatch Books.

29 Maltz, W. (2010). 'The Porn Trap', *Therapy Today*, 21(1).

30 McGilchrist, I. (2009). *The Master and His Emissary: The Divided Brain and the Making of the Western World*. New Haven, CT: Yale University Press.

31 Carnes, P., Delmonico, D. & Griffin, E. (2007). *In The Shadows of the Net*. Center City, MN: Hazelden.

32 Hall, P.; Paula Hall (2018). *Books & Writing*. Available at: https://www.paulahall.co.uk/books/ (Accessed: 23 August 2022).

33 Neves, S. (2021). *Compulsive Sexual Behaviours*. Routledge.

34 Braun-Harvey, D and Vigorito, M. (2015). *Treating Out of Control Sexual Behavior: Rethinking Sex Addiction*. Springer.

35 Gerhardt, S. (2004). *Why Love Matters: How Affection Shapes a Baby's Brain*. Routledge.

36 Martin-Sperry, C. (2003). *Couples and Sex: An Introduction to Relationship Dynamics and Psychosexual Concepts*. Radcliffe medical press.

37 Rape Crisis (2022). *our Annual Stats 2020–21*. Available at: https://rapecrisis.org.uk/get-informed/rcew-statistics/ (Accessed: 3 September 2022).

38 Topping, A. (2021). 'Four-fifths of young women in the UK have been sexually harassed, survey finds', *The Guardian*, 10 March. Available at: https://www.theguardian.com/world/2021/mar/10/almost-all-young-women-in-the-uk-have-been-sexually-harassed-survey-finds. (Accessed: 4 September 2022).

39 Safeline (2022). *National Male Survivor Helpline and Online Support Service*. Available at: https://safeline.org.uk/services/national-male-helpline/ (Accessed: 4 September 2022).

40 SurvivorsUK (2022). Available at: https://www.survivorsuk.org/ (Accessed: 4 September 2022).

41 Rape Crisis (2022). *Rape Reports Hit Record High.* Available at: https:// rapecrisis.org.uk/news/rape-reports-hit-record-high/ (Accessed: 4 August 2022).
42 Rape Crisis (2022). *Annual Rape Prosecutions Fall Again.* Available at: https:// rapecrisis.org.uk/news/annual-rape-prosecutions-fall-again/ (Accessed: 4 September 2022).
43 End Violence Against Women (2022). *Major New YouGov Survey for EVAW: Many People Still Unclear What Rape Is.* 6 December 2018. Available at: https:// www.endviolenceagainstwomen.org.uk/major-new-survey-many-still-unclear-what-rape-is/ (Accessed: 23 August 2022).
44 Amnesty International UK (2017). *UK: New Poll Finds a Third of People Believe Women Who Flirt Partially Responsible for Being Raped.* 21 November 2005. Available at: https://www.amnesty.org.uk/press-releases/uk-new-poll-finds-third-people-believe-women-who-flirt-partially-responsible-being (Accessed: 23 August 2022).
45 Rothschild, B. (2000). *The Body Remembers.* New York: W. W. Norton.
46 James, S. E., Herman, J. L., Rankin, S., Keisling, M., Mottet, L., & Anafi, M. (2016). *The Report of the 2015 U.S. Transgender Survey.* Washington, DC: National Center for Transgender Equality.
47 Office for National Statistics (2022). *Dataset: Nature of Sexual Assault by Rape or Penetration, England and Wales.* Available at: https://www.ons. gov.uk/peoplepopulationandcommunity/crimeandjustice/datasets/natureofsexualassaultbyrapeorpenetrationenglandandwales (Accessed: 4 September 2022).
48 Bass, E., & Davis, L. (1990). *The Courage to Heal.* London: Harper & Row.
49 Haines, S. (1999). *The Survivor's Guide to Sex.* San Francisco, CA: Cleis Press.
50 Lew, M. (2004). *Victims No Longer.* New York: Harper Collins.
51 Kelly, R., & Maxted, F. (2005). *The Survivors Guide.* Rugby, Warks, UK: RoSA.
52 American Association of Sexuality Educators, Counselors and Therapists (no date). *Wendy Maltz Releases Free Sexual Healing and Intimacy Videos.* Available at: https://www.aasect.org/blog/wendy-maltz-releases-free-sexual-healing-and-intimacy-videos (Accessed: 4 September 2022).
53 Herman, J. (1993). *Trauma and Recovery.* New York: Basic Books.
54 Sensorimotor Psychotherapy Institute (2020). *Dr. Pat Ogden: Window of Tolerance,* 27 July. Available at: https://www.youtube.com/watch?v=wIosUotibEs (Accessed: 4 September 2022).
55 Kauppi, M. (2021). *Polyamory: A Toolkit for Therapists (and Their Clients).* Rowman and Littlefield.
56 Fern, J. (2020). *Polysecure: Attachment, Trauma and Consensual Nonmonogamy.* Thorntree Press.
57 Easton, D. & Hardy, J. (2017). *The Ethical Slut, third edition: A Practical Guide to Polyamory, Open Relationships, and Other Freedoms in Sex and Love* Ten Speed Press.
58 Bader, E. (2022). *Differentiation in Couples Relationships.* Available at: https://www.couplesinstitute.com/differentiation-couples-relationships/ (Accessed: 4 September 2022).
59 Conflict Resolution Network (2020). *Learn, Reinforce and Teach Conflict Resolution Skills with Our Definitive Resources.* Available at: www.crnhq.org (Accessed: 4 September 2022).
60 Perel, E. (2007). *Mating in Captivity.* London: Hodder.

61 Schnarch, D. (1998). *Passionate Marriage*. New York: Owl Books.
    Schnarch, D. (2002). *Resurrecting Sex*. New York: Harper Collins.
62 Love, P., & Robinson, J. (1995). *Hot Monogamy*. New York: Plume, Penguin.
63 Lightwoman, L. (2012). *Tantra: The Path to Blissful Sex*. Piatkus.
64 Carellas, B. (2007). *Urban Tantra: Sacred Sex for the Twenty-first Century*. Ten Speed Press.
65 Gerhardt, S. (2003). *Why Love Matters: How Affection Shapes a Baby's Brain*. Routledge.
66 Brown, B.; TEDx Talks (2010). *The Power of Vulnerability: Brené Brown at TEDxHouston*. December. Available at: https://www.ted.com/talks/brene_brown_the_power_of_vulnerability (Accessed: 4 September 2022).
67 Macy, J. & Young Brown, M. (1998). *Coming Back to Life*. New Society Publishers.

Conclusion

We have explored many topics in this book. Hopefully the Homeodynamic Model with its focus on social and cultural factors and the pleasure principle has helped you to think differently – in a more empowered, joyful way – about yourself as a sexual person, and about your sex life. Hopefully, you have done some of the exercises, and found that they have helped you become more intimate with yourself and your own sensual and sexual pleasure, and if you have been doing some of them with a partner or partners, deepened your understanding and enjoyment of each other as well.

To recap one last time – the Mind section explored our beliefs and sexual values and how they may have been influenced by religion, shame and a cultural exploitation of sexuality, as well as what we learnt as children. We explored the power of creating and choosing our own sexual values. The Body section described sexual functioning, including how the vulva, not the vagina, is the primary female sex organ. The roles of the nervous system, endocrine system and respiratory system in the sexual arousal process were also explained. This knowledge can move us away from thinking of intercourse as 'real sex' with everything else as 'just foreplay', into valuing all the sexual behaviours we may want to express. The Brain section explored our passion, urges and sexual desire. It outlined the role of neurochemicals in sexual functioning, and described the difference between the survival and the socialising brain circuits: the former activating the adrenal system and the latter, activating 'feel good' substances instead. How childhood experiences impact our reflexive reactions was discussed, and how we can use our thinking capabilities to make choices about how we behave. The section on Emotion explored emotional intelligence and outlined the impacts of trauma on our bodies and hearts, as well as diving into what it takes to sustain loving and intimate relationships of all types and flavours. As we have said, these four quadrants of the Homeodynamic Model are all in constant interplay with each other. Considering them separately helps us understand how each is constantly impacting, and being impacted by, the others, and how this plays out in our unique sexual selves and sexual experiences.

DOI: 10.4324/9781003322405-9

This is just a model, a way of thinking about these different elements to try to understand better what may be the ingredients for a healthy sexual self-esteem. Please feel free to use this as you wish and discard anything that does not work for you. There may be other elements you wish to add or topics that have not been included that are of interest to you. There are many resources, some included here and others in books or on the internet, for you to explore further.

Reclaiming Sex

Throughout this book, we have invited an evaluation of our social and cultural relationship with sexuality, a consideration of what we are teaching our children, discussing in the media and viewing on the internet.

This free, amazing gift for fun and pleasure does not get the good press it should; we do not seem to be at peace with this aspect of humanity, and we certainly do not celebrate our sexual potential. In the West, we are encouraged to want *things* rather than relationships; to have attachments to and value objects (cars, phones, etc.), rather than people. We have developed an objectified relationship to our sexuality. Our bodies, rather than being honoured as a free source of sensual and sexual pleasure, are offered up to be pruned and plucked; starved, shaved and cut, to be altered into a mono-cultured image of beauty, and then and only then, 'made sexy'.

If we are to reclaim sex for our own authentic fun, pleasure and bonding, we need to become more comfortable seeing ourselves as sexual beings, sexual subjectivities, and allowing ourselves to be seen that way by others. We need the confidence to make our own sexual stories, fine-tuned to our own desires and specific tastes and preferences, based on our knowledge of ourselves. We need the clarity to place the responsibility for sexual violence firmly on the perpetrators. We need to demand sex-affirmative resources and products that help us feel proud of our own unique sexual arousal and pleasure; resources that spark our imaginations and creativity whatever we look like and whatever we enjoy. What if we start seeing sexual pleasure as a soothing, rejuvenating, ecstatic, free way to counterbalance the pains and struggles of human existence? What if we reclaim the pleasure principle: that we have as much right to fun and play, as the demands put on us to work?

Hopefully, the tide is turning in our attitudes to sex and sexuality. It would be wonderful for us to break out of our cultural shame; to stop focusing on sex as something we perform, to honour our relational needs and develop an ease about being emotional, sensual and sexual beings.

The Food Analogy

We know we have needs for sex like we have for food. In recent years we have changed our cultural attitudes to food; we are becoming much more aware of what foods are healthy, and what are not. We know we need proteins, complex carbohydrates, vitamins and minerals. We know that processed foods are often stripped of ingredients needed for good digestion; and that junk foods might be convenient but are high in saturated fats, salt and sugar, with all the associated health implications. We have become more aware of our nutritional needs, both for our physical and emotional well-being. So what if we were to consider the same for our sexual needs; what would be the equivalence? Like healthy food, satisfying sex triggers the release of feel-good chemicals like oxytocin, dopamine and serotonin. It allows us to play, gives us pleasure and relieves pain. It is good for our physical, mental and emotional health.

Many of the exercises in this book have encouraged you to explore what sexual nutrients you want and value; and also to evaluate what of your thinking and behaviour is nutritious, in that it satiates you; body, mind and soul. Does your sexual life leave you feeling good, in a state of physical, psychological and emotional well-being?

This is not about judging certain sexual behaviours as unhealthy. We can have fast sex or slow sex. We can be a gourmet cook and still sometimes just want a snack. Our tastes and preferences may vary. It is not a hierarchy of what is best; it is a circular view of sex.

The Heart

The heart is very connected to sexuality as the heart and the genitals both have smooth muscle, which responds differently to other muscles in the body. Buhner (2004)[1] explains how the heart can be seen as so much more than a pump for our circulatory system: it is also an endocrine gland, making and releasing numerous hormones; a generator of electromagnetic messages and a part of the central nervous system, with direct links to the limbic system. He goes further to describe how the heart is an organ of perception and communication. The heart is also our metaphorical place of love, and for many sharing sexual expression in the context of love, is where the delights of passion can be experienced at their most exquisite. This is not to imply that such experiences can only happen in committed long-term relationships; this is about a relationship with the self. Being conscious, present and open can bring sexual delights through self-pleasuring or in an encounter with someone you have met for the first time.

Figure 8.1 considers the Homeodynamic Model in alignment with the elements of fire, air, earth and water used within many spiritual traditions, and asks what is at the heart? Each individual is seen to have differing amounts of all of these qualities within them. If we consider all the elements of our sexuality, what is the synergy created when we bring them all together?

And beyond our individual selves, how are we impacted by the wider world, and what do we want to contribute to it? This book has foregrounded

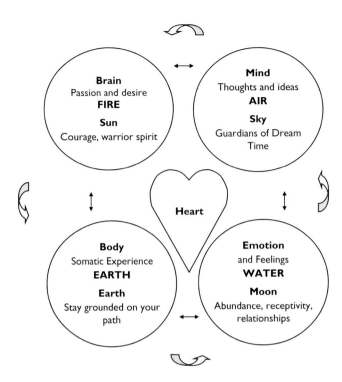

Figure 8.1 The Elemental Homeodynamic Model.

the importance of differentiation within romantic relationships. We believe this can be extrapolated to wider society relationships – how crucial it is that more broadly we welcome and are curious about different opinions, beliefs and values; that people coming from different places can truly hear each other and take each other's needs into account. May you feel empowered to use and develop the relational skills you have honed reading this book and doing the exercises, to also foster dialogue around some of the many social issues urgently requiring attention.

We hope *LoveSex and Relationships* has provided an opportunity for you to re-evaluate your sexuality. We hope that you now feel more empowered to enjoy sexual nourishment that suits your own preferences and tastes; that you can love and honour your sexuality, that you can love sex, respect those you share your body with and feel good about yourself.

Note

1 Buhner, S. (2004). *The Secret Teachings of Plants*. Rochester, VT: Bear and Company.

About the Authors

Over a 30-year career, Cabby Laffy has worked as a psychosexual psycho-therapist with individuals and those in relationships. She has facilitated training in a diverse range of settings on issues relating to Psychosexual Health. She has supervised therapists trained in counselling and psycho-therapy, and also many trained in Bodywork and a wide range of comple-mentary and alternative health therapies. Drawing on her professional experience and studies in Neuroscience she has developed the integrative Homeodynamic Model. Cabby's passions include being at the coast, social justice and getting time to write her novel.

Polly likewise offers individual and relationship psychosexual therapy. She's also passionate about group work as a modality for enhancing sexual empowerment and pleasure. As well as her training in counselling and psychotherapy she has studied with the Institute of Group Analysis, Pink Therapy, the Gestalt Centre, Barbara Carellas, Nick Totton, Layla Martin and Spectrum Therapy. Polly used to be a literary translator (from French), and lives on Dartmoor with her wife, three children and a lot of animals. She loves reading fiction, growing vegetables and dancing.

Cabby and Polly are co-directors of the Center for Psychosexual Health (https://psychosexualhealth.org.uk/) and until recently have taught a two-year Diploma in Integrative Psychosexual Therapy, devised around the Homeodynamic Model. In conjunction with The Grove they are now offering an eight-day Certificate in Psychosexual Therapy and other one-day CPD events. Cabby also co-facilitates an eight-day Certificate in Working with Couples and other Relationships, with her daughter Shana Laffy, via their joint enterprise Heartful Therapy Training (https://www.heartfultherapy.co.uk/training/).

References

ABLEize. (2019) *Disability & Special Needs Products & Services*. Available at: https://www.ableize.com/ (Accessed: 16 Aug 2022).

Active Pause. (no date) *Scientific Evidence for the Polyvagal Theory*. Available at: https://activepause.com/polyvagal-theory-evidence/ (Accessed: 23 August 2022).

American Association of Sexuality Educators, Counselors and Therapists. (no date) *Wendy Maltz Releases Free Sexual Healing and Intimacy Videos*. Available at: https://www.aasect.org/blog/wendy-maltz-releases-free-sexual-healing-and-intimacy-videos (Accessed: 4 September 2022).

Amnesty International UK. (2017) *UK: New Poll Finds a Third of People Believe Women Who Flirt Partially Responsible For Being Raped*. 21 November 2005. Available at: https://www.amnesty.org.uk/press-releases/uk-new-poll-finds-third-people-believe-women-who-flirt-partially-responsible-being (Accessed: 23 August 2022).

Anzani, A. (2020) 'Sexual Fantasy Across Gender Identity: A Qualitative Investigation of Differences Between Cisgender and Non-binary People's Imagery', *Sexual and Relationship Therapy*, February. Available at: https://www.researchgate.net/publication/339567666_Sexual_fantasy_across_gender_identity_a_qualitative_investigation_of_differences_between_cisgender_and_non-binary_people's_imagery (Accessed: 7 September 2022).

Arthur, K., & Arthur, Karen. (2022) *Menopause Whilst Black*. Available at: https://www.thekarenarthur.com/menopausewhilstblack (Accessed: 10 September 2022).

Attwood, F. (ed.) (2010) *Porn.Com: Making Sense of Online Pornography*. New York: PeterLang Pub Inc.

Bader, E. (2022) *Differentiation in Couples Relationships*. Available at: https://www.couplesinstitute.com/differentiation-couples-relationships/ (Accessed: 4 September 2022).

Banks, S. (2011) 'Understanding Despair, Denial, Power and Emotions in the Context of Climate Change', *Transformations*. Winter 2011/2012.

Barker, M. J. (2018) *Rewriting the Rules*. Routledge; Meg-John Barker (2016) *Rewriting the Rules*. Available at: https://www.rewriting-the-rules.com/meg-john-barker/ (Accessed: 4 Sept 2022).

Barker, M. J., & Langridge, D. (eds.) (2007) *Safe, Sane & Consensual: Contemporary Perspectives on Sadomasochism*. UK: Palgrave Macmillan.

Barrett, L. F. (2021) 'Your Brain Predicts (Almost) Everything You Do'. Available at: https://www.mindful.org/your-brain-predicts-almost-everything-you-do/ (Accessed: 23 August 2022).

Bass, E., & Davis, L. (1990) *The Courage to Heal*. London: Harper & Row.

Basson, R. (2000) 'The Female Sexual Response: A Different Model', *Journal of Sex and Marital Therapy*, 26(1), pp. 51–65.

Batmanghelidjh, C. (2007) *Shattered Lives*. London: Jessica Kingsley.

BBC News. (2022) *Why Do So Few Rape Cases Go To Court?* 27 May. Available at: https://www.bbc.co.uk/news/uk-48095118 (Accessed: 23 August 2022).

Bennett, J., & Pope, A. (2008) *The Pill*. New South Wales, Australia: Allen & Unwin.

Berne, E. (1961) *Transactional Analysis in Psychotherapy*. MN: Condor Books.

Biddulph, S. (2004) *Manhood*. London: Vermillion.

BISH. (2022) *A Guide to Sex, Love and You*. Available at: https://www.bishuk.com/ (Accessed: 21 August 2022).

Bowlby, J. (1988) *A Secure Base*. Abingdon, Oxon: Routledge.

Bowlby, R. (2004) *Fifty Years of Attachment Theory*. London: Karnac.

Boyd, C. (2020) 'Children Who Lived in Deprived Orphanages in Romania Have Brains That Arealmost 10% SMALLER than English Adoptees', *Times of Naukri*, 7 January. Available at: https://ukraine.timesofnews.com/health-care/children-who-lived-in-deprived-orphanages-in-romania-have-brains-10-smaller-than-english-adoptees.html (Accessed: 25 August 2022).

Bradshaw, J. (2005) *Healing the Shame That Binds You*. Deerfield Beach, FL: Health Communications Inc.

Braun-Harvey, D., & Vigorito, M. (2015) *Treating Out of Control Sexual Behavior: Rethinking Sex Addiction*. New York, NY: Springer.

Briden, L. (2021) *Hormone Repair Manual: Every Woman's Guide to Healthy Hormones After 40*. GreenPeak Publishing.

Brown, A., Barker, E., & Rahman, Q. (2020) 'A Systematic Scoping Review of the Prevalence, Etiological, Psychological, and Interpersonal Factors Associated with BDSM', *Journal of Sex Research*, 57(6), pp. 781–811.

Brown, B., & TEDx Talks (2010) *The Power of Vulnerability: Brené Brown at TEDxHouston*. December. Available at: https://www.ted.com/talks/brene_brown_the_power_of_vulnerability (Accessed: 4 September 2022).

Callaway, E. (2010) 'Human Facial Expressions Aren't Universal,' *New Scientist*, 19 March. Available at: www.newscientist.com/article/dn17605-human-facial-expressions-arent universal.html (Accessed: 23 August 2022).

Cancer Research UK. (2022) *Cancer Incidence for Common Cancers*. Available at: https://www.cancerresearchuk.org/health-professional/cancer-statistics/incidence/common-cancers-compared#heading-One (Accessed: 21 August 2022).

Candida Royalle. (2022) *Feminist Porn*. Available at: http://candidaroyalle.com/feminist-porn/ (Accessed: 23 August 2022).

Carnes, P., Delmonico, D., & Griffin, E. (2007) *In The Shadows of the Net*. Center City, MN: Hazelden.

Carrellas, B. (2007) *Urban Tantra*. New York: Celestial Arts.

Carrington, D. (2022) 'Cocktail of Chemical Pollutants Linked to Falling Sperm Quality in Research', *The Guardian*, 10 June. Available at: https://www.theguardian.com/environment/2022/jun/10/cocktail-of-chemical-pollutants-linked-to-falling-sperm-quality-in-research?CMP=Share_iOSApp_Other (Accessed: 21 August 2022).

Chalker, R. (2000) *The Clitoral Truth*. New York: Seven Stories.

Charura, D., & Lago, C. (eds.) (2021) *Black Identities & White Therapies: Race, respect and diversity*. PCCS Books.

Chia, M., & Abrams, D. (2002a) *The Multi Orgasmic Couple*. London: Thorsons.

Chia, M., & Abrams, D. (2002b) *The Multi Orgasmic Man*. London: Thorsons.

Chia, M., & Carlton Abrams, R. (2005) *The Multi Orgasmic Woman*. Emmaus, PA: Rodale.

Childline. (2022) Available at: https://www.childline.org.uk/ (Accessed: 4 September 2022).

Chödrön, P., & The Pema Chödrön Foundation. (2022) Available at: https://pemachodronfoundation.org/ (Accessed: 23 August 2022).

Conflict Resolution Network. (2020a) *Conflict Is the Stuff of Life*. Available at: https://www.crnhq.org/cr-kit/ (Accessed: 29 August 2022).

Conflict Resolution Network. (2020b) *Learn, Reinforce and Teach Conflict Resolution Skills With Our Definitive Resources*. Available at: www.crnhq.org (Accessed: 4 September 2022).

Consent Is Everything. (no date) *Consent – It's Simple as Tea*. Available at: http://www.consentiseverything.com/ (Accessed: 4 September 2022).

Cook, S. M. C. et al. (2015) 'Social Issues of Teenage Pregnancy', *Obstetrics, Gynaecology and Reproductive Medicine*, 25(9), pp. 243–248.

Corinna, H. (2016) *S.E.X: The All-You-Need-To-Know Sexuality Guide to Get You Through Your Teens and Twenties*. Available at: https://uk.bookshop.org/books/s-e-x-second-edition-the-all-you-need-to-know-sexuality-guide-to-get-you-through-your-teens-and-twenties/9780738218847 (Accessed: 22 August 2022).

Corinna, H. (2021) *What Fresh Hell Is This? Perimenopause, Menopause, Other Indignities and You*. USA: Piatkus.

Couples Institute. (2022) *For Couples*. Available at: https://www.couplesinstitute.com/for-couples/ (Accessed: 19 August 2020).

CrashPadSeries. (2022) Available at: https://crashpadseries.com (Accessed: 23 August 2022).

Crenshaw, K., & TEDx Talks. (2016) *The Urgency of Intersectionality: Kimberlé Crenshaw at TEDWomen*. Available at: https://www.ted.com/talks/kimberle_crenshaw_the_urgency_of_intersectionality (Accessed: 16 August 2022).

Crenshaw, T. (1997) *The Alchemy of Love and Lust*. New York: Pocket Books.

Crown Prosecution Service, The. (2022) *Rape and Sexual Offences - Chapter 6: Consent, 21 May 2021|Legal Guidance, Sexual offences*. Available at: https://www.cps.gov.uk/legal-guidance/rape-and-sexual-offences-chapter-6-consent (Accessed: 4 Sept 2022).

Dana, D. (2018) *The Polyvagal Theory in Therapy: Engaging the Rhythm of Regulation*. New York: W.W. Norton.

Davis, A. et al. (2018) 'What Behaviors Do Young Heterosexual Australians See in Pornography? A Cross-Sectional Study', *Journal of Sex Research*, 55(3), pp. 310–319.

Davis, N. (2019) 'Sexual Dysfunction Cuts Risk 'Leaving Thousands in UK Without Help'', *The Guardian*, 22 April. Available at: https://www.theguardian.com/society/2019/apr/22/sexual-dysfunction-cuts-risk-leaving-thousands-in-uk-without-help (Accessed: 16 August 2022).

DeGruy, J. *Post Traumatic Slave Syndrome (P.T.S.S.)*. Available at: https://www.joydegruy.com/ (Accessed: 29 August 2022).

Diamond, L. (2008) *Sexual Fluidity*. Boston, MA: Harvard University Press.

Dipsea. (2022) *Let Us Tell You A Sexy Story*. Available at: https://www.dipseastories. com (Accessed: 23 August 2022).

Disabilities-R-Us. (2022) *Disability Sexuality Resources*. Available at: https://www. disabilities-r-us.com/sexuality resources/ (2022) (Accessed: 16 Aug 2022).

Dodsworth, L. (2017) *Manhood: The Bare Reality*. London: Pinter and Martin.

Dodsworth, L. (2019) *'Womanhood: The Bare Reality'*. London: Pinter and Martin.

Dodsworth, L. (no date) *Bare Reality*. Available at: https://www.lauradodsworth. com/bare-reality-photography/ (Accessed: 22 August 2022).

Easton, D., & Hardy, J. (2017) *The Ethical Slut, Third Edition: A Practical Guide to Polyamory, Open Relationships, and Other Freedoms in Sex and Love*. New York: Ten Speed Press.

Ejegård, H. et al. (2008) 'Sexuality After Delivery with Episiotomy: A Long-term Follow-up', *Gynecologic and Obstetric Investigation*, 66(1), pp. 1–7.

Ekman, P., & Paul Ekman Group. (1954–2018a). About. Available at: https://www. paulekman.com/about/paul-ekman/ (Accessed: 27 August 2022).

Ekman, P., & Paul Ekman Group. (2018b). *Are Facial Expressions Universal or Culturally Specific?* Available at: https://www.paulekman.com/blog/facial-expressions-universal-culturally-specific/ (Accessed: 25 August 2022).

End Violence Against Women. (2022a) *Attitudes to Sexual Consent, Research by YouGov*, December 2018. Available at: https://www.endviolenceagainstwomen.org. uk/wp-content/uploads/1-Attitudes-to-sexual-consent-Research-findings-FINAL.pdf (Accessed: 11 September 2022).

End Violence Against Women. (2022b) *Major New YouGov Survey for EVAW: Many People Still Unclear What Rape Is*, 6 December 2018. Available at: https://www. endviolenceagainstwomen.org.uk/major-new-survey-many-still-unclear-what-rape-is/ (Accessed: 23 August 2022).

ErikaLust. (2022) Available at: https://erikalust.com (Accessed: 23 August 2022).

Erotic Blueprint Breakthrough. (2022) About. Available at: https://missjaiya.com/ about/ (Accessed: 11 September 2022).

Federation of Feminist Women's Health Centres (FFWHC). (1995) *A New View of a Woman's Body*. Los Angeles, CA: Feminist Health Press.

Feldman Barrett, L. (2022) *Seven and a Half Lessons About the Brain*. Available at: https://lisafeldmanbarrett.com/ (Accessed: 23 August 2022).

Fern, J. (2020) *Polysecure: Attachment, Trauma and Consensual Non Monogamy*. Portland, OR (USA): Thorntree Press.

Fielding, L. (2021) *Trans Sex: Clinical Approaches to Trans Sexualities and Erotic Embodiments*. New York: Routledge.

French, R. (2018) 'Sexual & Reproductive Health', *BMJ*, 44(1), January. Available at: https://srh.bmj.com/content/44/1/16 (Accessed: 7 September 2022).

Fromm, E. (1995) *The Art of Loving*. London: Thorsons.

Frothingham, S. (2018) 'Excitatory Neurotransmitters', *Healthline*, 12 December. Available at: https://www.healthline.com/health/excitatory-neurotransmitters# excitatory-neurotransmitters (Accessed: 11 September 2022).

Gabriel, A. (2021) 'Trauma: How It Gets Passed On and Breaking the Cycle', *Counselling Directory*, 26 October. Available at: https://www.counselling-directory. org.uk/memberarticles/trauma-how-it-gets-passed-on-and-breaking-the-cycle (Accessed: 29 August 2022).

Garcia, M., & Zalizynak, M. (2020) 'Effects of Feminizing Hormone Treatment on Sexual Function of Transgender Women', *Journal of Urology*, 1 April, pp. 203–204.

Gerhardt, S. (2004) *Why Love Matters*. Hove, Brighton, UK: Brunner- Routledge.

Gibb, B. J. (2015) 'A Quick Guide to Drugs, the Brain and Brain Chemistry', *Welcome Collection*, 1 November. Available at: https://wellcomecollection.org/articles/W9hIBBAAAHAb74ma (Accessed: 11 September 2022).

Goldhor Lerner, H. (1990) *The Dance of Intimacy*. Ontario, Canada: Pandora.

Gottman, J. (2015) *The Seven Principles for Making Marriage Work*. Random House.

Gottman Institute, The. (2022) *Couples*. Available at: https://www.gottman.com/couples/ (Accessed: 6 September 2022).

Grigg, K. (2021) 'Record Rise in Young Adults Living with Their Parents', *Richard Nelson LLP*, 20 April. Available at: https://www.richardnelsonllp.co.uk/record-number-young-adults-living-with-parents/ (Accessed: 29 August 2022).

Gurney, K. (2020) *Mind the Gap: The Truth About Desire and How to Futureproof Your Sex Life*. UK: Headline.

Gurney, K., & TEDx Talks. (2020) *The Surprising Truth About Desire Everyone Needs to Know: Karen Gurney at TEDxRoyalTunbridgeWells*. 17 July. Available at: https://www.youtube.com/watch?v=krA8-_iXptE (Accessed: 10 September 2022).

Gurney, K., & TEDx Talks. (2022) *The Power of Orgasms to Address Gender Inequality: Karen* Gurney at TEDxLondonWomen. 31 March. Available at: https://www.youtube.com/watch?v=4oy7UH9rNl4 (Accessed: 22 August 2022).

Haines, S. (1999) *The Survivor's Guide to Sex*. San Fransisco, CA: Cleis Press.

Hall, P., & Paula Hall (2018) *Books & Writing*. Available at: https://www.paulahall.co.uk/books/ (Accessed: 23 August 2022).

Hanson, E. (2020) 'What Is the IMPACT of Pornography on Young People?', *NHS UK*. Available at: https://sexualhealth.cht.nhs.uk/fileadmin/sexualHealth/contentUploads/Documents/What_is_the_impact_of_pornography_on_young_people_-_A_research_briefing_for_educators.pdf (Accessed: 21 August 2022).

Harper, C. (2022) 'Why Fairer Relationships Lead to Better Sex Lives', *Psychology Today*, 15 July. Available at: https://www.psychologytoday.com/gb/blog/articles-heterodoxy/202207/why-fairer-relationships-lead-better-sex-lives (Accessed: 19 August 2022).

Harvey, D. B., & Vigorito, M. A. (2016) *Treating Out of Control Sexual Behavior: Rethinking Sex Addition*. New York, NY: Springer.

Harville, & Helen. (no date) Available at: https://harvilleandhelen.com/ (Accessed: 19 August 2022).

Havelock Clinic, The. (no date) *Conditions for Good Sex.pdf*. Available at: https://drive.google.com/file/d/1oFcK755Ne-0hcIOuQ5futwDgruxgnkyt/view (Accessed: 23 August 2022).

Havelock Clinic, The. (2022) *Courses*. Available at: https://havelockonlineworkshops.teachable.com/courses (Accessed: 10 September 2022).

Hawkins, R., & Neves, S. (2020) 'Integrating Diversity into Therapy', *COSRT Online Seminar*, 26 August.

Hendrix, H. (1993) *Getting the Love You Want: A Guide for Couples*. London: Pocket Books.

Hendrix, H. (1995) *Keeping the Love You Find*. London: Pocket Books.

Herman, J. (1993) *Trauma and Recovery*. New York: Basic Books.

Hite, S. (1976) *The Hite Report.* New York: Dell.

Hite, S. (1994) *The Hite Report on the Family.* London: Bloomsbury.

Home Office. (2022) *Female Genital Mutilation Resource Pack.* Available at: https://www.gov.uk/government/publications/female-genital-mutilation-resource-pack/female-genital-mutilation-resource-pack (Accessed: 22 August 2022).

Hunter, M. (2019) 'Understanding Menopause with Professor Myra Hunter', *Unmind,* 30 September. Available at: https://blog.unmind.com/menopause-with-professor-myra-hunter (Accessed: 10 September 2022).

Hunter, M., & Smith, M. (2021) *Living Well Through the Menopause: An Evidence-based Cognitive Behavioural Guide.* London: Robinson- Hachette.

Imagoworks. (no date) *Imago Dialogue: The Basic Steps.* Available at: http://imagoworks.com/the-imago-dialogue/steps/ (Accessed: 19 August 2022).

IPSOS. (2022) 'LGBT & Pride 2021 Global Survey'. Available at: https://www.ipsos.com/sites/default/files/LGBT%20Pride%202021%20Global%20Survey%20Report%20-%20US%20Version.pdf (Accessed: 21 August 2022).

James, S. E., Herman, J. L., Rankin, S., Keisling, M., Mottet, L., & Anafi, M. (2016) *The Report of the 2015 U.S. Transgender Survey.* Washington, DC: National Center for Transgender Equality.

Kahr, B. (2007) *Sex and the Psyche.* New York: Penguin.

Karpman, S., & Karpman Drama Triangle. Available at: https://www.karpmandramatriangle.com/ (Accessed: 22 August 2022).

Kaschak, & Tiefer. (2001) *A New View of Women's Sexual Problems.* New York: Routledge.

Kaufman, G., & Rafael, L. (1996) *Coming Out of Shame: Transforming Gay and Lesbian.* Lives Doubleday.

Kaufman, M., Odette, O., & Silverberg, C. (2005) *Ultimate Guide to Sex and Disability: For All of Us Who Live with Disabilities, Chronic Pain and Illness.* San Francisco: Cleis Press.

Kauppi, M. (2021) *Polyamory: A Clinical Toolkit for Therapists (and Their Clients).* Rowman & Littlefield.

Kelly, R., & Maxted, F. (2005) *The Survivors Guide.* Rugby, Warks, UK: RoSA.

Kessler, D. (2010) 'Obesity: The Killer Combination of Salt, Fat and Sugar', *The Guardian,* 13 March. Available at: https://www.theguardian.com/lifeandstyle/2010/mar/13/obesity-salt-fat sugar-kessler (Accessed: 23 August 2022).

Kinsey, A., Wardell, P., & Martin, C. (1948) *Sexual Behaviour in the Human Male.* Philadelphia: WB Saunders.

Kinsey, A., Wardell, P., & Martin, C. (1953) *Sexual Behaviour in the Human Female.* Philadelphia: WB Saunders.

Kitzinger, S. (1985) *Women's Experience of Sex.* New York: Penguin.

Komisaruk, B., Beyer-Flores, C., & Whipple, B. (2006) *The Science of Orgasm.* Baltimore, MD: John Hopkins University Press.

Krupnick, M. (2022) 'More than 3,000 Potentially Harmful Chemicals Found in Food Packaging', *The Guardian,* 19 May. Available at: https://www.theguardian.com/world/2022/may/19/more-than-3000-potentially-harmful-chemicals-food-packaging-report-shows (Accessed: 21 August 2022).

Laffy, C. (2013) *LoveSex: An Integrative Model for Sexual Education.* London: Routledge.

Lee, R. G. (2008) *The Secret Language of Intimacy*. Perth, Western Australia: Gestalt Press.

Lehmiller, J. (2018a) *Tell Me What You Want: the science of sexual desire and how it can help you improve your sex life*. London: Robinson - Hachette.

Lehmiller, J. (2018b) 'The Science of Sexual Fantasy and Desire: Part 1', *Sexual Health Alliance*. Available at: https://sexualhealthalliance.com/justin-lehmiller-science-of-fantasy (Accessed: 22 August 2022).

Levine, P. (1997) *Waking the Tiger*. Berkeley, CA: North Atlantic Books.

Lew, M. (2004) *Victims No Longer*. New York: Harper Collins.

Lewis, R. et al. (2017) 'Heterosexual Practices Among Young People in Britain: Evidence from Three National Surveys of Sexual Attitudes and Lifestyles', *Journal of Adolescent Health*, 61(6), pp. 694–702.

Li, W. (2022) *Current Biology*. Available at: https://neurosciencenews.com/fear-sensory-cortex-20250/ (Accessed: 7 August 2022).

Lightwoman, L. (2012). *Tantra: The Path to Blissful Sex*. London: Piatkus.

Lisitsa, E. (2013) 'The Four Horsemen: Criticism, Contempt, Defensiveness, and Stonewalling', *The Gottman Institute*, 23 April. Available at: https://www.gottman.com/blog/the-four-horsemen-recognizing-criticism-contempt-defensiveness-and-stonewalling/ (Accessed: 16 August 2022).

Lisitsa, E. (no date) 'The Four Horsemen: The Antidotes', *The Gottman Institute*. Available at: https://www.gottman.com/blog/the-four-horsemen-the-antidotes/ (Accessed: 19 August 2022).

Love, P., & Robinson, J. (1995) *Hot Monogamy*. New York: Plume, Penguin.

Macfarlane, A., & Dorkenoo, E. (2017) 'Prevalence of Female Genital Mutilation in England and Wales National and Local Estimate', *UK Data Service*, October. Available at: https://ukdataservice.ac.uk/case-study/prevalence-of-female-genital-mutilation-in-england-and-wales-national-and-local-estimates/ (Accessed: 22 August 2022).

Macy, J., & Young Brown, M. (1998) *Coming Back to Life*. Canada: New Society.

Maltz, W. (1991) *The Sexual Healing Journey*. New York: Harper Collins.

Maltz, W. (2010) 'The Porn Trap', *Therapy Today*, 21(1).

Martin-Sperry, C. (2003) *Couples and Sex: An Introduction to Relationship Dynamics and Psychosexual Concepts*. London: Radcliffe Medical Press.

Masters, W. H., & Johnson, V. E. (1966) *Human Sexual Responses*. New York: Little Brown.

Masters, W., Johnson, V., & Kolodny, R. (1994) *Heterosexuality*. London: Thorsons.

McCarthy, B. & E. (2020) *Contemporary Male Sexuality: Confronting Myths and Promoting Change*. New York: Routledge.

McGilchrist, I. (2009) *The Master and His Emissary: The Divided Brain and the Making of the Western World*. NewHaven, CT: Yale University Press.

McKee, A., Albury, K., & Lumby, C. (2008) *The Porn Report*. Melbourne, Australia: Melbourne University Press.

McKenzie-Mavinga (2016) *The Challenge of Racism in Therapeutic Practice*. London: Palgrave.

Menopause matters. (no date) *CBT for Menopausal Symptoms*. Available at: https://www.menopausematters.co.uk/cbt_for_menopause.php (Accessed: 10 September 2022).

Meston, C., & Buss, D. (2007) *Why Humans Have Sex*. Available at: https://labs.la.utexas.edu/mestonlab/files/2016/05/WhyHaveSex.pdf (Accessed: 21 August 2022).

Mindell, Amy and Arnold. (2008). *Deep Democracy*. Available at: http://www.aamindell.net/worldwork?rq=Power%2C%20Rank%20and%20Privilege%20 (Accessed: 4 September 2022).

Mindell, Amy and Arnold. (1986). *Process-Oriented Psychology*. Available at: http://www.aamindell.net/process-work (Accessed: 4 September 2022).

Montañez, A. (2017) 'Beyond XX and XY: The Extraordinary Complexity of Sex Determination', *Scientific American*, 1 September.

Morgenroth, T., Pliskin, R., & van der Toorn, J. (2020) 'Not Quite Over the Rainbow: The Unrelenting and Insidious Nature of Heteronormative Ideology', *Current Opinion in Behavioural Sciences*, 34, pp. 160–165. Available at: https://www.sciencedirect.com/science/article/pii/S2352154620300383 (Accessed: 23 August 2022).

Morin, J. (1996) *The Erotic Mind*. New York: Harper Collins.

My Pleasure. (2022) Available at: https://mypleasure.com/ (Accessed: 16 August 2022).

Nagoski, E. (2015) *Come as You Are: The Surprising New Science that Will Transform Your Sex Life*. New York: Simon Schuster.

Nagoski, E., & TEDx Talks. (2018) *The Truth About Unwanted Arousal: Emily Nagoski at TEDxVancouver*, 4 June. Available at: https://www.youtube.com/watch?v=L-q-tSHo9Ho (Accessed: 10 September 2022).

Nathanson, D. (1992) *Shame and Pride: Affect and the Birth of Self*. New York: W. W. Norton.

National Archives, The. (2022) *Prohibition of Female Circumcision Act*. Available at: https://www.legislation.gov.uk/ukpga/1985/38/contents (Accessed: 22 August 2022).

National Maternity and Perinatal Audit (NMPA). (2022) Clinical Report 2019. Based on Births in NHS Maternity Services Between 1 April 2016 and 31 March 2017. Available at: https://maternityaudit.org.uk/filesUploaded/NMPA%20Clinical%20Report%202019.pdf (Accessed: 11 September 2022).

NETFLIX. (2022) *Sex Education* (2019). Available at: https://www.netflix.com/gb/title/80197526 (Accessed: 22 August 2022).

Neves, S. (2021) *Compulsive Sexual Behaviours*. London: Routledge.

NHS. (no date) *What Are Pelvic Floor Exercises?* Available at: https://www.nhs.uk/common-health-questions/womens-health/what-are-pelvic-floor-exercises/ (Accessed: 23 August 2022).

NoFap. (2022) *Get a New Grip on Life*. Available at: https://nofap.com (Accessed: 23 August 2022).

Nordling, N., Sandnabba, N. K., & Santtila, P. (2000) 'The Prevalence and Effects of Self-reported Childhood Sexual Abuse Among Sadomasochistically Oriented Males and Females', *Journal of Child Sexual Abuse: Research, Treatment, & Program Innovations for Victims, Survivors, & Offenders*, 9(1), pp. 53–63.

Northrup, C. (1995) *Women's Bodies, Women's Wisdom*. London: Piatkus.

Northrup, C. (2003) *The Wisdom of the Menopause*. New York: Bantam.

NSPCC. (2022) *How Safe Are Our Children?* Available at: https://learning.nspcc.org.uk/research-resources/how-safe-are-our-children (Accessed: 21 August 2022).

O'Conner, K. (2020) 'What Is Code-Switching?', *Psychology Today*, 3 December. Available at: https://www.psychologytoday.com/us/blog/achieving-health-equity/202012/what-is-code-switching (Accessed: 29 August 2022).

Odent, M. (1999) *The Scientification of Love*. London: Free Association Books.

O'Dwyer, K. (2011) 'Can We Learn How to Love? An Exploration of Eric Fromm's The Art of Loving', *Self and Society*, 39(2).

Office for National Statistics. (2022) *Dataset: Nature of Sexual Assault by Rape or Penetration, England and Wales.* Available at: https://www.ons.gov.uk/people populationandcommunity/crimeandjustice/datasets/natureofsexualassaultbyrape orpenetrationenglandandwales (Accessed: 4 September 2022).

Ogden, P. (2021a) *The Pocket Guide to Sensorimotor Psychotherapy in Context.* United States: W.W. Norton & Company.

Ogden, P. (2021b) *Window of Tolerance.* Available at: https://www.youtube.com/watch?v=wIosUotibEs (Accessed: 13 September 2022).

Outsiders Trust, The. (no date) *The Outsiders Club.* Available at: https://outsiders.org.uk/club/the-outsiders-club/ (Accessed: 22 August 2022).

Panksepp, J. (1998) *Affective Neuroscience.* New York: Oxford University Press.

Paslakis et al. (2020) 'Associations Between Pornography Exposure, Body Image and Sexual Body Image: A Systematic Review', *Journal of Health Psychology*, 27 October. Available at: https://journals.sagepub.com/doi/abs/10.1177/135910532 0967085?journalCode=hpqa& (Accessed: 22 August 2022).

Perel, E. (2007) *Mating in Captivity.* USA: Hodder & Stoughton.

Pert, C. (1998) *Molecules of Emotion.* New York: Simon and Schuster.

Philips, L., & Philips, Dr Lee. (2022) *Psychotherapy and Sex Therapy.* Available at: https://www.drleephillips.com/ (Accessed: 22 August 2022).

Poole Heller, D. (2022) *Attachment Styles Test.* Available at: https://dianepooleheller.com/attachment-test/ (Accessed: 16 August 2022).

Pope, A., & Hugo Wurlitzer, S. (2022) *Wise Power: Discover the Liberating Power of Menopause to Awaken Authority, Purpose and Belonging.* London: Hay House.

Porges, S. (2007) 'The Polyvagal Perspective', *Biological Psychology*, 74, pp. 116–143.

Porges, S. (2017) *The Pocket Guide to the Polyvagal Theory: The Transformative Power of Feeling Safe.* New York: W.W. Norton.

Porges, Stephen W. (2022) *Polyvagal Theory.* Available at: https://www.stephenporges.com/ (Accessed: 23 August 2022).

Porn Hub. (2022) *2021 Year in Review.* Available at: https://www.pornhub.com/insights/yir-2021#top-20-countries (Accessed: 22 August 2022).

QMC. (no date) *Resources.* Available at: https://www.queermenopause.com/resources (Accessed: 23 August 2022).

Quinn, J. (2020) '3 Realms of ACEs – Updated!', *PACEs Connection*, 7 October. Available at: https://www.pacesconnection.com/g/hutchinson-ks-aces-connection/blog/3-realms-of-aces-updated (Accessed: 5 August 2022).

Rape Crisis. (2022a) *Annual Rape Prosecutions Fall Again.* Available at: https://rapecrisis.org.uk/news/annual-rape-prosecutions-fall-again/ (Accessed: 4 September 2022).

Rape Crisis. (2022b) *Rape Reports Hit Record High.* Available at: https://rapecrisis.org.uk/news/rape-reports-hit-record-high/ (Accessed: 4 August 2022).

Rape Crisis. (2022c) *What Is Sexual Violence?* Available at: https://rapecrisis.org.uk/get-informed/about-sexual-violence/what-is-sexual-violence/ (Accessed: 3 September 2022).

RedSchool. (no date) *Women's Stories.* Available at: https://www.redschool.net/categories/womens-stories (Accessed: 23 August 2022).

Rewriting the Rules. (2016) *The Consent Checklist*. Available at: https://www.rewriting-the-rules.com/wp-content/uploads/2019/10/Consent-Checklist-1.pdf (Accessed: 4 September 2022).

Richters, J. et al. (2008) 'Demographic and Psychosocial Features of Participants in Bondage and Discipline, Sadomasochism or Dominance and Submission (BDSM): Data from a National Survey', *Journal of Sexual Medicine*, 5(7), pp. 1660–1668.

Robinson, E., & Aveyard, P. (2017) 'Emaciated Mannequins: A Study of Mannequin Body Size in High Street Fashion Stores', *Journal of Eating Disorders*, 5(1). Available at: https://www.researchgate.net/publication/316631986_Emaciated_mannequins_A_study_of_mannequin_body_size_in_high_street_fashion_stores (Accessed: 6 September 2022).

Robinson-Wood, T. (2017) *The Convergence of Race, Ethnicity and Gender*. California: Sage.

Rose, S. (1999) *The Chemistry of Life*. New York: Penguin.

Rothschild, B. (2000) *The Body Remembers*. New York: W. W. Norton.

Royal College of Obstetricians and Gynaecologists, Working Party. (2008) *Standards for Maternity Care*. Available at: https://rcog.org.uk/media/wispcst3/wprmaternitystandards2008.pdf (Accessed: 22 August 2022).

Safeline. (2022) *National Male Survivor Helpline and Online Support Service*. Available at: https://safeline.org.uk/services/national-male-helpline/ (Accessed: 4 September 2022).

Savage, D. (2021) *Savage Love from A to Z: Advice on Sex and Relationships, Dating and Mating, Exes and Extras: Straight Talk on Love, Sex, and Intimacy*. USA: Sasquatch Books.

Scarleteen. (no date) *Sex Ed for the Real World*. Available at: https://www.scarleteen.com (Accessed: 22 August 2022).

Schnarch, D. (1998) *Passionate Marriage*. New York: Owl Books.

Schnarch, D. (2002) *Resurrecting Sex*. New York: Harper Collins.

School of Sexuality Education. (2021) *Sex Ed: An Inclusive Teenage Guide to Sex and Relationships*. Available at: https://uk.bookshop.org/books/sex-ed-an-inclusive-teenage-guide-to-sex-and-relationships/9781406399080 (Accessed: 22 August 2022).

Sensorimotor Psychotherapy Institute. (2020) *Dr. Pat Ogden: Window of Tolerance*, 27 July. Available at: https://www.youtube.com/watch?v=wIosUotibEs (Accessed: 4 September 2022).

Sensorimotor Psychotherapy Institute. (2022) *Pat Ogden, PhD*. Available at: https://sensorimotorpsychotherapy.org/therapist-directory/pat-ogden-phd/ (Accessed: 19 August 2022).

Sex Positive Families. Available at: https://sexpositivefamilies.com (Accessed: 22 August 2022).

Sh!. (2022) *Lubricant*. Available at: https://www.sh-womenstore.com/catalogsearch/result/?q=lubricant (Accessed: 23 August 2022).

Shapiro, R. (1987) *Contraception: A Practical and Political Guide*. London: Virago.

Sherwin, A. (2011) 'Sex Isn't Such a Straight Choice Anymore for Brits', *i Newspaper*, 29 September.

Silverberg, C. (2013) *What Makes a Baby*. New York City: Seven Stories Press.

Silverberg, C. (2015) *Sex Is a Funny Word: A Book About Bodies, Feelings, and You*. New York City: Seven Stories Press.

Silverberg, C. (2022) *You Know, Sex: Bodies, Gender, Puberty, and Other Things*. New York City: Seven Stories Press.

SPOKZ. (2020) *Sex Aids*. Available at: https://www.spokz.co.uk/sex-aids.html (Accessed: 22 August 2022).

Spring, C. (2015) 'The Trauma Traffic Light', *Carolyn Spring*, 1 June. Available at: https://www.carolynspring.com/blog/the-trauma-traffic-light/ (Accessed: 29 August 2022).

Spring, C. (2021) *Shame Is the Handbrake on Anger*. Available at: https://www.carolynspring.com/blog/shame-is-the-handbrake-on-anger/ (Accessed: 29 August 2022).

Sunderland, M. (2007) *What Every Parent Needs to Know*. London: Dorling Kindersley.

SurvivorsUK. (2022) Available at: https://www.survivorsuk.org/ (Accessed: 4 September 2022).

Swami, V., & Furnham, A. (2008) *The Psychology of Physical Attraction*. London: Routledge.

Thames Valley Police. (2022) *Consent Is Everything*. Available at: https://www.thamesvalley.police.uk/police-forces/thames-valley-police/areas/c/2017/consent-is-everything/ (Accessed: 4 September 2022).

Tomkins Institute, The. (2022) *Affect Imagery Consciousness (Vol I-IV)*. Available at: https://www.tomkins.org/what-tomkins-said/books-and-articles/affect-imagery-consciousness-vol-i-iv/ (Accessed: 23 August 2022).

Tomkins, S. (1962) *Affect Imagery Consciousness. Vol I: The Positive Affects*. New York: Springer.

Tomkins, S. (1963) *Affect Imagery Consciousness. Vol II: The Negative Affects*. New York: Springer.

Tomkins, S. (1991) *Affect Imagery Consciousness. Vol III: The Negative Affects: Anger and Fear*. New York: Springer.

Tomkins, S. (1992) *Affect Imagery Consciousness. Vol IV: Cognition: Duplication and Transformation of Information*. New York: Springer.

Tonegawa, S. (2017) 'Brain Circuit That Drives Pleasure Inducing Behavior Identified', *Neuroscience News*. Available at: https://neurosciencenews.com/pleasure-amygdala-neuroscience-6286/ (Accessed: 23 August 2022).

Topping, A. (2021) 'Four-fifths of Young Women in the UK Have Been Sexually Harassed, Survey Finds', *The Guardian*, 10 March. Available at: https://www.theguardian.com/world/2021/mar/10/almost-all-young-women-in-the-uk-have-been-sexually-harassed-survey-finds (Accessed: 4 September 2022).

Turner, D., & Dwight Turner Counselling. (no date) Available at: https://www.dwightturnercounselling.co.uk/ (Accessed: 29 August 2022).

Underwood, S. (2003) *Gay Men and Anal Eroticism*. New York: Routledge.

Vance, T. (2019) *Very Grand Emotions: How Autistics and Neurotypicals Experience Emotions Differently*. Available at: https://neuroclastic.com/very-grand-emotions/ (Accessed: 23 August 2022).

Veale, D. et al. (2015) 'Am I Normal? A Systematic Review and Construction of Nomograms for Flaccid and Erect Penis Length and Circumference in up to 15 521 Men', *British Journal of Urology International (BJUI)*, 115(6), pp. 978–986.

WebMD. (2022) *Hands Free Orgasm: What It Is*. Available at: https://www.webmd.com/sex/hands-free-orgasm (Accessed: 23 August 2022).

Women's Environmental Network. (2022) Available at: https://www.wen.org.uk/ (Accessed: 23 August 2022).

Women's Environmental Network. (no date) *Seeing Red*. Available at: https://www.yumpu.com/en/document/read/29560735/download-seeing-red-womens-environmental-network (Accessed: 23 August 2022).

Wu, J. (2020) 'How Does Your Attachment Style Impact Your Relationships?', *Psychology Today*, 8 April. Available at: https://www.psychologytoday.com/us/blog/the-savvy-psychologist/202004/how-does-your-attachment-style-impact-your-relationships (Accessed: 4 September 2022).

Zilbergeld, B. (1999) *The New Male Sexuality: The Truth About Men, Sex, and Pleasure*. New York: Bantam Doubleday Dell Publishing.

Index

Note: **Bold** page numbers refer to tables and *italic* page numbers refer to figures.